Working in Aviation

Working in Aviation

Verité Reily Collins

Distributed in the USA by
The Globe Pequot Press, Guilford, Connecticut

Published by Vacation Work, 9 Park End Street, Oxford
www.vacationwork.co.uk

WORKING IN AVIATION
by Verité Reily Collins

First edition 2004

Copyright © Vacation Work 2004

ISBN 1-85458-322-0

Publicity by Roger Musker

Cover design by mccdesign ltd

Illustrations by Mick Siddens

Typeset by Brendan Cole

Printed and bound in Italy by Legoprint SpA, Trento

CONTENTS

ACKNOWLEDGMENTS

This is an enormous thank you to the friends, acquaintances and friends-of-friends who gladly gave hours of their time, helping me put together this book and cheerfully answering yet another question. It was great to meet Mark Anderson, General Manager World Duty Free Terminal 3 Heathrow, who is so enthusiastic about his job, and showed me around 'his' terminal shops with such pride; Captain Ed Davidson, Director of Safety at IATA set me straight about important safety issues; and Joe Desmond of Gatwick Aviation Training and Roy Drummer (ex BA Engineering) patiently tried to explain the way the route in to engineering qualifications is changing.

James Banerjee of BA not only gave me an insight into cabin crew rostering, but also patiently answered continuous frantic e-mails and clarified a multitude of obscure points. Rory Galway, Equal Opportunities Manager with Bombardier gave so much of his time; I used to work for this company, when they were known as Shorts Aviation, and as usual they were helpful and informative. Alex Brown, MA Frameworks Co-ordinator SEMTA and David Stewart of the Department for Transport cheerfully answered my questions when I couldn't understand new regulations and qualifications, and David Wilson and Emirates Airlines Press Office at QBO Bell Pottinger Public Relations were stars; they managed to produce answers almost before I had sent the questions – time and time again.

Thank you also to all the staff at Anne Kavanagh PR who found some marvelous enthusiasts for me to interview and were always helpful; to Robert Rogers, whose IT expertise discovered many obscure but useful websites, and Jason Wakeford of Consol PR for arranging some fascinating interviews with KLM. And to Vikram Sinha – a hero of Microsoft's helpline. As usual, BA press office, and in particular Nicola Dunbar-Newman, put up with constant questions on obscure subjects – and came up with answers.

And everyone at Vacation Work publishers, especially Charles, David, Anne-Marie and Roger, with thanks for being so understanding when I delivered copy so late.

PREFACE

Within the last century the aviation industry has become part of the lives of millions of people around the world, from holidaymakers and business travellers flying to their destinations, to the world's poorest people relying on aid supplies air-lifted to their countries.

Working in aviation is like working for an enormous global family, and an airport is like a small town, where your friends and colleagues work together to give the best possible service when handling passengers or cargo. The industry requires vastly different skills and experience in hundreds of different jobs, but once part of the workforce you will generally find it easy to work in different countries, or at least visit them as part of your job.

It's not only cabin crew and pilots who travel as part of their jobs, but engineers, retail assistants in airport shops, sales and marketing executives, aid workers, logistics experts, security staff, caterers and thousands of people in other jobs. Once in, you will find that air travel has become part of your working life, with your passport always in your pocket in case you suddenly have to fly abroad.

This industry demands perfection, not least because you have people's lives in your hands, but salaries are good for those who obtain the relevant qualifications.

For me there is still a thrill arriving at an airport, and I hope it will always be the same for you.

Verité Reily Collins
London 2004

Introduction

HISTORY

When first Orville, then Wilbur Wright took off in a tiny aeroplane from Kill Devil Hill, near Kitty Hawk in North Carolina on December 17th 1903, man could at last fly like the birds. As their flights captured the public's interest, a new industry and a new way to travel was born. Manufacturers started making planes commercially, and companies offered people the chance to fly as passengers; first for joy-rides, and then as a means of travelling from A to B. Today there is hardly a country that doesn't have its own airline and airport.

Flying became a hobby for the rich, and a way to increase circulation figures for newspapers. Britain's Daily Mail in particular was in the forefront of the publicity bandwagon, offering prize money for every possible 'first flight'. In 1909 the Frenchman Louis Blériot claimed their £1,000 prize for being the first man to fly the English Channel in a powered flight.

The First World War acted as a catalyst for the fledgling industry; until then flying had been for rich enthusiasts, but the need to fight meant governments were prepared to spend money developing war machines and give pilots training – albeit this was often very basic. After the war was over, two British aviators, John Alcock and Arthur Whitten Brown, both ex-wartime flyers and prisoners of war, were the first to fly the Atlantic in a converted Vickers Vimy bomber, powered by a Rolls-Royce Eagle engine. They took off from Lester's Field, St. Johns', Newfoundland on 14th June 1919, along with toy cat mascots and a bottle of whisky. During the flight they encountering dense icy fog, sheet ice dangerously weighed down the planes fragile wings and at times they were flying upside down. Eventually they touched down at Clifden Wireless Station in Ireland, having flown 1,980miles in 16 hrs 12 mins. This time the Daily Mail came up with £10,000, Alcock and Brown were knighted, and today there is a statue to them at Heathrow Airport.

Eight years later, on May 20th 1927, the American Charles A. Lindberg took off from Roosevelt Field near New York City in his plane, the Spirit of St. Louis. Flying solo, 33 hrs and 30 mins later he landed at Le Bourget Airfield, Paris, to a hero's welcome.

KLM, the Royal Dutch airline, started the world's first and oldest commercial flight on 17th May, 1920, between Croydon in London and Amsterdam in the Netherlands, when pilots navigated by following railway tracks between cities. When Imperial Airways started flying routes across the world, they needed some way of navigating across the trackless desert between Palestine and Baghdad. Their solution was to plough a furrow several hundred miles long across the sand, so pilots could follow this route. Imperial flew the first commercial flight across the Atlantic on July 21st, 1938, but shortly afterwards World War II broke out and commercial flights were suspended.

World War II acted as catalyst similar to the First World War in developing fighter planes. Governments realised their potential and developed huge planes to carry out bombing raids and act as troop carriers. Frank Whittle invented the jet aeroplane; Rolls-Royce were converting his designs into production engines and set the foundation for the company that still makes jet engines for the world's aeroplanes today. After the war was over there were all these large transport planes lying idle, and it wasn't long before entrepreneurs such as Vladimir Raitz (founder of Horizon Travel) realised they could be utilised to fly passengers quickly to holiday destinations.

The Berlin airlift in 1948 helped more with development. Surrounded by a Russian blockade, the Allies were desperately trying to fly in supplies to keep Berlin supplied with food. This non-stop 'air bridge' between the eventual nine airfields in the British sector of Germany provided superb training for pilots, many of whom joined commercial airlines when discharged. It also proved a marvellous shop window for the ubiquitous DC3, a workhorse aircraft developed by the Douglas company in the US, and so popular and efficient that over sixty years after its first flight in 1935 there are still over 1000 flying, carrying cargo and also passengers on nostalgia flights.

The DC3 was so useful that it was used by fledgling airlines all over the world; it was the first plane built that was a commercial success as it was cheap enough to fly and not need mail or other cargo to make it viable. Although officially it carried up to 32 passengers, one flight in the China-Burma-India war zone took off with 73 refugees on board – and landed with a baby born on the way, making 74.

After the war, BOAC took over Imperial's pioneering routes. Imperial had developed a highly complex spider's web of connecting flights across the globe, making it sensible for other airlines to feed in to their timetable system, so it was easier for passengers to connect up with flights. Eventually, even though today other airlines might want to change the original system, it would be far too difficult to untangle all the connections. Hence the world's airline timetables are descended from these original timings, and Asian and other airlines start their long-haul flights to Europe in the middle of their night, since Heathrow Airport only allows a minimum of night flights.

Vladimir Raitz, a Russian refugee working in the British tourist industry, was the next big influence on flying. Up until his time, flying was for the rich, but in the early 1950s he realised the ex-war planes could be flown relatively cheaply, and it would be possible for British holidaymakers to fly off to the sun at an affordable price. Hence the start of the package holiday, and the world's love affair with flying – or perhaps one should say 'tolerance', since today's planes are nothing like as comfortable as the pioneering airlines, which had large seats, plenty of leg-room and even beds. But cramming in seats means cheaper flights, and that's what counts with the majority of today's passengers.

Recently the aviation world held its breath after the events of September 11th 2001, and bookings dipped. But people have to travel, cargo has to be delivered, and airlines that survived are back recording record numbers of passengers.

All these people need looking after – in the air and on the ground. Which means jobs, jobs and more jobs. Whilst most people think of jobs as being with flight crew, there are literally thousands of vacancies in administration, engineering, sales and marketing for airlines, with many jobs at airports, which are often the size of a small city.

There is something exciting about the buzz of working at an airport, and as someone once said 'Jobs in offices may offer free coffee. Airline jobs may offer free travel'.

It is said that Sir George Cayley, an Englishman from Brompton in York-shire, invented the aeroplane in 1799, according to Wilbur Wright – and he should have known. According to Roger Highfield, Science Editor of the Daily Telegraph, in 1909 Wright said: 'About 100 years ago, an Eng-lishman carried the science of flight to a point which it had never matched before and which it scarcely reached again during the last century'.

WHY THE INDUSTRY NEEDS YOU

People have been moaning since the 1920s that running an airline is the easiest way to lose a fortune, and there have been spectacular bankruptcies, often leaving passengers stranded. But manufacturers are still building planes and they are still flying. Now financiers have worked out better solutions to making airlines profitable, the job scene is improving every day.

The recent rise of low cost airlines in Europe has certainly added to the jobs' pool. For years European entrepreneurs looked at ways of operating low cost airlines, on the lines of Southwest Airlines in the USA. Freddie Laker tried and failed with Skytrain – but then hard-headed businessmen who weren't interested in the 'romance' of flying, but more in analysing costs, worked out that instead of looking to save money in the air, they could negotiate cheaper landing fees at airports, cut out frills such as free food, not guarantee to look after you if a flight was cancelled (a huge cost to airlines), cut out tickets, use the internet to sell seats instead of agents who needed commission, reduce the luggage allowance, etc. These cost-saving ideas worked, and now Europe is criss-crossed by low-cost carriers. Every day my e-mails seem to carry the announcement of yet another airline start-up. These airlines have their ups-and-downs, but with low operating and administration costs, if one route has to be closed, it is cheap to open up another and keep planes flying.

The traditional airlines are still operating, providing flights for passengers who demand better service, particularly business clients – a very profitable market. Another profitable side is air cargo – and the big parcel carriers have come in to this market and are flying more and more planes.

Airlines are in the middle of a busy job circle: banks lend money to aviation companies to run an airline, which then has to make a profit to service this loan. So staff are needed in sales and marketing departments to encourage people to fly or send goods by air; more staff are then needed to sell tickets to prospective passengers, operate a website, or sell space for freight in a cargo plane; ground staff are needed for checking-in flyers and luggage handling; engineers to service the aircraft; retail staff are required to sell gifts and goods at the airport; backroom staff who keep airports operational, and cabin crew and pilots ensuring that planes fly to their destination with safety and as much comfort as possible for passengers. Whilst in the air, Air Traffic Control act as the 'sky police', monitoring and assisting flights to cross their territory. Once landed, an aircraft needs ground crew to help the plane dock; meet passengers and off-load baggage, before they arrive in the Customs Hall for Immigration and Customs checks. Then there are the service outlets that will hire passengers a car, book an hotel or change money once passengers have arrived at an airport. The only problem with this book has been to leave out some of the many jobs in aviation – so apologies if you work in aviation and think I should have mentioned yours!

The BAA (British Airports Authority) runs Heathrow Airport, the world's busiest international airport (not the biggest airport – that is O'Hare in Chicago), plus Gatwick (fourth busiest), Stansted, Glasgow, Edinburgh, Aberdeen (world's busiest commercial heliport) and Southampton. They are major employers in Britain, so we have used them for case studies in many cases. British Airways (BA) is one of the world's largest and busiest airlines, and although their slogan 'the world's favourite airline' was a clever advertising ploy, they fly routes across the world, and are very popular with non-British customers. Although there are stories that passengers are deserting airlines for various reasons, Marketing Departments are remarkably resilient – and they will keep on plugging at selling aircraft seats – meaning more and more work for you.

Incidentally, if you want to travel and live in another country, many airlines recruit staff from outside their country to work from their bases.

Airline Jobs

In this book I have tended to concentrate on the major international airlines such as AA, BA, Emirates, KLM, SAS etc. but smaller companies will offer similar jobs – although not so many! The jobs available include:

- Administration and Marketing.
- Customer / Passenger Service Agents.
- Jobs in the USA.
- Finance and Accounts.
- Ground Handling.
- Pilots.
- Rostering.
- Sky Nannies.
- Ticket Sales.
- Working on Private Jets.
- Working in Cargo.
- Loyalty programmes.
- Career Progression.

There is also work for cabin crew, engineers and in security; which are major sources of jobs and are covered in other chapters.

ADMINISTRATION

Airlines don't make money when their planes are sitting on the tarmac; they need to be flying in the air, carrying passengers or cargo to keep in profit. So the job of those in administration, marketing seats or selling cargo space, is what keeps planes flying, and hopefully making a profit.

Like an iceberg, an airline's administration is generally not visible to the general public. Offices may even be situated well away from airports, because office space at airports is often very expensive. There will be a small operations office at an airport, but the main offices or buildings will be well away – possibly even on a business site.

An airline will have all of the following administration departments – and probably some more eg:

- Customer Services/Complaints.

- Engineering/Administration.
- Finance and Accounts.
- Forward Planning (different titles according airline).
- Human Resources (personnel).
- Legal.
- Marketing.
- Rostering.
- Ticket Sales.
- Training.

For all of these jobs you will need good IT skills. For some you will need a good speaking voice, for others the right qualifications in accountancy or law.

To find out more, look up major airlines' websites – and be astonished at the different job titles that come under Administration. Don't let this worry you – they are all aiming at the same thing – making money for the backers/shareholders in as legal and efficient a manner as possible, by flying people or cargo from one destination to another.

Customer Services/Complaints

Sadly you cannot please all of the people all of the time – and sometimes a budget airline doesn't even try. However, major airlines will have large customer service departments, not only to handle complaints, but also to play a pro-active part in helping passengers by providing wheelchairs, special diets, etc.

Engineering Administration

See the *Engineering* chapter.

Finance and Accounts

This is equally as important as the Sales and Marketing departments – many would say the most important department, particularly in low cost airlines. Not only can you not fly aircraft if the company is bankrupt, but unless revenue is handled efficiently the civil aviation authority that licenses the airline will step in and suspend operations. In the past many airlines went bankrupt because the people running them were more concerned with flying – and the fun of flying – than in making sure funds were in place to make this happen. Luckily, thanks to efficient financial departments this is less likely to happen today.

Later on you will read about one airline where the CEO asks his staff to use pens they find in hotels, etc. He won't buy them as stationery – that's how tight cost control is today.

If cost analysis, budget forecasts, etc. thrill you, you will be fascinated by the work that goes on behind the scenes in an airline. You will constantly be looking for ways to reduce costs, and of course you will travel 'down the line' as an integral part of your job.

Forward Planning

This department is known by so many different names it would take the whole book to list them! Basically it is the department that has to predict what the travelling public will want in eighteen months time, so the airline can plan its routes and services to attract passengers. This can be a fascinating area in which to work. Currently the major airlines have two things in mind; the rise of low cost airlines, and the demise of Concorde.

Everyone is trying to outdo the low cost airlines, but most airlines will admit that their large administration departments cost too much to run budget operations. So what must they come up with to counter the commercial threat? That is what they are trying to find out, and working with the financial deparments they will agonise over ways of cutting costs that will still keep customers booking.

When three Concordes landed at Heathrow for the last time, not only was super-luxury travel the poorer, but the best way for the mega-rich and stars to travel across the Atlantic had come to an end. Airlines around the world are now looking at ways of attracting these passengers onto their airline to spend some of their millions.

When it comes to low cost carriers, their forward planning departments play a dominant part in the airline's administration. These airlines may charge low fares, but generally pay good salaries to those whom they do employ, especially on the all-important administration side.

Recent Jobs with easyJet

easyJet (www.easyJet.com) based in Luton, currently has 75 aircraft with more on order, so its administration staff needs are increasing. Some of the jobs recently on offer for degree-calibre staff are:

○ Senior Negotiators to secure and manage high value commercial contracts. This means dealing with aircraft manufacturers, ground handling companies, engineering facilities etc. to get the best contract deals possible for the airline. Salary £45,000 + bonus.

○ European Airports Commercial managers to assist the Airports Commercial Manager to obtain best value and service from a range of long term contracts with airports throughout the easyJet network.

○ You don't even have to work your way up through the airline; they look for potential staff who have been working for other companies in purchasing or supply chain management, with a reputation for optimising value from suppliers.

Human Resources (Personnel)

This department will advertise and interview prospective staff, and liaise with the training department to organise or supervise training courses.

Legal

This department will be concerned with liaising with the relevant Civil Aviation authority, IATA, insurance companies, etc. and checking that appropriate permission has been obtained to fly over new routes and sensitive areas, etc.

Marketing

There are many different marketing jobs, and each airline seems to have a different name for the same job.

It is the job of this department to keep the name of the airline in front of that sector of the public who will actually be buying seats on their aircraft. Compare advertising from low cost airlines, with that appearing in the glossy magazines – totally different markets, but each carefully aimed at the appropriate readers.

Job opportunities can occur when an airline decides to develop a different brand name – such as British Midland's off-shoot bmibaby – which has been developed to fight off competition from the low cost carriers. Each time any airline decides to invest in a new brand, more people are hired to develop the identity.

Work in this sector follows the life cycle of a brand, from research and development to putting together business cases and developing brands.

The larger the airline, the more frustrating this work can sometimes be, and staff complain of the time it can take for a new product to be launched. But then if you have a good idea, which is adopted, you know your idea or suggestion is flying around the world.

Everyone who works in this sector says one thing – 'the diversity, the commitment to doing an outstanding job, and the talented people here make the job fascinating'.

Rostering Department

This department will be concerned in ensuring that the right amount of pilots and cabin crew are available to fly on each flight. Organising who goes where and deciding who flies on long haul/short haul flights is one of the most important jobs. Most international trans-continental airlines will have a local division that flies on domestic and short haul flights. New crew or those who want to return home at night will fly on short haul routes.

Generally, another department trains and looks after crew who fly long haul flights. Usually the planes are different (long haul cabin seats will have slightly more legroom, etc) so crew have to be checked out on the different types, as emergency exits will vary.

But at the end of the day you go where you are sent. Sometimes the administration might try merging long and short haul, deeming that if crew are trained to fly the appropriate planes, they can muck in and swop roles for the good of airline. This can cause problems; no one wants to give up their hard-won perks.

Training

It is a legal requirement that cabin crew are trained up to a high international standard, and most airlines will carry out this training themselves. Admin. staff will interview, select and train the crews. For more details see chapter on Cabin Crew.

There may also be marketing, sales and other types of training handled in-house.

Some airlines offer a general training scheme which covers accounts, cargo, reservations, passenger services, computer operations and personnel.

Recent jobs ads in the BA (www.britishairwaysjobs.com) house magazine included:

○ Network Analyst delivering revenue forecasts, commercial business insights and analysis, Excel capability.
○ Finance Managers to support the business simplification programme and provide quality analytical and strategic support.
○ Key Account Manager in New York to develop strategic partnerships to deliver value to BA and its highest-value corporate customers.
○ Support Account Managers to join Corporate Sales, to service a portfolio of top corporate accounts.
○ Senior World Sales Analyst to take a global view of sales performance and act as a focal point for change.

CUSTOMER/PASSENGER SERVICE AGENTS – CSA/ PSA

The **Customer Service Agent** (CSA) is generally the first airline person passengers see, and therefore the staff mostly likely to experience customers' bad temper and sadly, rudeness. Due to current anti-terrorism measures, passengers will generally have to queue before checking in, and staff say the length of the queue affects people's tempers. Many airlines work a filter system; you join a general queue, and when you reach the top you go to the next available agent, rather than joining the shortest queue, only to find there is someone with a problem in front of you, and you could end up missing your flight.

Francesca Freeland, the MD of KLM Ground Services at Heathrow, is in charge of a team which includes:

○ Customer Service Agents (were known as Passenger Service Agents).
○ Senior Customer Service Agents.

○ Passenger Services Controllers.
○ Ground Services Duty Managers.

At check-in, the CSA :

○ Welcomes the passenger.
○ Asks security questions.
○ Checks ticket, destination and weight of luggage.
○ If luggage is overweight they explain where/how to pay excess (this is one of today's major problems, but since Sept. 11th airlines are much stricter).
○ Labels luggage securely and sends it down to baggage hall.
○ Confirm where passenger wishes to sit.
○ Checks passport and any visas necessary.
○ Issues boarding pass.
○ Hands over documentation and wishes passenger a pleasant flight.

Once the flight is closed (usually 30 minutes before departure) staff go down to the gate ready to supervise boarding passengers.

Those passengers with problem check-ins are usually the least trouble. Arrive with a shotgun (legitimately) and the CSA will take the passenger around to customs to complete the paperwork. But if it is a firearm then it is the police who will deal with the paperwork. Passengers with excess luggage such as sports equipment or bicycles fall into two categories: those who have phoned ahead, warned the airline and followed their advice about packing, etc. – no trouble at all. And those who haven't given any thought to the problems of getting their belongings into an aircraft hold, and often arrive at the last minute. Guess what the staff think of them – but they are too professional to say so! Then there are:

○ Baggage Service Agents.
○ Senior Baggage Service Agents.
○ Controllers.

And *Ramp* jobs which include:

○ Drivers.
○ Loaders.
○ Ramp Service Agents.
○ Ramp Services Controllers.
○ Special Service Maintenance Mechanics.

However, other airlines use different job titles. British Midland (bmi) uses:

○ Customer Service Agent.
○ Lead Agent.

O Assistant.
O Supervisor.

With KLM, staff at junior level have to be multi-functional; this makes work more interesting as they have the power to make many decisions without referring to anyone else. Other airlines and ground handling companies will insist that CSAs refer to senior management if there is any problem, but at KLM 'we try to encourage them to do as much as possible'.

Baggage Service Agents do an invaluable job, which is very much more customer-oriented: mis-route a bag, and you have a very unhappy client. The bags come down a chute from the check-in desk, their labels are scanned, and agents collect and take them away to the appropriate flight. Label scanning means the airline has a complete record if a bag needs to be off-loaded before departure – e.g. if a passenger misses the flight. When a flight arrives at its destination, label scanning means the agents have a complete record of which bags were loaded in the unlikely event one isn't on the flight.

Ramp Service Agents; during their first six months as staff will be taught to drive an HGV (Heavy Goods Vehicle), and take a test to enable them to drive specialist equipment such as tractors to tow aircraft (there is no reverse gear on an aircraft – it has to be pushed back from the ramp before it can taxi out for take-off). They also receive instruction on using specialist equipment such as de-icing machinery.

To service this equipment there are specialist **Maintenance Mechanics**. And staff learn the signals needed when they guide in the aircraft to dock at the ramp.

Useful Address
www.KLM.com

JOBS IN THE USA

In Europe most passengers want to buy their tickets in advance; they don't go for 'turn up and fly', but would rather have a confirmed seat. In the States, many passengers buy tickets at the airport, so American Airlines (AA)'s CSAs carry out jobs across the spectrum:

O Preparing and issuing tickets.
O Computing fares.
O Checking passports and refunds.
O Checking baggage.
O Working at arrival and departure gates, ensuring on-time departures.
O Providing assistance, answering general travel enquiries and successfully resolving customer issues.

AA also employs **Passenger Service Representatives**, working side-by-side with CSAs. They may also handle customer flow at check-ins, co-ordinating special assistance services, etc. The US airlines started this concept at other airports to assist passengers at long check-in queues. This job can often offer temporary work at peak holiday times at any airport with direct flights to the USA.

Useful Address
www.aacareers.com or www.myAAjob.com

FLIGHT SERVICES

Most airlines will have a Flight Services department, whose **Flight Dispatchers** weigh and balance all the cargo and luggage going onto an aircraft. Once they did complicated sums with average passenger weight, plus weight of luggage etc. then had to say where it should be stowed.

Now airlines such as KLM feed the details into their computer at base (in the Netherlands for KLM, Lufthansa's is in Frankfurt) to give 24 hour cover; back comes the instantaneous answer (one hopes) and the aircraft's load sheet is printed out on the flight deck.

Mrs Freeland of KLM muses that these people may eventually be replaced by 'gate runners' – who will do the Flight Dispatchers job, but as the mathematical element will disappear, the job will need a different kind of personality. In future their work will probably be more problem solving, but they must still be able to understand deadlines and the importance of getting cargo, luggage, catering, services and passengers on board in time for departure.

Station Managers

In the past **Station Managers** would have worked up from being Flight Dispatchers, but have the qualities of a gate runner. Mrs Freeland believes in the future everyone in this department will have the same skills; talentwise this is going to help a lot; putting 10-12 people in the department who are all possible Station Managers.

'It's a wonderful industry to work in', says Mrs Freeland
I came from working in TV – both industries do attract the same kind of extrovert personalities'. Starting out with GB Airways at Manchester Airport in Sales and Marketing and Customer Services, she then realised she was much happier on the administration side and went to work for KLM in Manchester as Station Manager. After 20 months they closed down, and she transferred to Air UK. Then she 'decided to take a chance and joined KLM at Heathrow, and the industry just has not stopped changing.

Really, I don't think we can do anything more. People are working harder and some of the glamour has gone. To some extent it's travel concessions that keep staff in the industry, plus the glamour of the uniform'.

Salaries

At KLM the starting salary for a CSA is £12,500 p.a. plus shift pay (around £4,000 p.a.) and 22 days leave per year.

A recent advert for Singapore Airlines at Heathrow asked for excellent communication skills, both face-to-face and on the telephone, previous customer service experience, ideally with another airline; ticketing and baggage knowledge would be a plus. Shift work. Salary around £16,500 p.a. plus shift allowance.

British Midland (bmi) pay £16,500 p.a. for a 37.5 hour week for shift work at Heathrow. Shifts start at 5am and late finishes are 11.45pm – but if handling charter aircraft at other airports this could be throughout the night. Shifts will include a mixture of early starts and late finishes.

Criteria

So what do airlines look for? British Midland (bmi) ask for:

○ Age 18-65.
○ 4 GCSEs at grade A-C including Maths and English, or equivalent.
○ Must hold a 10 year British or EU passport or have indefinite right to work in UK.
○ Full clean driving licence.
○ Minimum 12 months in a customer service job.
○ Good standard of English.
○ Immaculate appearance.

Useful Address
British Midland recruitment: www.flybmi.com

Speech Recognition
However, CSAs days could be numbered – at least if an idea being trialled by SAS (Scandinavian Airlines System) works. The airline claims they are the first with check-in via speech recognition, and explain:

Voice Check-in

2.8 million travellers now have the option of checking in on SAS with the help of a mobile phone and a speech recognition service called Voice Check-in. SAS has become the first in the world to offer customers a reminder by SMS and then the possibility to check in via speech recognition. The traveller subscribes to a 'check-in notification' in her/his profile at scandinavian.net, inserts a mobile phone number and their SAS EuroBonus or Travel Pass card number. About 22 hours prior to departure these travellers receive an SMS to their mobile phone informing them that the flight is now open for check-in via speech recognition or the Internet.

Travellers who call the Voice Check-in service answer a few simple questions, such as whether they prefer an aisle or window seat. In the dialogue the mobile phone number functions as the key to the reservation. The service can be used by all travellers with an SAS EuroBonus card or Travel Pass when travelling with up to two pieces of baggage in addition to hand baggage. When the check-in process is completed confirmation is sent via SMS to the traveller's mobile phone.

Travellers who prefer to check in via the Internet can choose a seat on the site and, when holding a ticket that permits booking changes, can also opt to check in for an earlier or later flight if space is available. 'By being ready to fly when they arrive at the airport, travellers avoid any queues', says **Martina Samuelsson**, responsible for self-service on-ground at SAS. 'Our aim is to simplify travel and give the customer freedom of choice regarding how and when he/she wishes to check in.' After the check-in, travellers with hand baggage only can go directly to the gate at the airport. Travellers with checked baggage are issued with baggage tags by an SAS Self Service automat. Currently languages used in the speech recognition service are Danish, Norwegian, Swedish and English; determined by the country code of the mobile phone number. The caller can change the Danish, Norwegian or Swedish dialogue to English if desired.

PASSENGER DUTY OFFICER

Passenger Duty Officers are further up the career ladder.

Ex-Policeman David Cook has been with KLM for 25 years.
Brimming over with enthusiasm for his job, he is in charge of 28 staff. He is responsible for the smooth running of his shift, which includes supervising staff on the check-in desk. It is up to David to ensure that:

○ All passengers from the incoming flight are off the plane, all baggage unloaded, and cleaners on board are ready to give a 40 minute turn-around.
○ Departing passengers are checked in smoothly.
○ They receive good customer service.
○ The flight is all checked-in and 'closed' (ready to fly) on time.
○ Every passenger's luggage gets to the aircraft on time.
○ Passengers board on time.

He likens this to the old circus trick of spinning plates on poles, and seeing that none fall off! Not easy, especially coming up to departure, when all the staff swarm around the aircraft like bees around a honeypot.

David's biggest problem is bad weather causing delays, and when this happens he believes in telling passengers the truth. It is an old airline custom to shorten waiting times i.e. say there will be a half hour delay, when in reality it will be at least an hour. He always gives as accurate a picture as he can, believing passengers are intelligent enough that they would rather hear the truth, than be fobbed off.

Today, everyone seems to demand more from the aviation industry – perhaps because airlines allow passengers to book tickets, not turn up, and if they are full-fare tickets give a refund. Musing about passengers, he remembered a famous rock band who were a bit fresh with the CSA at check-in. When they returned from their concert in Amsterdam, they arrived with a huge bunch of flowers and four tickets for their next concert to apologise to the check-in girl. And they hadn't been that much of a problem.

The behaviour of today's passengers has got worse since Airline, the TV docu-soap which highlights passengers losing their temper. Younger staff can get intimidated, so David steps in to defuse the situation. There isn't time '*to provide the same quality of service as when I started, but I think staff today do a good job. It's a shame more people don't come in to the job; the days are never dull*'.

You shouldn't go into the industry unless you are prepared for a lot of grief; if you don't want to deal with people don't go into the airline business. But David never hears complaints about salaries, and the job is always interesting; you walk in to the airport at 5 am – and when it's one o'clock you wonder where the day has gone.

GROUND HANDLING

See also Customer Service Agents' information above.

As well as the airlines, there are ground handling companies (see the *Airport* chapter) who supply services for airlines if they don't have enough flights to warrant setting up their own ground handling. Working for a ground handling company might mean working for different airlines every day, generally it is full-time shift work.

Many people who work for ground handling companies come in from other industries, finding their management expertise and experience are what is wanted when working, and juggling, with different client requirements. Groundstar is a major company offering ground handling services at airports and their recruitment site highlights two staff who came from varying backgrounds:

Groundstar's General Manager, Birmingham, is Caroline Thaw, who has worked in the travel industry for 27 years; for Ellerman Sunflight, Wings Holidays, Horizon and Thomson. She then ran a pub, and joined Birmingham Airport in 1991 working for Ogden Aviation as a passenger services assistant, was promoted to supervisor, then passenger services manager and eventually to station manager. She then left Servisair in Sept 2001 and joined Groundstar as general manager at Birmingham.

Rhonda McLaren Anderson – General Manager Newcastle – has worked in aviation for over thirty years, first for Gill Aviation which later became Gill Air. Held posts as operations manager, business aviation manager in-flight services manager for UK & Europe. She then worked for Barratt Developments controlling the operation of their 2 corporate helicopters and aircraft. (You may remember they used their helicopters in some very effective TV commercials). She then joined Northeast Aviation as station manager, becoming general manager when the company became Groundstar.

> **Swissport, the ground handling company, recently advertised for a station manager:**
> Station Manager for Luxembourg to support existing customers, help acquire new customers, supervise quality standards, handle accounting, financial reporting, profitability etc. Must be able to speak English, French, and possibly German.

Useful Addresses
www.aena.es
www.fraport.com
www.servisair.com
www.swissport.com. (UK HR-Department paulina.parara@swissport.com)

Ramp Officers/Dispatch Co-ordinators

These come under Customer Service or Airside Services Dept. and basically liaise with the customer service staff checking in passengers, and with the onboard cabin crew and pilots. They are in charge of overseeing the arrival and departure process, and are the link between central load planning, the flight crew, other internal departments, caterers, fuelling bowsers and other suppliers (newspapers, magazines, etc). They also play an important role as 'piggy in the middle' when a passenger gets 'lost' in the departures lounge, which might cause the captain to delay departure and miss their take-off time slot.

> **Overseas airlines will almost certainly recruit ramp staff locally – not from their own country**
> American Airlines recently advertised for Duty Managers ramp service, Heathrow, *'to be responsible for the safe and timely load-unload of freight and luggage to strict and rigid deadlines. Graduate calibre or similar strong personality and leadership skills. As a decision maker you'll need to think on your feet, train, develop and motivate your staff.*

PILOTS

An aircraft captain's authority is the same as a ship's captain: total. The

CAA's Air Navigation Order says 'every person in an aircraft shall obey all lawful commands which the commander of that aircraft may give for the purposes of securing the safety of the aircraft.... or the efficiency or regularity of air navigation'. This order is most frequently used to bar drunken passengers from boarding an aircraft – potentially they could be a hazard if a plane ditches and they don't obey orders, but in truth other passengers don't pay good money to sit next to someone who might make their journey unpleasant.

Once airlines trained their own pilots, and/or took ex-Forces personnel. Today, the major carriers can no longer afford to run training schools, and rely on one or all of the following:

1. Applicants who fund their own training.
2. Offer limited sponsorship to selected candidates.
3. Or employ ex-services personnel.

1. *If your parents can help you fund training*, or you can obtain funding, you will find details of some courses in the Training Chapter.

Lufthansa make a very sensible suggestion: check out if you are medically fit to work as a pilot, before signing up and paying for a course. This means obtaining what is known as a Class 1 Medical Certificate, plus an eye test for visual acuity corrected to 20/20. You are allowed to wear glasses. It is NOT a 'pop into the surgery and I will give you a going over' medical, but a very, very thorough investigation into your health. Your doctor will be able to arrange this, but it is undertaken by specialised doctors – who can't be fooled! If successful, you will have to take many such medicals throughout your working life.

2. *Sponsorship scholarships* are offered to a very, very few applicants by some airlines. The best way to find out which ones currently offer these is to go to all the major airlines' websites – they will say if they are offering any partial or full sponsorships (as rare as the proverbial hens' teeth, and you will have to overcome massive competition). Today, the cost of sponsorship is often deducted from your salary once working for the airline.

3. *If you qualify for entry into the forces*, many pilots use this as a stepping stone to commercial flying.

Even if you have paid for your own training, you then have to produce evidence you have a CPL/IR (Commercial Pilot's Licence/Instrument Rating) to work for the major airlines, and generally around 200 hours logged flying time to be interviewed as a Second Officer (junior pilot).

Difficult – but not impossible, and the rewards are a fantastic job with good pay. Start browsing the web now!

Frustrations

There are frustrations galore in this job, which you have to overcome and put behind you. Sitting on the tarmac at Barcelona, the Iberia Captain's voice came over the system, full of frustration, to announce the aircraft would be subject to delay whilst the baggage belonging to someone who didn't have the correct visa for entry into Britain was off-loaded. Once that was found, we then had to wait for Air Traffic Control to allocate a new take-off time. (You will find a glossary of aviation terms at the end of the book).

Arriving at Heathrow, the captain's voice was heard again – this time ATC had told him the airport was so congested we would have to circle around waiting for a landing slot. Once landed, his voice came on again – full of disbelief. 'You are never going to believe this, but there isn't a ramp available for us to park'. All the delays meant he and his crew were out of hours, and another crew would have to take over the return flight.

There is work for Helicopter Pilots (see Training Chapter) and a small amount for balloonists who hold a Pilot's Licence.

When it comes to looking for work, don't forget the massive cargo airline industry, today worth a massive $46 billion per annum a year. '40% of world trade value is carried by commercial aircraft' according to Dora Kay, President of the International Air Cargo Association.

It all started when William Boeing and Eddie Hubbard flew the first international airmail service from Vancouver to Seattle in a Boeing Model C (a modified World War I trainer). Today Boeing predict world air cargo traffic will triple over the next 20 years and freighter fleets will double, mostly using the massive and efficient 747.

Useful Address
www.boeing.com

Hours

The number of hours that crew can work are strictly regulated by government authorities. This ensures that:

○ Pilots are alert and fit to fly aircraft.
○ Cabin attendants are fit and able to supervise emergency procedures.

Pilots' and flight attendants' working hours in domestic flying service are normally calculated in one of two ways, although many airlines use a combination of regulations and have several limits that include:

1. From the time of reporting to the airport until departing from the airport

(Duty Hours).

2. From the time the aircraft pushes back from the gate until it arrives at the gate in the destination airport (Flight Time or Hard hours).

Airline limits above are further defined by their individual State's regulatory body and/or a labour contract that may be more limiting than the State's rules. For instance, in the United States and Canada, the Regulators limit hours in number 2 above to 100 per month and 1,000 per year. However few, if any, major North American carrier labour agreements allow for more than 85 hours worked per month that includes both 1 and 2 above.

International flying has different rules applied based on the country of registry of the airline. Hours in international flying are necessarily higher to accommodate the longer stage lengths of the flying performed. Additional rules by regulators or contracts further limits the number of hours in a seven-day period (usually no more than 30) and in a single twenty-four hour day (typically no more than eight, however longer hours may apply in international flying).

There have been rumblings recently that some low cost airlines are making pilots work longer hours than they should. Although they may not actually be physically working sitting in the cockpit, by working a complex mixture of early and late shifts their sleep patterns are disrupted.

The University of Leicester has recently conducted research into this topic, which found keeping to tight schedules could mean taking off without crew meals onboard, 'making pilots dash to change aircraft ... and refusing them time to complete flight safety records'. The author of the report, Simon Bennett, urged airlines to listen to pilots because they were 'safety barometers'.

Female Pilots

BA has around 100 women pilots – other airlines, particularly those in Scandinavia, seem to have a higher percentage. BALPA say the industry would welcome more female pilots, but no-one seems to know why so few women apply.

As a woman, and author, I can probably be allowed to say that perhaps not enough specific gender-based research has been carried out to fit the person to the job. All research tends equally to be across the male and female spectrum, but in the back of my mind is the understanding that men and women are different – in case you hadn't noticed! And I can't help wondering if our female bodies (particular internal organs) take an even bigger pounding from jet lag and airline stress, than male colleagues; therefore many women decide that a job on the ground is likely to be more what they want.

So, if you are a female reading this, BALPA will welcome you. Just realise that criteria for pilot selection is so rigorous that you have the same chance as a man to be accepted – and competition is fierce. Go For It!

Salaries

As in real life, you get what you pay for. Junior pilots can earn up to £50,000 a year, a captain's salary starts at £80,000, and in airlines like Ryanair it goes up to £120,000 a year, for this airlines expect you to fund your own training – a huge sum.

Rostering; Long Haul/Short Haul

Or why you go where you are sent: this department could be said to be the hub of an airline. Without crew no airline would work, but you are dealing with human beings, not engines, and they can't just be programmed to fly – their needs have to be taken into account.

So the Rostering department will look at a flight going out and ask:

- ○ What type of aircraft?
- ○ Have crew received appropriate training or are licenced to fly that type?
- ○ How many hours/days is the aircraft away from base?
- ○ Will they need to arrange for crew to 'slip' and new crew take over?
- ○ Where is it flying – i.e. will they need to ensure crew have correct vaccinations and immunisations?

Then comes the chess game. They have to take into account any time that crew have asked to be stood down. This might be for medical reasons – perhaps they are to have an operation. Their child might have a very important date coming up, which they have promised they will try to be there for (but cabin crew kids have to learn that this might not happen). Are they allergic to certain vaccinations, so the company doctor has said they are not to fly to certain countries. Are they due an official medical check-up. etc. etc.

Then the rostering team start planning – and eventually issue the roster sheet with names of crew detailed for that flight. That is why, if you work for a large airline, you may not know any of the other crew.

Communications Manager – Inflight Service James Banerjee says:

- ○ I manage the department that issues all communications to the cabin crew. The communication ranges from work instructions, changes in regulations, company business information to product information.
- ○ I am responsible for the design and implementation of the communication plan for the Inflight Service business plan.
- ○ I support the senior management team to improve communications capabilities across the management community and work with other departmental communications managers to ensure our messages are consistent.
- ○ Through bench marking and keeping updated with the latest industry thinking, I identify best practice in communication and implement these in Inflight Service.

> ○ I manage a small team of 5 people who all work at rostering.
> ○ The bit I like the most? It's hard to say. Communication is a truly interesting area to work in. You get to know almost everything that is happening in the company. The hours can be long, but there's never a dull moment.

At bmi airline crew receive their roster 4-8 weeks in advance, which will include flying duties, and also periods where they come in ready for work, and wait to go out if someone reports in sick. These duties are extremely important, as no airline wants to have staff hanging around – they are not proving cost effective!

Virgin Atlantic passengers turned up recently to return to Britain, and found their pilot had been taken off the flight. There was no-one else to cover, so passengers had to be put up in hotels and fly out a day late – very expensive both in money and goodwill.

Stand-by duties are not popular with staff, not knowing if and when they are going to fly or where.

SKY NANNIES

A **Sky Nanny** service is available on all Gulf Air flights between London and Abu Dhabi or Sydney. Over time, the plan is to put sky nannies on all Gulf Air flights, as more sky nannies are trained through Norland College (www.norland.co.uk) in Britain. Norland train nannies (male and female) for royalty, Mick Jagger, pop stars' families, etc. and have developed a childcare training course for Gulf Air's in-flight nanny service. Thirty cabin crew took the original course, which covered dealing with demands of children up to the age of 12. One nanny per flight will look after children on board, check on dietary requirements, and keep them amused with toys, videos and games.

> **Sarah Armitage has worked for Gulf Air for nine and a half years**.
> *I was taken on from the United Kingdom, where I was working in Insurance. There are 64 nationalities working at Gulf Air, and I can't wait to get on board and start looking after my 'charges'. I love children, and was delighted to be one of the original thirty crew trained by Norland to be a Flying Nanny.*

The job a Sky Nanny does is quite simple; to do anything and everything to make life easier for parents travelling with children. From helping with boarding and disembarkation to giving parents a break during a long flight.

Gulf Air says the job of a Sky Nanny isn't confined to just helping onboard. 'When passengers arrive at the airport your Sky Nanny will be at the boarding gate to meet and escort the family onto the aircraft and take them to a dedicated seating area in the aircraft. Onboard she will then outline her role and check things like required dining times for children and any special dietary requirements arranged beforehand. She can also suggest separate dining times for children to leave parents free to enjoy their own meals.

After take-off the Sky Nanny really comes into her own, as your children now become the centre of her attention. If you're travelling with a baby your Sky Nanny will set up the bassinet. Younger children will also be handed special Gulf Air welcome packs that include various activities.

They will also organise drinks for children and do their meal service during the main bar service so you're free to assist your children if necessary – without interrupting your own meal. They'll also find lots of things to keep your children occupied throughout the journey. They even have games they can loan them. And of course it's very reassuring to know a Sky Nanny will be keeping a watchful eye on your child should you doze off or just want to get engrossed in a book or a movie.

Sarah says that the next step will be to train up to 100 cabin crew. 'We will work through the parents to entertain the children and help with meal service. On our training course we were taught about traits of children at certain ages and what we can do to keep them entertained. I love my job, and really look forward to meeting lots of children'. She was bubbling over with enthusiasm when we met, and obviously loves being with children.

BA's system is to have a dedicated lounge for Skyfliers (their name for junior fliers) who are travelling alone at Heathrow's Terminal 3. Skyfliers are well-travelled kids of ex-pats and diplomats, most of whom travel home for holidays from boarding school in Britain. Some flights to and from popular ex-pat homes such as Hong Kong can have 50 – 60 kids per flight at the start and end of holidays.

BA has lounge staff who check Skyfliers in, check their documentation to see where they are flying, if anyone is meeting them, etc. and check their ages if very young – if aged 5 they can only fly one sector – otherwise they must be aged 6-17. As you would expect the lounge has playstations, games and so many interesting things to occupy a kid's mind that sometimes they have trouble getting them on to the aircraft.

On the popular school holidays' flights BA will fly out extra staff (who actually volunteer for the job) to supervise the Skyfliers, and lend a hand to Cabin Crew. Just as well, as these kids can be a handful – not in the usual sense, but they are so 'savvy' it can be frightening. One eight year old known to the author know held up a complete plane load; he wasn't going to go on board until he had eaten the full breakfast he had been promised during a delay – and had the whole crew running after him to ensure he was properly fed.

Useful Address
www.sniperhire.net/gulfair/careers

TICKET SALES

Telesales sales staff working in Call Centres are often based in large complexes on industrial estates, in places like Glasgow and Newcastle-upon-Tyne; well away from airports and cities, as it's cheaper for the airline. There is work for anyone with a good telephone manner, and one advantage is that hours are often flexible, so this suits students and those wanting part-time work. If you are disabled, particularly wheelchair bound, this is an area which might well give you a job where you can use your skills without needing to be mobile.

If you speak a language fluently many US airlines now employ staff in British Call Centres to handle telephone bookings Europe-wide. e.g. someone in Spain phones to book a flight from Madrid to the USA. They call a local telephone number in their country, which automatically re-routes them to an office in Britain (they pay the local call charge, with the airline picking up the difference). In Britain they are answered by someone speaking fluent Spanish, and probably never know where their booking is handled. Computers linked with Spain, Germany, France, etc. will automatically issue the ticket.

In the USA, AA's call centres are currently based in Cincinnati, Cary NC, Dallas, Hartford, Honolulu, Tuscon, etc.

Useful Addresses
www.Delta.com
www.aacareers.com

Ticketing Service Agents

These are the staff who sell tickets at an airport; insiders say their days are numbered, as so many passengers now book over the web. Currently theirs is a very complex job, having to understand and quote the right fares across different sectors; but soon all they will have to do is tap in the details and print out the ticket.

Currently one reason why these staff are still so important is the inability for most airlines to interline with e-ticketing (when one airline sells a ticket whose use will mean passengers have to start their journey with their airline, then fly onward with another one or more different airlines). One airline's computer may not be able to 'communicate' with another airline; but the IT boys are working on it. However, airlines constantly tear out their hair as these staff, as soon as they are trained, then go to work for travel agents where they get the same travel concessions, but often pay is better.

WORKING ON PRIVATE JETS

There has been a remarkable increase in companies offering to hire planes and helicopters for politicians. Pop stars, musicians, royalty, prize winners, sportsmen and business people are finding that not only does your private jet give you privacy, but it can even be cheaper. Companies worried about security of their personnel, either because they are going to an area notorious for terrorism or hijacking, or because they are worried their top people might get kidnapped and held to ransom, are massive users of chartered jets. Recently one firm, Air Charter, has been awarded a Royal Warrant for organising planes for The Queen and the royal family.

Generally cabin crew and pilots will come to work for the small private companies that make up this sector, after they have worked in commercial aviation. And as one executive said 'we headhunt the staff we want', so there is no set application procedure. All you can do is find out which are the firms that operate near you, then apply to them – and wait.

> **It's not just rock stars and royalty who make use of private planes.**
> Small firms as well as big businesses can find it makes commercial sense to hire a plane with crew for a day, as it works out cheaper. Hallidays Antiques is one such small firm, which has a workshop making room panelling for private houses, restoring old buildings, etc. and is based in Dorchester-on-Thames. Their carpenters have to measure up any room that is to be panelled (a very exact process), wherever it is. They then take the measurements back to the workshop and build up the room on a plan marked on the floor – 'a bit like up-market MFI' as their MD describes it. Once the room panelling is finished, it is dismantled, flat-packed and flown to the room, where the craftsmen who have carved the wood will re-assemble their work.
>
> Hallidays often uses a private plane, flying from White Waltham near their workshop. The planes take up to six craftsmen, who can fly to most places in Europe in the day, do the measurements or re-assemble the panelling, and get back at night. In total it works out much cheaper than buying plane tickets on a scheduled flight, having to travel the extra mileage to Heathrow, then travel from an international airport rather than a local one, plus the cost of hotel rooms.

WORKING IN CARGO

There are dedicated cargo airlines, such as Federal Express, DHL,TNT, etc. Most large airlines also have their own cargo divisions to handle the business to this lucrative side.

BA World Cargo is the world's fifth largest international cargo carrier; they have around 3,000 people working at Ascentis, their cargo centre near Heathrow, with one of the largest automated freight depots in the world.

BAA's airports handle around 30% of UK cargo exports, valued around £50 billion. Fruit and vegetables are now major cargos, but until a few years ago no-one would have thought it worthwhile flying strawberries or cherries half way around the world. It all started when TWA (the US airline) wanted to utilise spare capacity, and offered the fruit growers of Florida cheap space in cargo holds to export all their spare grapefruit across the Atlantic to what, in those days, were new markets in Europe. The idea took off, and now countries such as Kenya depend on their exports of beans, mange-tout, baby sweetcorn, etc to the UK. Over 250,000 tons of fresh goods came in from Africa in 2002, although one wonders how long this will last; these countries emphasise they can supply organic produce, but shoppers are beginning to question how 'organic' something is that has had to pollute the atmosphere travelling half way across the world. However, it is certain that cargo airlines will keep on searching for new goods to carry, so pilots working for these airlines would seem to have a relatively secure future.

One expanding market is the courier and parcel delivery services offered by airlines such as DHL, Federal Express, UPS, TNT, etc. To deliver the massive amount of goods and parcels they handle every day, each company has their own cargo airline, dedicated to delivering your goods across the globe. Even the Royal Mail has its own fleet of planes.

Useful Addresses
www.dhl.com
www.emerald-airways.co.uk
www.fedex.com
www.tnt.com
www.ups.com

Aid Crisis

Whenever there is an aid crisis – war, famine, earthquake etc. – TV shows pictures of aircraft being loaded with relief supplies. These aircraft are generally giant Antonovov aircraft, possibly operated by specialist companies such as Antonov Airlines or Volga Dnepr. Volga Dnepr was the first private all-cargo carrier in Russia, operating nine AN-124 100 'Ruslan' aircraft, with a load lifting capacity of 120 tons in its 1,100 cubic metre hold.

Recently Antonov Airlines, based at Kiev in the Ukraine, entered the Guinness World of Records with a giant load of a Siemens power generator, weighing 135.2 tons. This was airlifted from Dusseldorf in Germany to Delhi in India. Shortly afterwards they transported 270 tonnes of excavating equipment from St. Petersburg to Novosibirsk in Siberia.

Planning how and where to carry this cargo took the airline's logistics experts three months. Originally the cargo, equipment for constructing an underground railway, was built in Canada, then transported by sea to St.Petersburg. Then the only way for it to reach its destination was by plane, and two AN-124-100 aircraft were used, each taking a 135 ton load.

Stansted Airport is the fastest growing airport in Europe, and has over 30 dedicated cargo airlines operating out of it, largely because of good connections to Britain's motorway network and London. This cargo is as diverse as Formula One racing cars, flowers and racehorses (the airport is near Newmarket, HQ of British racing).

There is so much parcel traffic in and out of Stansted that Federal Express has its own dedicated unit with aircraft stands; TNT and DHL also have a considerable presence.

LOYALTY PROGRAMMES

These started in the States, where airlines decided that it was cheaper to keep current customers flying with them, than go out and advertise for new clients. So someone had the bright idea that as there were often empty seats on aircraft, it made sense to offer these as a bonus to frequent fliers.

These fliers could build up 'air miles' every time they flew, and cash these in when they had enough to give them a free flight. American Airlines were the first to launch a scheme in 1981 and now has the largest scheme in the world with more than 45 million members. According to The Times, 'the world's second biggest currency .... is the air mile. Worldwide stock of unused air miles is currently standing at about eight trillion'. Many airlines now report unused miles as a liability on balance sheets, and use is rising around 7 – 9% a year.

For some airlines, their only profitable section is their air miles scheme, which today is usually franchised out to separate companies who are experts in administering these schemes. On behalf of airlines they also make money by 'selling' miles to credit card companies and other firms, which then award air miles to clients.

In Britain, The AirMiles Travel Company is a full service travel company, needing staff whose expertise is available to everybody who collects air miles. These staff will be offering people who telephone their company the chance to fly with over 18 airlines, with access to 20,000 hotels worldwide and over 50 of the UK's top travel operators.

Recently BAA announced they had joined up with the AirMiles Travel Company.
BAA's customer loyalty programme WorldPoints enables members, who include the highest spending most frequent fliers, to collect points on almost all airport spending and redeem them for a range of rewards. They also receive regular communications updating them on the latest news and offers in airport shopping and travel. WorldPoints members can now redeem 250 WorldPoints for 30 air miles which can then be used in isolation or combined with cash to pay for holidays, flights and car hire.

At the launch, Drew Thomson, MD of AirMiles, announced plans 'to treble in size by 2005. Over 120 million people pass through BAA's seven

UK airports annually and our partnership with them sets us well on the road to achieving this goal'.

There are a number of ways AirMiles recruit people for their travel centre in Birchwood: recruitment campaigns with the aim of 100-150 new travel experts; Open Days in Manchester; adverts in local press and travel trade press. The recruitment number is 01925- 848614, or e-mail travelexperts@airmiles.co.uk.

CAREER PROGRESSION

British airline companies are amongst the largest, most efficient, and most profitable in the world. Generally an airline starts you with an induction programme, the length of which depends upon the type of work you choose to do. Most airlines have a well defined career structure and are particularly good at training.

Ground staff at airports with efficient management skills and qualifications can progress to become airport managers. These usually have responsibility for specific areas such as security, safety, and operations at the airport.

There will also be opportunities at the airline offices requiring supervisory staff for reservations teams, sales and marketing managers, and business planning and development role.

Useful Addresses
www.firstchoice.co.uk
www.britanniaairways.com
www.britishairwaysjobs.com
www.flybmi.com
www.easyJet.com
www.monarch-airlines.com
www.scotways.co.uk
www.virgin-atlantic.com, etc

For more contacts see the *Web Addresses* chapter.

Cabin Crew

Where Are the Jobs and What are They?

On board any commercial passenger-carrying aircraft there will be a flight crew of pilot/s and cabin crew, sometimes known as **Flight Attendants** or **Stewards/ Stewardesses** (or even Trolley Dollies), to fly with passengers to their destination, and look after their needs whilst flying. Cabin crew ensure safety announcements and demonstrations are given; they see that passengers are looked after, given food and drinks where appropriate, sold duty free goods and appropriate customs paperwork is filled out, give out appropriate immigration forms, look after children, the disabled and elderly passengers, ensure the film and/or videos are running properly, etc. The number one reason why cabin crew *have* to be on board is safety. If IATA and international law suddenly declared there was no need for cabin crew to be there to supervise emergency landings, most airlines would decide to dispense with them on short haul flights – at least in the economy section. Even on long haul flights numbers would be reduced.

Once the aircraft arrives at its destination, there will be a team of ground handling staff to meet the aircraft, liaise with cabin crew and arrange transfers, sort out wheelchairs and disabled transport, supervise luggage arrival – and possibly deal with lost (or in airline-speak – misrouted) luggage.

Meanwhile an army of cleaners come on board to clean the plane (cabin crew may have to do this with some airlines), cabin crew have to check that food has arrived from caterers and that a bowser comes out to re-fuel the aircraft ready for turn-around and the next load of passengers.

Facing Facts

Without doubt the highest-profile job in aviation is that of cabin crew. Perhaps you want to fly around the world, and quite fancy stopovers in tropical locations. You imagine being a cabin crew member will give you such an exotic life-style.

When you start out you are far more likely to be working on internal or domestic flights (those inside a country). Instead of lolling beside a swimming pool, you will be rushing to clean the aircraft before the next lot of passengers. Having said that, it still beats the rush hour commute, for variety and interest if nothing else.

Any airline work involves shifts (even though many British airports theoretically shut down at night to give locals a chance to sleep). If you are abroad flying into Britain, you have to take off in the middle of the night to enable flights to arrive whilst UK airports are open. Unfair, but historically this happens because between the two world wars Imperial Airways started a worldwide network connecting the old British Empire. It stretched around the globe. Other airlines 'fed' into their system, and so developed an interlocking network, which would be next to impossible to dismantle today.

Cabin crew hate the erratic hours; go to the BA website and you see Vanessa saying she hates the instability of the life and the roster (timetable) changes. Joanne, a Cabin Services Director, says she dislikes the constant tiredness due to jetlag. If local public transport is erratic, or doesn't start early enough (and you have to report several hours before a flight takes off) you may have to have access to a car.

Low cost airlines have opened up new routes, encouraging many more people to fly regularly. Because they are low cost, these airlines have cut costs to the bone, flying into small airports with cheaper landing fees scattered around Europe, that not many people have heard of. But this is good for local business, and eventually good for local jobs. However, if a new route is not as profitable as hoped – then it is chopped, and you may lose your job.

However, on the plus side even if airlines drop a route, they have to keep their aircraft flying, so they will look for new routes, and will then need staff to work on these aircraft.

Working Conditions

All airlines have to employ several crews for each aircraft they own (pilot/s and cabin crew). For safety reasons IATA (International Air Transport Association, the worldwide regulatory body) state that crew are only allowed to work a certain number of hours per year. So this means changes of crew if the planes are to keep flying.

With most airlines crew will be allocated to a certain type (Airbus, 747, etc.) because they have been trained in emergency procedures for that type of aircraft. Different planes have their emergency exits in different areas – and it wouldn't do in an emergency to have to go looking to find the exit doors. This means that cabin staff will be allocated work according to which aircraft they have been checked out on. It can mean working with a different crew every time you fly, so you have to be a good team worker.

Some airlines may employ less than 1,000 staff, but the giant companies such as British Airways (BA) employ upwards of 13,000 cabin crew. When there is a downturn in bookings and you read stories saying '1000 cabin crew to be sacked', what this usually means is that the airline mentioned will halt recruitment and rely on natural wastage to bring down numbers; until bookings rise and recruitment starts again.

The majority of BA staff are based at Heathrow and Gatwick, but there are small teams at Manchester and Glasgow. In addition, BA teams are based at strategic overseas locations such as Buenos Aires, Delhi and Bahrain. As BA say, working for them '*is about delivering outstanding customer service in all* conditions. *At its most fundamental level, you are responsible for passenger safety in the cabin. Beyond that, crews share a common goal – to see British Airways customers walk away at the end of a flight contented'.* Crew members are expected to be totally flexible as to where they are based and which routes they fly.

A Typical Day for Cabin Crew

The day begins when cabin crew arrive at their reporting centre. If they work for British Airways or similar airlines that use IT for crew contact, they will use their pass to swipe through a slot at a bank of computers. Once the computer has identified them, confirmation details and e-mail messages come up on the screen. By checking in for their flight they confirm they have read and understood all safety messages. At this point they find out which room to go to for their pre-flight briefing, where the cabin crew team meet up with the Cabin Service Director (CSD) who goes over the flight details and assigns the crew to their working positions on board. Each crew member knows from his or her working position which emergency exit he or she is responsible for during take-off and landing. A Purser (supervisory crew member) is also assigned for each class, and crew assigned to the First Class cabin will generally have received additional training.

At the briefing the crew are told about VIPs and special passengers, such as disabled, children etc. Any modifications to the aircraft type or schedule are discussed and every crew member is tested on their knowledge of aviation safety and first aid, before everyone boards the bus to take them to the aircraft. Anyone who is unable to answer their safety and first aid questions correctly is offloaded and is replaced by a crewmember on standby. Not being up-to-date with safety and first aid is a serious matter and usually means the person concerned must be re-trained, and continued failure may lead to being declared unfit for the role.

James Banerjee, who worked for Air Cabin Crew with British Airways long haul based at Gatwick, explains, 'before the passengers arrive, you go over safety procedures, checking equipment in the cabin. The pursers liaise with the catering staff to ensure sufficient meals are loaded (and as a precaution that there are different meals for the captain and co-pilot).

By now the passengers are beginning to board and you have already positioned yourself in the cabin ready to greet them with a smile. You help them find seats and show them where to place their hand baggage (being careful as you are not covered by insurance if you hurt yourself when lifting heavy bags for passengers). On a short flight there are a huge number of tasks that have to be completed within tight timescales, from safety demonstrations to serving meals and selling duty free. On longer sectors other challenges, like restless children and jetlag, will test your ability to handle the pressure.

Once the plane takes off, the bars are opened for passengers; Customs regulations prevent them from being opened any earlier. The drinks service is set up and the crew go into the cabins and offer the passengers a drink from the bar. Depending on the length of the flight they may go out again and do another drinks service before the meal. While the crew are serving drinks, the purser prepares the meals. After they have cleared up the bottles, cans and glasses from the drinks service, the crew then take out the main meal, and serve these to the passengers. A little while later tea and coffee is served, followed by another clear up. Once all the used trays have been collected in and the passengers have settled down again, the duty free trolley is checked (very important, as crew will often receive a percentage of sales, which adds to take home pay) and wheeled out. Sales are higher on some sectors and low on others. For example you may not sell much on a flight to New York, but on the run to Lagos you could sell everything and have to be careful to leave some stock for the return crew to sell – otherwise you won't be very popular. The crew share approximately 10% of the sales as commission, but this varies according to which airline you work for.

By now you are famished, so as the passengers settle down you are ready for your own meal. Crew meals are usually different from those provided for passengers. You then set out snacks in the galleys, particularly in Club Class (First Class has à la carte service). For safety reasons you have to patrol the cabins every twenty minutes. You use this time wisely to provide additional customer service, for example by taking out drinks to people. You will also find people will take the time to talk to you about everything – in a short space of time they can reveal their life history.

Then it is time to prepare for landing; once landed James and his colleagues take a well-earned rest. They have been on their feet for hours and time changes can make you very tired. Time changes and dehydration are two of the biggest challenges and can make you very light-headed, even though BA provides bottles of water for the crew. It takes longer to get over jet lag when flying across time zones, rather than runs to Africa when there won't be more than one or two hours' change. Therefore on a flight to New York the crew will have 24 hours off before their return flight, and three days off when they return home. To Lagos they still have 24 hours off, but only two days rest on their return.

As BA say, '*Working as a member of our Cabin Crew is not so much a job as a way of life. In many ways it's a privileged life, with opportunities to visit places and experience cultures that are beyond most people's reach*'.

Before reading further, see if you match up to a sample job advert for a recent job with BA. Most airlines will require many if not all of the same criteria, so you should think about what you need to know, such as any training that will add to your skills, etc.

Sample Advertisement from British Airways

AIR CABIN CREW – CCSLHR103
Location: *London, Heathrow,*
Dept: *In-flight Services*
Status: *Permanent /Full-Time*
Uniform: *Yes*
Shift Work: *Yes*
Closing: *No closing date*

The Role
Representing British Airways as a member of our Cabin Crew is a unique experience. Our customers have their own unique needs and require-ments. You'll find every day holds a different challenge. From the moment you welcome our customers aboard the aircraft, their safety and comfort are your responsibility. Your role includes all aspects of customer care from communication to serving refreshments. You will hold the key to our customers having a fantastic flight and most importantly, wanting to fly with us again. There are vacancies at both London, Gatwick and London, Heathrow.

APPLICATION CRITERIA:

- Age 19 or over at time of application.
- At least 5ft 2in (11.58 metres).
- Educated to GCSE standard or equivalent with passes at C or above in English and Maths.
- High standard of written and spoken English.
- Complete a comprehensive medical questionnaire.
- Hold an EU Passport with unrestricted worldwide travel.
- A GNVQ or equivalent qualification in Nursing/Hospitality/Travel.
- Tourism or Care Services plus 12 months customer service experi-ence or 2 years consecutive airline customer service experience.

Legislation controlling access to restricted zones at all UK airports (known as 'airside access') requires British Airways to carry out additional back-ground checks for all new employees requiring a permanent restricted zone security pass. As part of these background checks, British Airways will require you to successfully complete a criminal record check at basic disclosure level before you can commence employment. This is in addition to references that we will also need to obtain from previous employers.

Desired Skills:

O Motivation to deliver excellent customer service.
O Emotional resilience.
O Interpersonal skills.
O Team skills.
O Commercial Awareness.

You as a person:

O Friendly and caring personality.
O Competent in handling difficult situations.
O Confident communicator and great listener.
O Supportive of colleagues and a team player.
O Able to remain calm and efficient under pressure.
O Willing to treat everyone as an individual.
O Satisfy current BA/CAA health requirements.
O Take pride in personal grooming with no visible tattoos or piercings.

Education:

O Educated to GCSE standard or equivalent with passes at C or above in English and Maths.
O Good standard of written and spoken English.
O Ability to converse in a second language is desirable.

Experience Required:
A GNVQ or equivalent qualification in Nursing/Hospitality/Travel & Tourism or Care Services plus 12 months customer service experience OR 2 years consecutive airline customer service experience.

The Benefits

O Full time basic starting salary £9,210 per annum.
O Flying allowances variable and can vary each month depending on trip allocation.
O Typical new entrant cabin crew member can expect to earn in the region of £500 per month additional flying allowances.
O Holiday entitlement is 30 days (including public holidays pro-rated in first year).
O Hotel accommodation whilst on flying duty.
O Free Uniform, worn in accordance with uniform regulations.
O Profit share scheme.
O Bonus.

- Employee share scheme.
- Car park, subsided catering, sports and social facilities.
- Choice of contributory pension and private healthcare schemes.
- Opportunities for reduced air fare travel and travel discounts (at the company's discretion).

But remember

- As the flying operation is 365 days a year, Cabin Crew must be able to fly on public holidays and religious festivals.
- Your remuneration package will be determined by your individual contract of employment.

Nice things

BA staff, like other cabin crew, have positive things to say about their jobs. They wouldn't stay in the job if the benefits didn't outweigh the disadvantages. Vanessa likes 'the people I work with'; Yumiko from the team based in Japan loves seeing different countries and exploring their cultures. 'I am always excited when I open my roster to discover my forthcoming trips'. Joanne says she welcomes the opportunity to fly all around the world, stay in beautiful hotels, and meet fascinating new people. On a flight to Johannesburg she looked after Nelson Mandela. It was wonderful to meet someone I had admired and respected for so long. He was everything I expected him to be – quietly spoken, polite, with the most amusing face full of character'.

WHAT COMPANIES LOOK FOR

Some companies' requirements are easy to understand, but you may wonder why they are so specific about things like height. This is for safety reasons – you must be able to reach up to lockers to bring out life-saving equipment, but not so tall that you can't stand up straight without hitting the ceiling. There was a wonderful airline called Suckling Airways operating out of East Anglia, who specified short cabin crew because they flew small planes with low headroom. You could also phone Mrs. Suckling and tell her what you wanted in your sandwiches – those were the days! They were taken over by ScotAirways, who say we have a maximum height restriction of 5ft 11ins, but do not specify a minimum height, though staff members would have to be able to reach the overhead lockers.

ScotAirways say it would like the opportunity for people not quite reaching 5ft 2ins, to get an airline job, 'if there was more knowledge of the fact that we recruit 'shorties'. The only issue with giving shorter people a chance to fly is that their progression as far as a career is concerned is limited. ScotAirways have bases at Edinburgh, Dundee, London City and Southampton Airports. Employees would have to live within a 30 minute radius of their chosen base.

We are not a huge recruiter of staff. We only recruit when someone leaves'.

Personal qualities required:

○ Able to work well in a team.
○ Stamina.
○ Smart appearance.
○ Ability to 'think on your feet'.
○ Good communication skills.
○ Customer service abilities.
○ Common sense.
○ Literacy and numeracy.
○ Outgoing personality.
○ Enthusiasm and flexible approach.
○ Experience of dealing with the general public.

You will need a happy personality that can give everyone a smile at the end of an 18 hour duty session. And the ability to ignore the fact that your feet have no feeling at the end of a long day!

Cabin Crew Requirements

There are specific requirements for people applying for jobs as cabin crew – some of them are subject to international regulations:

○ Minimum age for cabin crew is generally 20+ (but not with BA; see above).
○ Excellent health and good eye sight is needed, but contact lenses are usually accepted.
○ Height generally from 5ft 2ins-6ft 2ins (1.57m-1.87m) with weight in proportion.
○ Cabin crew MUST be able to swim – this is a legal requirement as officially crew are on an aircraft to help passengers in the event of an accident, which might mean ditching into water.
○ Good standard of general education.
○ Clear speech and good spoken English (even if you are working for a non-British or US airline, if airlines fly internationally you HAVE to be able to speak English as aviation's international language).
○ Other languages are an asset, including sign language.
○ Some airlines will require specific languages.
○ Customer service experience.
○ Passport that can be validated for travel to all countries covered by an airline's routes.
○ Car driver and owner or have means of 24 hour transport to base.

We have included British Airway's requirements as it is one of the world's major airlines; most airlines have the same requirements, the only addition being that a few airlines will only recruit their own nationals, and some require you must speak the airline's 'home' language.

An Airline's Mission Statement

Lisa Ulberg from Scandinavian Airlines System (SAS) kindly sent us their 'mission statement'

We view each customer as an individual with personal needs and desires, which it is our task to fulfil.

Our service must be characterised by simplicity, freedom of choice and consideration. We must be the equals of our passengers and have them feel that they are being well cared for, while at the same time we stand for absolute safety and punctuality.

SAS is a Scandinavian company working in an international environment. We view cultural/ethnic diversity as an asset and strive for a working environment which is characterised by knowledge, respect and tolerance towards other cultures.

The vision of SAS is to make Scandinavians proud of their airline and as an employee you are an important and self-evident part of that process.

We fly about 20 million customers per year and each customer has on the average ten contacts with some of us during their journey. It is on these occasions that the customer's good impression of SAS can be reinforced and hence where you as an employee become our greatest competitive advantage.

As an employee onboard, you need to possess qualities which at times can seem to be the direct opposites of each other. For example, this means that along with having to be sensitive and service-minded you must also be an authoritarian leader in an emergency situation. You must also like intensive contact with people, while at the same time being able to manage things on your own when you find yourself in a different place, often in a different country. Your schedule is given to you roughly 14 days in advance and it includes standby obligations. Standby means that you are on-call and can be called upon to work at short notice.

The work is characterised by a large degree of irregularity and a fast pace. It involves contact with many people and new colleagues each and every day.

Different duties onboard

Onboard in the cabin, there are a number of occupational groups. To begin with, you will work as a flight attendant or steward. After a number of years in the profession and additional training from

SAS, you will eventually have the opportunity to become a purser, in other words the cabin manager.

As a flight attendant you will work with safety onboard, help the passengers feel at home, serve beverages and meals, assist with possible sales and see to it that our customers are looked after and generally feel happy.

As a steward, you have by and large the same tasks to perform, however with a special focus on food.

At every departure you work with representatives of other departments. This involves technicians, personnel at the gate, cargo handlers and many others. When you work onboard, you are a part of an entire team, working for optimum safety, punctuality and service.

Safety, punctuality and service

Safety, punctuality and service are the three cornerstones of our company, they are the baseline level of our quality. When you work onboard, you are involved with all of them.

The foundation of this baseline quality level is always safety onboard. You will thus be trained in managing an emergency situation and be able to convey knowledge and confidence to those passengers who possibly are ill at ease over the prospect of flying.

The second part of the baseline quality level is punctuality. It can perhaps appear difficult to influence when you work onboard, however there are many things to contribute.

Helping the passengers to find their seats quickly and to stow away their carry-on baggage in the proper manner is just one example.

The third part of the baseline quality level, service, is what makes the passengers feel good when they fly with us – to feel at home and well attended to.

Training under the auspices of SAS

The training lasts for approx. six weeks and is held at the SAS Flight Academy in either Stockholm or Copenhagen.

Safety routines and first aid are important factors in the part of the training involving safety. Among other things, you will experience simulated emergency situations and practice extinguishing fires.

In the service part of the training, passenger psychology is also included. You will also receive training in preparing and serving meals both in training cabins at the school as well as in the air.

During the training, which is free, there are no wages and after its completion you will be offered a trial employment position for six months. Welcome to Scandinavian Airlines.

(N.B. Some airlines pay a small retainer during training, others pay nothing).

CAREER PROGRESSION

Wherever you live, generally an airline starts you with an induction programme, the length of which depends upon the type of work you choose to do. Most airlines have a well-defined career structure and are particularly good at training. With a small airline, you may have to wait until someone leaves before you can take the next step and join the flying crew, but with major airlines there is a well-defined path to the top. However, as you progress up the career ladder you find there is more paperwork; sometimes cabin crew don't want to bother so prefer to stay at entry grades.

Career Ladder

In general cabin crew with major airlines start off by working on older aircraft, progressing up to larger/more modern aircraft by taking the appropriate training. Eventually you become a team leader, known as **Purser** or **Cabin Service Director** (but different airlines have different job titles).

Once cabin crew decide they have had enough of flying, they often take a job on the ground training new cabin crew. This is always a large section of the personnel department in an airline, as not only do new staff need training, but current staff have to have their training up-dated at frequent intervals for safety reasons.

Air Cabin Crew Vocational Qualification

Recently this new qualification has been developed by Pan Aviation Training, and is being offered in colleges in Britain. Devised by cabin crew, the training includes a day in a simulator at a local airport where you 'ditch' into water, and carry out emergency evacuation procedures in a full-size replica aircraft.

This training has been very successful; airlines are pleased that it gives applicants a good idea of what they want, plus teaching the basics of safety such as smoke procedures and ditching drill. Many airlines now contact the colleges running the course to give their students first chance at job vacancies, and have asked for more recruits via this course.

WHEN DO AIRLINES RECRUIT?

Airline recruitment is almost continuous, with most airlines having large personnel departments or agencies to handle their interviewing. If large amounts of staff are required you may well see adverts in national newspapers or in trade magazines. If you have access to the Internet it is well worth trawling the recruitment sites in the *Web Addresses* chapter who post new job opportunities on a daily basis.

Do realise that from the time you go for your first interview until the time you take-off on your first flight can take six months or more.

If you want to work for an airline and live in another country, watch Emirates website for recruitment Open Days in London, Birmingham, Leeds, Milan, Paris, Berlin, Brisbane, Cairns, Melbourne, Auckland, Cape Town, Tokyo, Vancouver, Dublin, Romania, Brazil, Argentina, etc.

They require 1,000 extra cabin crew in the next two years, to be based in Dubai, along with crew from over 100 countries.

Emirates' Vice Chairman and Group President Maurice Flanagan, says

The Open Day is aimed at attracting top quality employees from the UK as part of a drive to double the airline's workforce by the end of the decade.

One of the many reasons why people from the UK are so sought after and excellent at this job is because they are well-known for their warm personalities and gracious hospitality. Being an employee-focused company, we are committed to providing staff with competitive salaries, attractive benefits and excellent working conditions.

Useful Address
www.emiratesgroupcareers.com

Under Eighteen?

You can still prepare for working by taking courses that will be useful and look good on your CV:

1. Take a First Aid Course run by organisations such as the Red Cross or Red Crescent, St. John's Ambulance or a hospital.
2. In Britain take the four-day course in Health and Safety offered by many Environmental Health Departments at Town Halls; similar courses are run by local authorities in other countries.
3. Start reading a quality newspaper. You will be asked questions on general knowledge at your interview, and reading a newspaper is excellent preparation.
4. If you are taking a GNVQ make sure it includes the Travel Geography option.
5. Help out with a local charity looking after children, disabled or older people. At a recent interview of 300 people, all the 19 accepted had done some kind of community or voluntary charity work.
6. Take a one-day course that tells you what airlines are looking for, interview techniques, etc.

The Downside

There is nothing more tiring than working some days as cabin crew. Either you are criss-crossing Europe on short-haul flights with hardly time to off-load one lot of passengers before the next arrives on board, or you are on your feet for a long-haul flight for hour upon hour. Everyone will tell you this is when gripes come to the fore – and to avoid getting a reputation as the crew-member they dislike flying with – just take a deep breath and remember:

1. Always muck in. If your job is done, help out a colleague.
2. Stay out of on-board politics.
3. Complaints have a ripple effect. Don't be a goody-goody who can find something nice to say about every problem, but do remember that a sympathetic presence and no grumbles makes you more popular with fellow workers.
4. If a passenger annoys you – follow the advice of my favourite Purser; 'just take a deep breath and smile. It might make them stop – on the other hand it might annoy the hell out of them, but there is nothing they can do'.

EXECUTIVE JETS

Many companies own their own corporate jets, which need cabin crew of a very high standard. The work sounds glamorous, and it is – but it can also mean starting work very early in the morning as the directors jet off for a business meeting, then waiting all day on a cold, wet and windy airfield (and once the directors have been whisked away in the company limousine, there is often no other transport into the local town), then having to be all smiling when they return late.

It isn't only the jet set that uses these planes. Many companies find it cheaper to hire their own plane if several executives have to attend the same meeting. If you are unlucky enough to have an accident abroad, and you carry insurance, you may be repatriated home on a private jet. This will be staffed by freelance nurses who are on constant call for emergencies.

An Unusual Job

In the words of Liz, the **Corporate Jet Stewardess:** *you could say I fell into this work by accident. I was feeling pretty miserable – the low cost airline I worked for had just gone bust (too low cost to keep the bank happy), leaving over 300 of us looking for jobs. My sister had a boyfriend who worked for the local oil company as a pilot for their corporate jet and said their regular stewardess was pregnant, and as soon as the company doctor knew this she would be grounded. Was I interested in her job? Was I! I was down to the offices faster than Concorde. They roared with laughter when I turned up on a bike – saying it would do their corporate eco-friendly image a lot of good – and somehow after that, even though my interview lasted almost all day, and was far more searching than when I applied to my previous employers, it was interesting. They phoned as soon as I arrived home to offer me the job.*

I soon realised that the searching questions were the first of very, very thorough security checks. I had to fill out forms detailing every member of the family, where they were born, etc. Then it was off to a very smart

London tailors for a beautiful uniform which I love wearing. I was warned that the job was not glamorous – and when you are serving coffee (no alcohol on oil companies' jets) to a team of roustabouts dressed in creased overalls at 5 am, I can see their point. But we work as a team, and often have to go to France to an installation in the Bay of Biscay. I have discovered there is a marvellous market in the local town; the airport bus takes me there, and all my employers give me shopping lists to fill. Friends think I am stupid to do shopping for others – I say it helps pass the time and as I order such vast amounts of food the stall keepers usually give me my own goods for free.

Liz works a shift system; she looks after the executives as they fly between Aberdeen and Scandinavia, when she often has to stay away in very comfortable hotels; if a worker is injured the plane might be sent to pick them up and Liz will have a registered nurse and sometimes a doctor working as part of the crew. Liz loves these flights —the look of relief on the worker's face when they turn up is worth a lot.

She has to organise the catering on board, which means liaising with a catering company, and ensuring that they take along all the favourite foods of the various executives – she once forgot to order the Chairman's Smarties – never again! He still teases her unmercifully by 'refusing' to allow the pilot to take off until Liz has presented him with his tube on a silver salver.

Every so often she has to go on refresher courses for safety training, and she has taken a catering course which helped her serve food in a more appetising way. Recently the company has bought another jet, capable of flying as far as the Middle East. This entailed Liz going on a Foreign Office course learning about local etiquette, such as presenting food with the right hand. She has started to teach herself Arabic, and enjoys welcoming local staff in their own language. She is thinking about her next career move, but enjoys being part of a company team – so it's not just yet!

WHAT NEXT?

Other airlines have tried to copy the successful formula adopted by Southwest Airlines in the States, famous for procedures such as staff 'camping up' safety announcements; apparently everyone listened as they didn't want to miss any of the jokes (one way of ensuring passengers listen to safety announcements). However, what works for this airline might not work for others.

Recently First Choice Airways in the UK decided that cabin crew should be 'more flirty and fluffy' by creating a 'playful' cabin culture to combat the sterile impersonal atmosphere on many airlines. According to newspaper reports, crew members will be dubbed 'starlets' and will spend more time storytelling and giving informative descriptions of meals. Sounds interesting – to say the least – but open to misinterpretation?

Airport Jobs

BACKGROUND TO AIRPORT OPERATIONS

Airports around the world have different owners. Airports can be owned, and sometimes run by a:

- ○ Government.
- ○ Public Limited Company.
- ○ Private Company.
- ○ Local Business.
- ○ Airline(s).
- ○ Local Chamber of Commerce.
- ○ Aircraft manufacturer.

Normally airports are public limited companies (or their equivalent) and are expected to make an operating profit, although if the Government owns the airport this might not be an important factor.

Airport size varies from small local airports operating limited hours, up to the mega-sized international venues open up to 24 hours a day, or as many hours as local amenity groups have negotiated.

Local airports are the lifeline of many local economies and local chambers of commerce and town halls are proud of them: as the Major of Stuttgart says 'more than seven million passengers, cargo to the value of over €8 billion and over 7,000 employees characterise the economic activity at the airport and underline its vital importance to industry in Baden-Würtemmberg' in Germany.

Airports are there to service travellers and/or goods imported and exported, and provide facilities to enable different types of aircraft to land and take off (airlines, private planes, helicopters, cargo airlines, etc).

Air traffic is expanding around the world, but many Airlines claim a major factor holding back their development is airport capacity. This means the number of flights that can land and take off during airport opening hours. There is a limit to the number of flights that can be handled in a terminal each day, and airlines don't like it if their aircraft are up in the sky circling around waiting for runway space to land (fuel costs money). So there is constant friction between local environmental groups, who want a peaceful life, and the demands of airport operators who want as many flights to land each day as possible.

When the first commercial flight from Heathrow took off for Buenos Aires in

1946, planners never imagined the number of passengers that would want to fly from the airport today, so built a relatively narrow approach road tunnel under the runway: they have been regretting the jams this causes ever since. So BAA opened the Heathrow Express, using the Underground tunnel, encourage passengers to come by train. Today 2% of BAA staff work on the Heathrow Express.

However, the good news is that most airports are now expanding once their owners realise the amount of revenue that can be made from airport retail, and local tourism businesses realise the revenue that comes from the spin-off due to increased visitors. Airports such as Charles de Gaulle in Paris, Frankfurt, Schiphol in the Netherlands etc. are vying to try to topple Heathrow from its position as the world's busiest international airport – all factors which will increase jobs.

Recently the UK Government announced proposed new runways for Stansted Airport, Heathrow, Birmingham and Edinburgh – so managing to alienate pressure groups across the country, who were hoping they had a 50/50 chance of avoiding a new runway in their back yard. However, politicians are always on the lookout for votes, and a new runway is a sure vote loser. Cynics say these plans will go to public consultation, locals will raise millions to fight the planners, and the end result will be that the runways will be built – eventually.

For Scotland, Donal Dowds, managing director of BAA Scotland, says: 'Passenger traffic at Edinburgh and Glasgow Airports continues to grow, reflecting recent positive trends, while Aberdeen remains affected by a steady reduction in the numbers of people travelling on oil-related services, particularly those served by helicopter. BAA Scotland is committed to developing and growing each of our airports in Scotland, working with all those concerned to ensure that our facilities support and promote local and national economic development.' In other words, BAA is committed to make certain more people fly, which means more jobs. BAA isn't the only airport operator in the UK. Other operators include local authorities, and TBI who own and run Luton Airport, Belfast and Cardiff, plus Skavsta, Stockholm, as well as operating, managing or providing services at airports in the US such as Orlando, and three in Bolivia. Many of TBI's airports are used by the 'no frills' airlines, who are expected to increase business in the next few years.

Airport rivalry is good for employment, and it looks as if this will continue for some time. In Britain Heathrow is being challenged by Luton, Gatwick and Stansted. Outside the London area, Birmingham, Manchester, Glasgow, Edinburgh etc. all have plans for expansion – and if they can persuade the trans-Atlantic carriers to make their airport a Gateway (entrance) airport, even more traffic could be generated. Abroad, demands from tourism and business fliers are driving airport expansion around the world. Sadly the only losers will be people living under airport approach flight paths – double-glazing salesmen must be in demand.

Airports are exciting places at which to work, with a huge demand for staff; over 70,000 people work at Heathrow Airport alone. Aéroports de Paris, the authority in charge of running the airports in the Paris region, say there are over

70,000 persons working at Roissy Charles de Gaulle. And O'Hare, Singapore, Dubai, Frankfurt, and hundreds of other airports around the world can similarly point to large working populations.

An International Airport is like a miniature city, containing everything from a Chapel to its own Police force. Every airport needs a small army of people doing different and exciting jobs.

Unlike the docu-soap 'Airline', the recent BBC TV series 'Airport' gave a very positive view of working at an airport, and skilful editing bought out the personal qualities needed from staff. Remember the Terminal Manager, always on the go? Her job was never boring, with new challenges every day.

A new job, but one that is becoming increasingly important is that of an airport's **Route Development Manager** – often in charge of a team supporting development. This job is particularly important for smaller, lesser-known airports, wanting to get on the bandwagon by encouraging low-cost airlines to use their airport. Attracting a low-cost carrier to your airport can increase annual passenger numbers by as much as 250,000 or more; a big increase in turnover. When a small airport such as Newquay started receiving flights operated by a low-cost carrier, traffic increased from a steady c.60,000 passengers a year to nearer 250,000.

Attracting low-cost carriers is good business for the whole area around the airport. They bring in more tourists, offer business travellers a greater choice of flights to fit in with meetings, and encourage people to buy properties and invest in the area. In some areas in France whole communities have been revived thanks to the influx of buyers looking for properties to buy and invest their money in restoring; craftsmen benefit – from builders to plumbers – and this keeps locals in work.

No longer is it up to Governments to decide where it would be a good idea to have a flight between one point and another. This worked in the past, but now Governments are no longer in the business of supporting an official carrier, new routes are only opened after a very thorough commercial evaluation.

To work at an Airport you have to be a good team member, particularly during peak times when delays can mean working late into the evening to clear a backlog. This can play havoc with your social life, but it also means that there is usually a strong team spirit amongst staff working at an airport.

JOBS AVAILABLE

To give you some idea of the diverse jobs available when working for airports (and an outline of the recruitment terminology) recent airport and administration jobs advertised in British Airways News ranged from :

- Newsdesk Manager to play a key role within Corporate Communications.
- Maintenance Planner to fill a new role within busy engineering department preparing short/long term fleet planning requirements.

○ Licensed Aircraft Engineer (Avionics and A&C) to work on the Isle of Man.

However, there are hundreds of different jobs at an airport. They include:

Administration
Air Traffic Controller
Bureaux de Change
Car Hire
Customer Reception
Customs and Excise
Emergency Services
Engineering
Ground Handlers
Hotel Booking Agencies
Immigration
Information
Lounges
Marketing
Tour Operators' Representatives
Travel Retail
Voluntary Sector *(Chaplain, charities dealing with passengers in trouble, etc)*

Office staff tend to work more regular hours but may need to provide cover during delays to support staff at the airport.

Not all the airports are the same, so jobs can vary as can their titles.

In some cases, it is the airport operator who is the employer (for management, administration, baggage handling, maintenance, cleaning, information, apron control, medical and emergency services). Other employers may be private companies based at an airport and operating a franchise on behalf of the Airport (employers in this section might include catering, car hire, etc).

Delays

In the TV series 'Airport', you may remember Jeremy, the Aeroflot Passenger Service Agent who had to cope with Russian passengers who thought the plane would wait for them whilst they finished their shopping? Would you have remained so good tempered and still got your point across? This job is vitally important, as delays have a knock-on effect down the line, and are NOT popular.

Angry passengers sometimes accuse airports of manufacturing delays, simply to keep passengers on the ground and buying in the shops. The reality is that if an airport becomes too congested, people can't move through the crush, and so less is sold. However, the public's perception that big airports equals potential for delays means that many small, local airports are gaining more travellers. Passengers like the ease and convenience of checking-in at a small airport and will forgo the massive duty free shops in return for less waiting time on the ground. Again, this means more jobs as small airports become busier.

Working at an airport will involve shifts, and you may need your own transport to cope with early or late starts. However, everyone will agree that there is a magic to working at an airport, particularly at night with the airport lights twinkling across the tarmac. You finish a long shift knowing you have helped countless people sort out their travel problems and seen them on their way.

Scope

To give you some idea of the scope, in their latest report the BAA said they earned:

- £450 million from duty, tax free and tax-paid shops
- £140 million from car parking
- £20 million from car rental
- £41 million from Bureaux de Change
- £38 million from catering
- £36 million from airport advertising
- £16 million from other sources

If you go to work for an airport company, you could easily find yourself working around the world. Now, when Governments want to expand their airports, they put the job out to tender; if your employer wins the contract you could be offered a transfer to the new site. For instance Bucharest Airport in Romania is run by an Italian company, and currently BAA manages contracts at Boston, Logan, Pittsburgh (USA), Naples (Italy), Oman, Salalah and Muscat in the Gulf, and Alice Springs, Darwin, Launceston, Melbourne, Perth and Tennant Creek in Australia. as well as its sites in Britain. By the time this book is printed they may have fewer or more contracts – but the chances are there will be more!

BAA recently carried out a survey of their 12,000 staff across the world, and found that:

- 60% are male 40% female.
- 66% of BAA's UK employees in management grades are male, 34% female.
- BAA offers employees over 600 different training and development schemes.
- Over half of BAA staff take up share offers in the company.

Of these employees:

- 66% work at Airports.

- 17% work in World Duty Free retail.
- 2% work for the Heathrow Express train (to and from Paddington in London).
- 15% work in corporate offices.
- More than one in three BAA UK employees work in security.

ADMINISTRATION

Like other airport operators around the world, BAA (British Airports Authority), recruits graduates for training in computing, finance and management services. If you visit their website you can see current jobs available, which might range from

Multi-skilled Technicians – Engineering – for Southampton Airport. HVAC and electromechanical experience, including 4 year apprenticeship in electro or mechanical engineering. c £21,000.

to:

Construction workers for Heathrow Terminal 5.

The CAA (Britain's Civil Aviation Authority) sometimes recruits people with previous experience in airport operation, for airport managerial positions.

If your aim is to become an **Airport Manager**, you might consider a diploma in business studies which includes transport options. Degree courses in transport administration, management and planning are offered by a number of universities. Contact the Chartered Institute of Transport for further information, or you can apply to the various airlines, franchises and service companies that hire their own staff at an airport.

Manager, Service Delivery Company

Natasha McGoldrick works as Manager, Service Delivery, for BAA
In my role of manager, service delivery (MSD) in Heathrow's Terminal 3, I am directly responsible for managing the terminal operation on a shift by shift basis, leading a cross functional team of operational staff who ensure we are providing service delivery to all terminal users.

The MSD works closely with the airlines and control authorities. In Terminal 3 we have 44 different airlines, with a variety of different cultures and requirements. In order to manage an operation and building the size of Terminal 3 you require a whole range of skills. The post requires excellent leadership and team working skills, sound judgement in order to deal with the diverse situations we as a team are often faced with, and a good all-round knowledge and understanding of the terminal operational

> *environment.*
>
> *I thoroughly enjoy my job as every shift is different, and you never know what situation or challenge you are going to be faced with.*

Natasha's principal accountabilities are to:

O Coach and develop the operational team by leading and managing as a role model, enabling individuals to achieve the required performance standards through the performance development process.

O Work closely with airlines, external and internal customers to meet common business objectives.

O Communicate effectively to the team on key business and operational issues, facilitating effective decision-making within the team to meet operational and business objectives.

O Deliver agreed levels of service through effective management of staff and overtime budgets.

O Advise the product and development teams to influence process improvement and ensure that developments do not compromise the operational effectiveness of the terminals.

O Maintain a safe and secure operation environment in line with safety management procedures, through: incident management, risk management, contingency planning and safety inspections.

AIRPORT DUTY MANAGER

As **Airport Duty Manager** (or ADM in Heathrow-speak), along with four colleagues, **Stephen Golden** is the senior operational manager at Heathrow with responsibility for the smooth running of the whole of the airport operation on a 24 hour basis.

> *Whatever the issue, whether out on the airfield, inside the terminal buildings or on any of the airport roads, it falls to me as the ADM to ensure that it is managed quickly and effectively so that the safety, security and efficiency of the airport is not compromised. The ADM is the senior incident manager for the airport. When any major incident, such as a serious fire, a total power failure, or an incident with an aircraft occurs, it is the ADM who implements the emergency procedures and co-ordinates the incident along with the police, the fire service and the duty teams in the terminals or on the airfield.*
>
> *I enjoy working at the airport because it is exciting and varied. No two shifts are the same and each day brings its challenges and rewards and I can never be sure exactly what might be the next thing I have to deal with. In the morning I can be assisting the special facilities team by meeting a*

Head of State from an early flight, while in the afternoon I can be coordinating the recovery from a major incident such as a runway closure. What skills do I need to do my job well? I have to be able to assess situations quickly, use sound judgement to manage major incidents – and I need a good sense of humour. I need to be organised and to be able to represent BAA in all kinds of situations.

Stephen's main responsibilities are to:

○ Maintain the total airport operation on a 24-hour basis. Also to be a role model, leader and performance coach, responsible for ensuring business recovery and shared learning following major incidents, as well as promoting the highest standards of safety, security and customer service to all airport users.

○ Establish and develop excellent customer and business partner relationships to gain full understanding of their needs, their business targets and their expectations of BAA. Communicating business partner and customer expectations to all other duty teams on the airport and to deliver excellent service.

○ Support and help Heathrow Airport business unit managers in identifying efficiency improvements and revenue generating opportunities for the business through input of expert operational knowledge.

○ Develop and maintain an effective communications strategy for ADMs to support business unit operations, ensuring critical and non-critical information is available to all airport users, as required.

○ Promote and develop best practice in airport operations and business performance across the company and actively seek new ideas and improvements for the airport industry.

○ Lead others through emergency situations, ensuring emergency services, control authorities, staff and all other airport users are fully briefed at all times. Co-ordinate business recovery and minimise the impact on all operations, ensuring that the safety and security of all airport users is maintained at all times. Manage post incident 'wash-ups' and shared learning for all involved.

○ Lead risk management through contingency planning with operational teams, regularly practicing plans and testing knowledge through exercises and actual incidents, coaching and support teams as appropriate.

CUSTOMER SERVICE DUTY MANAGER

Karen Jones says working as an airport Customer Service Duty Manager is a varied role which makes the job very interesting

From the minute you start your shift until you finish you just don't know what you're going to get called to: medical emergencies, fire alarm activations, unattended bags, check-in queue management, dealing with staffing issues and many others.

Due to the varied issues we have to deal with, you need to have excellent communication skills dealing with people at all levels and a wide variety of cultures. You need to be able to remain calm and show professionalism, emotional control and efficiency at all times. You have to think on your feet and deal with whatever situation the job throws at you, from sick passengers and emergencies to ensuring the smooth operation of passenger services and the information desk.

Karen's job is to provide high levels of customer service to all customers, i.e. passengers, airlines, control authorities etc, effectively managing operational issues during the course of the shift. She has to provide the highest level of service to the business units' customers both internal and external. Achieve key performance indicators and increase business unit profitability and airline efficiency through operational steering, whilst continually seeking improvements. She must: manage the terminal control centre through close supervision of the terminal – fire, security and safety systems; ensure compliance with current safety management systems procedures by undertaking regular safety inspections and risk assessments; respond effectively to emergency situations providing the highest levels of customer safety and security and to ensure that business recovery is expedient; provide leadership, identifying improvements and implementing change where appropriate.

In London, don't just think of working at Heathrow or Gatwick. There are Luton, London City and Stansted airports as well, and Stansted looks poised to increase its traffic dramatically. Back in 1986 BAA invested £400 million in this airport, built on an old wartime bomber base constructed by the USAAF. In a short time it has become the fastest growing airport in Europe. Not only for passenger traffic, but for over 30 dedicated cargo airlines operating here.

ROUTE DEVELOPMENT MANAGER

At the recent AirPolonia launch of their services between Poland and Stansted,Colin Oakley, Route Development Manager of Stansted Airport, was delighted that his hard work encouraging the airline to develop the route was paying off. Even before the start date the airline was reporting projected business for the first three months had been reached in the first month. Colin had warned AirPolonia that it wouldn't be Polish residents who would be the majority customers, but to expect more British passengers flying out. As we go to press the split is 60/40 UK passengers and Poles.

Developing a route means not only researching the viability of flying between one airport and another, but also promoting it to potential users. Colin was keen to tap in to the ethnic market of Poles resident in Britain, and to do this he was in contact with the Polish Embassy in London, local leaders of ethnic Polish communities, Polish language newspapers published in Britain, Polish restaurants such as the famous Daquise in London's South Kensington, etc. He tapped in to the large Polish communities in areas around World War II flying fields, where Polish Airman had been based and found themselves stranded and unable to return to Poland when the Communists moved in to their country.

AIR TRAFFIC CONTROLLER

Once ATCs (Air Traffic Controllers) worked at airports: seeing the high control tower as you approached the airport gave you a feeling of reassurance. Today, with modern IT communications, the control facility could be almost anywhere. In Britain, the centres are currently at Swanwick in Hampshire, West Drayton in Middlesex, Prestwick in Ayrshire and Manchester Airport. Eventually they will be based solely at Swanwick and Prestwick.

ATCs are needed for all airports, whether on-site or working at a control centre, handling air traffic control disciplines: aerodrome, approach and area (the section in between aerodromes). In other words, supervising the 'motorways' of the sky. IT engineers are also needed to service all the incredibly complicated computers that operate the systems.

Every plane flying in controlled airspace, whether it is a small helicopter or a big inter-continental 747, has to file a flight plan, which details the route where the plane is going. As the plane flies along this route, the pilot will make contact with the relevant control centre/s en-route. e.g. as Pilots fly along they will be talking constantly to an ATC assigned to supervise their plane whilst it is in their area and under his/her jurisdiction.

These routes are very well defined. You can't have planes wandering across busy airways at will; there would soon be a mid-air collision. To prevent this happening, the ATC will use a Radar screen to keep an eye on your plane, and also the planes flying near by, 'thinking in 3D' as they handle aircraft flying into their sector from different directions and at different levels: behind, in front, sideways and above and below. They track your plane whilst it is in 'their' area, then hand over the supervision to the next control centre once you fly out of their area.

In Britain Air Traffic Control comes under NATS (National Air Traffic Services). The 5000 people working for NATS handle flights carrying over 160 million passengers a year (soon expected to top 200 million), plus cargo flights. NATS say 'our most valuable asset is not our technology, but our people'. In this computerised age, it is nice to know that humans can still do some things better than technology.

To be an ATC, you need at least five GCSE/SCEs at Grade C or above, or equivalent, including Maths and English, and to have studied to A level standard, to start on the career path for this demanding job, and must be aged 18 – 29. Trainees are selected by tests and interviews. Work is shift work.

You also have to speak English. English was chosen as the worldwide language of aviation to ensure both pilots and controllers spoke the same language – otherwise it could be confusing, and confusion breeds crashes. There have been fatal accidents when a controller and a pilot couldn't understand each other.

Competition for ATC positions is fierce.

There is a Direct Entrant Graduate scheme for Systems Engineers, Software Engineers and Operations Research.

NATS' training facility is at Bournemouth Airport, where you are trained in a simulator and also with practical experience. Eventually you will be able to handle air traffic control across Britain, possibly the most complex airspace in the world.

Useful Address
www. nats.co.uk.

Incidentally, NATS (National Air Traffic Services) have started asking questions about types of aircraft and how they fly – so it is a good idea to get onto airline websites and learn the codes for different types of aircraft; find out what the numbers mean that are marked on runways, etc.

Once you have experience, the Royal Air Force occasionally recruits Aviation Officers Grade 2 (Air Traffic Controllers) to be employed within the Civil Service, and commissioned in to the RAF Reserve.

Useful Addresses:
In the UK: www.rafcareers.com
In the USA; www.fly.faa.gov

BUREAUX DE CHANGE

Most airports will have one or more money exchange bureaux needing cashiers. If you like dealing with money, contact companies such as International Currency Exchange. Generally you have to be 18+, reliable, with good customer service skills, numerate, accurate, responsible and used to handling money.

Useful Addresses
www.americanexpress.co.uk
www.thomascook.com
www.travelex.com

CAR HIRE

The major car rental companies such as Hertz, Avis, Budget, etc. will have desks at most airports. You must be able to drive, and languages are an advantage to work for these companies.

CUSTOMER SERVICE AGENTS/PASSENGER SERVICE AGENTS

When passengers arrive to catch a flight, probably the first person they will see standing behind the airline check-in desk is the CSA. All airlines need staff to check in passengers and their baggage, and meet incoming aircraft to supervise luggage collection, passengers with difficulties, etc. They are known by various titles; generally **Customer** or **Passenger Service Agents** (CSA/PSA).

Some airlines employ their own staff (see the *Airline Jobs* chapter), others will utilise a Ground Handling company's services (See the *Ground Handlers* section below), but either way the CSA's job is important as the 'face' of an airline, at the sharp end looking after passengers.

CUSTOMS AND EXCISE

Customs and Excise is probably the oldest Government force, dating back to at least 743 AD. Even today, if an officer wants to look up what duty is payable on an item, he uses a book of rates first published in 1506!

Duty free could be said to date from the Civil War, when Parliament imposed duty on beer and spirits (still there today). During the Napoleonic Wars smugglers gained sympathy from the gentry, who weren't averse to buying cognac and wines smuggled in from France (whose sale helped subsidise Napoleon's armies) and lace also became a smuggled commodity. One seized shipment of lace was worth over £1 million.

Working for Customs and Excise, a Government agency, you collect the duties/revenue on behalf of the Government. You are part of a team that provides 40% of the Government's revenue.

The major part of the work is dealing with VAT(value added tax) collection, but if you work at an airport you will be providing services to the travelling public. You handle legitimate import and exports of goods, detecting and assisting with investigation of offences arising from the import/export of prohibited and restricted goods (especially goods made from endangered species or materials such as ivory), and excise smuggling (trying to evade duty when you bring back goods from abroad, etc.).

At airports customs officers also collect revenue from other sources, such as VAT due from travellers. As a member of the travelling public, you might ask why you are charged VAT on presents you buy abroad above a certain value, but shopkeepers have to pay this tax legitimately, so it would be unfair competition for them if everyone were to go abroad to buy their goods. Other countries such as the USA apply the same taxes or tariffs to safeguard their factories and shops.

Over 23,000 officers work in the service in Britain, and as they say, 'the work can be physically demanding and at times unpleasant, but is always challenging and rewarding'. At the sharp end, you are responsible for the search of persons and the physical examination of passengers, baggage, freight, ships, cars, lorries, boats and aircraft. You might find yourself in a confrontational situation with angry members of the travelling public, especially smugglers, and it is up to you to handle them tactfully. Normal working is 5 days in a 7 day period, but this can be shifts around the clock.

To enter Her Majesty's Customs and Excise you must be a UK national (other countries have same stipulation for their nationals), and possess at least 5 GCE/GCSEs (grades A-C) including English language. IT skills are important, as much work is on projects worked out on computers. Disabled applicants are accepted, but you may be restricted as sometimes duties involve 'rummaging' in confined spaces in ship's holds, etc. Entry into Customs and Excise or immigration careers is also by the Civil Service entry exam, and there is a Graduate Fast Track Scheme which operates when staff are required.

Opportunities are limited for dog handlers to work with 'sniffer' detection dogs (anti-terrorist and drugs). You have to be a serving officer before you can apply to join the dog handling units.

History

Jobs are to be found all over Britain, at large and small airports. Work is very varied, and not many people know that these officers have the right to make arrests. Work covers VAT, Customs and Excise and Inland Customs. You generally start working doing VAT collection work, then go on to the other sections. Recent adverts for Anti-smuggling Assistant Officers stated salaries started at £14,327-£15,571.

For more information, look in your local telephone directory for the nearest International airport, or on www.hmce.gov.uk.

N.B.Customs and Excise and their equivalent organisations conduct stringent searches of personnel across the world. If you are working as airline crew and caught with illegal substances, you are subject to the laws of the country in question; in some countries this crime could carry the death sentence for drugs smuggling.

EMERGENCY SERVICES

Every airport has to have a fire service on duty all the hours the airport is open. Generally, these services are operated by the airport authorities, so they are the employers to apply to for work. A major part of any airport fire service department is training airport staff to handle potential emergencies; a very minor part is keeping birds away from the runways; specialists are employed for this!

Although most airports have a police presence, generally these are seconded from the local police force, and are not employed directly by the airport.

As fire-fighting and other emergency services provide increasingly sophisticated techniques to alleviate disasters, these services look more and more to recruiting career-minded people who intend to keep up-to-date with the latest technology.

If you have ever wondered how fire-fighters and safety staff are trained to face problems, a company called Willis (020-7488 8111) makes many of the videos used to train emergency services. These aren't cheap to buy, but do give an insight into how emergencies are tackled. One of their videos advises *'don't rush in – instead you are trained to think in steps – what to do first – what must you look out for – watch for, etc. Apparently the first person on the scene of an accident takes charge, until a more senior person arrives – so this could be you'.*

Generally, you will be employed by the airport operating company, so look on their websites for job opportunities.

At most airports there is a medical centre, employing nurses and often doctors. At major international airports this centre will often carry out inoculations and vaccinations for travellers. However, if anyone travelling by air needs to be met by an ambulance, this will normally be supplied by a private (off-airport) company, or a local hospital.

ENGINEERING

For information about opportunities in Engineering see the separate chapter below.

GROUND HANDLERS

Ground Handlers are companies that provide services 'on the ground' rather than in the air. If an airline doesn't have enough flights into an airport to justify employing their own full-time staff for check-in, maintenance, ramp duty, etc. they will hire a local ground handling company. You may never have heard of these companies, but working for them can provide an interesting career around the world. Some services these companies may provide are:

o Aircraft maintenance

- Aircraft servicing and cleaning
- Cargo and mail handling (on-/off-airport)
- Catering services
- Executive aviation services
- Flight operations and crew administration
- Fueling
- Load control and communications
- Operation of airport lounges
- Passenger and baggage handling
- Passenger document check
- Ramp services
- Representation and accommodation
- Security services for passengers, baggage, cargo and catering
- Station supervision and administration
- Surface transport of passengers and crews
- Unit Load Device control and management

Swissport

You may never have heard of Swissport, but last year their staff served more than 56 million airline passengers, provided ramp handling facilities for over 1,600,000 aircraft; and they aren't even an airline. What they are is a global ground and cargo handling business, with an annual turnover of over 1.2 billion Swiss Francs a year, working in over 150 airports. On their cargo side they helped import/export over 2.5 million metric tons.

Currently, Swissport operates in 29 countries: Argentina, Austria, Belgium, Brazil, Canada,Caribbean, Dominican Republic, France, Germany, Great Britain, Greece, Honduras, India, Israel, Italy, Kenya, Luxembourg, Mexico, Netherlands Antilles, Peru, the Philippines, Russia, South Africa, Spain, Switzerland, Tanzania, Turkey, Venezuela, and the United States. In some countries they are known as Aerogate, DAHACO, Havas, Miascor, Q.A.S. or Unitpool. In the USA look for Swissport, and also www.walshvisa@ngc.com.

Swissport are majority-owned by London-based Candover Partners Ltd. and are large enough to pledge their airline customers that they will make up for operational delays due to late landings. They even have their own internet platform for 'misdirected' luggage (luggage is never lost in airline-speak!): www.mylostbag.com.

Useful Addresses

www.swissport.com
www.groundstar.com
www.aviapartner.aero.com

HEATHROW EXPRESS

Because Heathrow Airport was planned in the days when flying was for a few rich people, the approach roads – especially the tunnel that goes under the runway to the termini in the centre – are too small and are frequently clogged with traffic.

To address the problem, BAA invested heavily in building a railway line from Paddington in central London to Heathrow. Now it is so popular that 2% of BAA's staff work for Heathrow Express.

As a Customer Service Representative working for Heathrow Express, Carol Arnold's shifts often start early.
Around 3.15 am I am up with the lark and raring to go to work, arriving at 4.40 am ready for the day ahead. As customer service representatives we cover various roles all involving assisting customers. These include dispatching trains (on time of course); working as on-board attendants checking and selling tickets on the trains; selling tickets in any one of our four ticket offices (three at Heathrow Airport and one at Paddington Station in London); and hosting and assisting passengers with the ticket machines. The location and duties vary depending on which shift you are working.

We are here first and foremost for the safety and well being of our customers and to help them in any way we can, which is the part of the job I enjoy most. As first point of contact for Heathrow Express customers we provide a comprehensive service enabling all customers' needs to be met from a single source.

I really do enjoy my job and the laughs I have with my colleagues, the staff are so friendly and very sociable. One of the benefits of shift work I find are the days off you get when everyone else is at work, and at 13.00 hours I will be finishing work and have the rest of the day to myself. Perhaps I will go back to bed!

Carole's duties include

- ⊙ Assisting customers with any aspect of the company's services.
- ⊙ Attending immediately to any apparent defect or shortcomings in station or train facilities and performing specified tasks at stations and on trains.
- ⊙ Advising customers on train times, fares and other service information.
- ⊙ Acting as on board attendant.
- ⊙ Checking tickets.
- ⊙ Assisting customers with awkward luggage and ensuring trolleys are readily available.
- ⊙ Reporting defects in train and station equipment.

o Removing litter, dirt and graffiti to provide customers with a clean and safe environment.

o Executing emergency plans for train and station evacuation to keep customers and staff safe in perilous situations.

o Dispatching trains in accordance with the timetable and safety procedures to avoid undue delay and ensuring customer safety, and reporting back to the customer services duty manager of opportunities for improvement in safety systems and of any aspect of human behaviour to prevent serious or minor incidents, etc.

o Full time salary £20,022 per annum (average 40 hours per week).

Useful Address
www.baa.com

THE USA

In the US the massive Port Authority of New York and New Jersey has signed an agreement with the City of New York to operate John F. Kennedy and LaGuardia airports until the year 2050 – for a payment of $700 million, and then another $5 billion between now and 2050. This should secure the future, and encourage job creation.

Useful Addresses
www.panynj.gov
www.ohare.com
www.aena.es
www.sea-aeroportimilano.it

HOTEL BOOKING AGENCIES

These are some of the service desks to be found at most airports. Some are operated by the local tourist board, some by hotel groups, others by a local chamber of commerce. Sometimes they are 'stand alone'; at other airports they will combine hotel bookings with providing tourist information. To find a job, ask the desk staff for employer details, or contact the Information Desks to ask for contacts.

IMMIGRATION AND NATIONALITY DIRECTORATE

In Britain, Immigration services are part of the Home Office, and an **Immigration Officer** is probably the first person a traveller meets when they arrive in a country. This officer will ask to see their passport, check they hold the correct visas (if needed) and that they have the right to enter the country. Officers also carry out checks, which are becoming more and more sophisticated, to see if a passport has been forged. If the officer believes the passport is forged, the passenger's visa is not in order, or for other reasons, if necessary, this officer has the power to decline to admit someone to a country, investigate and eventually return them to their point of origin.

Currently there are trials with various forms of facial and iris recognition, whose purpose is to make it harder for someone to enter a country with illegal documents – see the chapter on Security for more details.

The Immigration service also has responsibility for detecting illegal immigrants who have entered a country without passing immigration barriers, and remove them. To help them detect 'people smuggling' the Immigration service now has massive, sophisticated scanners. A lorry or other vehicle goes through the scanner which can detect the heat from a body which shows up on an X-ray screen.

With travel becoming easier, it is a constant battle to ensure that illegal immigrants don't enter a country undetected. If you have an enquiring mind, enjoy analysis and working with IT, then you could find this work unusual and interesting.

Useful Addresses
*For the UK:*www.ind.homeoffice.gov.uk
U.S. Immigration; www.ice.gov

INFORMATION ASSISTANTS

Wearing their smart airport uniform, **Information Assistants** are there to answer just about any question that makes life easier for the travelling public. Staff say a good sense of humour is a must; 'it helps to deal with some of our rather more 'interesting' members of the public!' Mind reading abilities would be useful too, or perhaps a crystal ball, to enable you to find out what passengers really want!

After long flights passengers can become disorientated, and a helpful approach with a smiling face can assist them smoothly through the airport. Assistants have a very difficult job to do at times, so you have to have your wits about you. Information Assistants can be called upon to assist the police, immigration or customs services with translation during their official enquiries, so foreign language speaking abilities are an absolute necessity as many passengers will not speak the local language. Knowing how to speak another language also gives you an insight to understand what the question being asked is really about, often nothing like the original query.

BAA say Assistants have to

O Provide and maintain a comprehensive, effective information service to all airport users, dealing with both personal and telephone enquiries.
O Provide information to the passengers and public, either face to face or via

the telephone, on a wide range of subjects.

O Enable speedy and satisfactory resolution of complaints.

O Ensure passenger welfare is maintained by giving reassurance and assistance when necessary.

O Provide and update flight information by inputting data to the computer which is sent to public visual display units throughout the terminals, ensuring that the latest flight information is easily accessible at all times.

O Make announcements in both English and foreign languages via the public address system, e.g. paging calls to locate passengers and their meeters/greeters, security announcements and general information announcements.

O Take custody of lost property items found in the terminal by logging items received and recording them on a computer system, before either ensuring their return to their rightful owner who may have claimed the property or awaiting collection by BAA's central lost property office.

O Assist with the evacuation of the terminal and with the emergency procedures on the instruction of the customer service duty manager or other senior management.

O Liaise and maintain good working relationships with the control authorities, airlines and other business partners.

O Undertake ad hoc projects in such areas as, information desk design, researching and providing information for future company publications/brochures and redesigning charts to show revised emergency exits/fire points.

Information Assistants have to be unflappable, and used to handling anything – you would be surprised what questions they can be asked by the travelling public. As well as spoken languages, sign language is very useful.

Current salary at London airports is c. £19,500 p.a.

Jose says a sense of humour is vitally important

In fact I would say this is the most important 'skill' needed by Information Staff. Then it would help if we were issued with a crystal ball, as people expect you to be able to read their minds. Every day someone will come up to ask – where is my mother/aunt/child? And expect you to know the answer without any more details. You need patience too, as you then have to unravel their demands and extract the information from them which will help you find out what has happened to their friend. Often it is just that their plane is delayed, but sometimes it is more serious. And the most frequently asked question? Easy, we are right under a sign pointing to Toilets, and passengers ask us constantly where can I find the toilets?

VIP AND OTHER LOUNGES

Sometimes these lounges are operated by an airline, sometimes provided by the airport operator, or a ground handler. Generally they are situated in the area beyond immigration control off departure lounges. However some airlines such as those that operate long haul flights will have their own dedicated lounges for incoming First and Business Class passengers, situated in the arrivals building, where they can have clothes pressed, take a shower or relax before starting work at their destination.

To work in these lounges you have to have good customer service skills, and be very presentable. Users are passengers entitled to the best service; generally they will have paid for a Business or First Class ticket, be a member of an airline's loyalty programme, be a guest of the airline, etc. so they expect a high level of service in return for paying 12 times the economy ticket price, or more. Needless to say low-cost airlines don't operate lounges – at the moment!

O You sit at a desk and scrutinise passengers' tickets or passes to ensure they have the right to enter the lounge. Generally these lounges are operated on a franchise from the airport authorities, so your company is charged a fee (around £10+) for each person who comes in, so your bosses won't be happy if you allow all and sundry to take advantage of the free drinks, snacks, newspapers and magazines.

O You have to act as a host/hostess – as though the lounge were your own home. Every so often if working in a small lounge you will pick up empty glasses, and tidy up papers, etc. In large lounges cleaners are employed and you have to ensure they do their job properly.

O Generally when you check the passenger's ticket you make a note of which flight they are catching, so you can make an announcement when boarding is happening, although in some large lounges this no longer happens – there are too many passengers so it would be too noisy for other users.

O If your passengers' flights are delayed, then you liaise with the airline to ensure that they are looked after as well as possible.

For certain lounges you may need extra job skills. Singapore Airport Services has opened a Rain Forest Lounge at Changi Airport, described as a 'walk-in sanctuary where passengers can rejuvenate themselves' in a copy of a tropical rainforest. It comes equipped with water features and a business centre – do hope they aren't in the same room as this will play havoc with computers.

MARKETING

The Press and Public Relations department of major, and some minor, airports is an important part of an airport's business strategy. The management strategy could be to increase passenger traffic by:

○ Highlighting new routes opening up.
○ Highlighting new destinations that local residents can reach.
○ Highlighting package holidays travelling from that airport and encourage the catchment area's population to fly by these tour operators.
○ Promoting visits to business exhibitions, conferences, etc.
○ Mentioning if a celebrity travels through (gives the airport a so-called glamorous image).

In fact anything that might encourage more travellers to use the local airport, and so produce more revenue, could be part of your marketing brief.

Some airports have huge marketing departments that have a countrywide or even global strategy. Singapore has targeted the lucrative stopover market for passengers on the long haul from Europe to Australia. If passengers break their flight en route for 24-48 hours in Singapore (so spending money in the country), the Government either picks up the hotel bill, or subsidises very much reduced hotel prices.

Marketing could also highlight duty free opportunities available at stopovers. Shannon Airport targeted bargain shoppers as a way to encourage transatlantic flights to refuel at its airport. The Gulf States such as Dubai have built enormous glitzy duty free shops, to keep passengers happy whilst their planes are being refueled.

Marketing Schiphol Airport

Amsterdam's Schiphol Airport Marketing department successfully targets British regional passengers to transit through their airport, rather than Heathrow or Gatwick.Once these regional passengers flew from their local airport in Britain to Heathrow or Gatwick to catch an onward flight abroad. KLM saw an opportunity, developed a strong regional network across Britain, and now an increasing number of passengers fly by KLM from British regional airports to Amsterdam, where they can catch intercontinental and international flights, so providing revenue for KLM rather than BA, British Midland, etc.

This has worked very successfully for Schiphol and KLM, and the next step in the marketing strategy is to give passengers something extra to do whilst they wait at Schiphol. One way is by offering shopping – and remember passengers may have flown out from regional airports with few shops, so this is an incentive. Schiphol's shopping slogan is Try–Buy–Fly; and seeing carrier bags printed with this slogan carried by returning passengers into UK airports must make BAA grit their teeth.

For intellectuals and culture vultures there is now an outpost of Amsterdam's world famous Rijksmuseum at the airport. Schiphol is the only airport in the world to have its own art museum, which is open to all passengers. The idea was a unique joint initiative by the Rijksmuseum Amsterdam and Amsterdam Airport Schiphol

Following the recent success of their Rembrandt exhibition, Schiphol's next exhibition is Van Gogh and The Modern Masters. Included in the exhibition are many famous paintings, including Van Gogh's Self-Portrait, painted in Paris in 1887. The chance to see this painting is a huge draw to many people, so they are happy to fly via Schiphol rather than a British airport.

As well as special exhibitions, ten works by famous masters of the Dutch Golden Age, such as Jacob van Ruisdael, Ferdinand Bol and Jan Steen are permanently on view in the museum. The Rijksmuseum Amsterdam Schiphol is located inside the airport terminal, after passport control, on Holland Boulevard in the corridor connecting Piers E and F. The museum is open daily from 7:00 am to 8:00 PM and admission is free.

In a recent survey more than 150 agencies based in the vicinity of regional airports, including Birmingham, Bristol, Edinburgh, Humberside, Leeds Bradford and Newcastle were quizzed on awareness of Schiphol Airport. Almost a third of them (31 per cent) said they 'always' recommended Schiphol to customers as first-choice airport at which to connect to a flight to their final destination. More than half (51 per cent) said they did so regularly. UK travel advisers were also asked to compare aspects of Schiphol and Heathrow facilities and ambience, rating them between 1 (poor) to 4 (good). Amsterdam Airport Schiphol won in all six categories: Customer friendliness (3.2 v 2.7); pleasant for business travellers (3.4 v 2.9); pleasant for tourists (3.2 v 2.5); clear (signage) and comfortable (3.2 v 2.4); efficient arrivals/departures (3.3 v 2.7); speedy transfer facilities (3.5 v 2.8) and tax-free shopping (3.3 v 3).

TOUR OPERATORS' REPRESENTATIVES

Airports that handle charter traffic will have **Tour Operators' Reps**. working at the airport, looking after their company's clients, handing out tickets and sorting out problems. Even major airports such as Heathrow will have a number of these staff, since more and more tour operators now send clients on scheduled flights. To work for these companies you apply to the tour operator. To find out which ones send clients through the airport, these are often listed on a board in the departures check-in area. If not, ask the Information Desk staff.

Thomas Cook say

As one of our Airport Services Representatives, you'll be surrounded by the sounds and excitement of travel – and with our range of benefits and discounted travel, you'll never be far from a dream holiday either! We need friendly, outgoing people with customer service experience to help at

> check-in and departures. Spending a lot of time on your feet (and thinking
> on them too!), you'll need energy, initiative and, ideally, airline or travel
> industry experience. A driving licence is essential, as is the willingness
> to work shifts, including weekends, nights and early starts. Your seasonal
> contract will run from April to October. Benefits include:

- Holidays from as little as £75
- Discounts on car hire
- Travel discounts of up to 50%
- Special rates for hotels – both in the UK and abroad
- 23 days holiday (pro-rata)
- Uniform

TRAVEL RETAIL

See the *Travel Retail* chapter.

MISCELLANEOUS AIRPORT JOBS

There are so many different jobs at today's airports, from the bird scarer who
keeps runways clear of birds (a major hazard for aircraft engines) to the VIP
'Meet and Greet' staff who welcome royalty, politicians, returning sportsmen
etc.

Valet Parking is becoming very popular, particularly with business clients
to whom time is money. Many companies offer some or all of the following
services:

- Drive up to the terminal.
- Hand over your car and keys to a parking valet in return for a receipt.
- When you return, you phone from the arrivals hall and the Valet has your car
  waiting for you to drive away.

Steve Waller, Sales & Marketing Director of Purple Parking says
*The chauffeur service has been running for 7 years. The qualities required
in chauffeurs are as follows:*

- Firstly and obviously a full clean driving licence – applicants will
  then undertake a purple parking separate driving test.
- 25 years plus – looking for a mature driver with experience.
- Ability to achieve high service industry standards.
- An understanding that the chauffeurs are at the customer interface.
- Ability to use initiative.

O Ability to make good initial and lasting impression.
O Communications skills.
O Ability to remain pleasant and work under difficult conditions.
O Diplomatic skills.

Purple Parking are the largest operator of chauffeur parking within the UK, employing over 300 chauffeurs at Heathrow Airport alone.

Useful Addresses

www.purpleparking.com
www.bluedogparking.co.uk

Useful Addresses

Amsterdam Airport Schiphol; www.schiphol.nl
Belfast City Airport; vacancies are generally advertised in the Belfast Telegraph on a Friday evening and also be posted on their website www.belfastcityairp ort.com for a period of 2 weeks.
Berlin Airport; www.berlin-airport.de
Bremen Airport www.airport-bremen.de
Cologne/Bonn; www.airport-cgn.de
Dortmund; www.flughafen-dortmund.de
Dresden; www.dresden-airport.de
Dusseldorf; www.duesseldorf-international.de
Frankfurt/Main; www.flughafen-frankfurt.de
Hamburg; www.ham.airport.de
Hannover; www.hannover-airport.de
Leipzig; www.leipzig-halle-airport.de
Munich; www.flughafen-muenchen.de
Munster; www.flughafen-fmo.de
Nurnberg; www.flughafen-nuernberg.de
Stuttgart; www.flughafen-stuttgart.de
Padeborn; www.flughafen-paderborn-lippstadt.de

Promotions Agencies:
www.kreatepromotions.co.uk
www.zoopeople.co.uk

Schedule or Charter Airlines

Today, the distinction between scheduled and charter airlines can be blurred.

SCHEDULED AIRLINES:

- Fly on a regular timetable.
- Passengers can book single or return tickets on flights on any planes flying to the airline's different destinations.

Most scheduled airlines will offer:

- A booking office, call centre reservations, internet booking or the option to go in to a high street travel agent and book any flight.
- Fully flexible fares that can be altered if wanted, with the option of changing flights if needed.
- Seat reservations.
- Service on board, from refreshments to newspapers, etc.
- Greater luggage allowance than a low cost airline.
- Assistance if there are delays or an aircraft is cancelled.
- Business and First Class options.
- Other benefits can include airport lounges, frequent flier schemes, etc.

CHARTER AIRLINES:

- Fly where their aircraft are chartered, or booked, to go.
- Generally the aircraft will be chartered by a tour operator to fly a regular series of flights during a summer or winter holiday season, carrying holiday-makers on package tours: according to Simon Buck of First Choice Holidays, a third of all UK airline passengers fly on charter flights.
- Charters may also be for single journeys such as taking spectators to a sporting event e.g. Monaco Grand Prix, positioning a ship's crew (when a new crew for cargo ships takes over from crew going on leave) or carrying horses to races.

One of the most famous charters carried the victorious English Rugby team, coming home to England from Australia, after they had won the Web Ellis Cup. British Airways even re-named their 747 aircraft Sweet Chariot, after the team's unofficial anthem, and reserved a seat for the trophy. The Airline were quick to let people know that the team were occupying Club Class World flat bed seats – together with quotes from the players saying how much they had enjoyed sleeping stretched out; a subtle reminder to business travellers that BA is fitting these seats in all its Club Class World cabins.

Disaster Relief Work

On a more serious note, one of the most frequently requested charters for flights today is to carry aid and relief workers to a disaster area, after an earthquake, famine, etc. Edi Bucher, Head Operations Leader for REDOG, the Swiss Disaster Dog Association, is used to flying out with his team of dogs to search for victims after earthquakes. He reports:

The Swiss are neutral, but as their contribution to world peace, if asked, Switzerland will always fund a disaster relief flight carrying a specialist rescue team. As soon as the call comes in to our headquarters from a country in distress, we assemble the team and the equipment we will need from stores ready in an airport hanger. The Government contacts airlines with large aircraft available, paying upwards of £500,000 to charter an appropriate plane.

Then we have a big logistics problem loading the equipment, ranging from forklift trucks and earth-moving equipment to heat-seeking cameras and first aid supplies. This has to be loaded in sequence, ready to come out of the plane in the correct order that we are going to need the equipment, so we can start work as soon as we arrive. In this job, time is valuable.

Last to be loaded are the REDOG team; up to 18 German Shepherd or similar dogs, trained not only to seek out humans by scent, but also to move incredibly gently over rubble and across planks or ladders in collapsed buildings. One false step by a dog could bring downs tons of rubble.

SEAT-ONLY TICKETS

To keep up with current demand, some charter airlines will offer single or return tickets to members of the general public:

○ If the airline hasn't sold enough seats to tour operators.
○ Or if a tour operator has not managed to sell all their package holidays and

has spare seats on the aircraft.

When a charter airline hasn't sold enough seats to operators, they will offer **seat-only** tickets for single or return flights, putting them in to competition with low cost and scheduled airlines.

Tour operators pay a lump sum to charter part or all of an aircraft, however many seats they fill. If they haven't sold all of their allocation, they will sell off the spare seats individually, thus making up the money they might have lost. These are known as **seat-only** sales.

On some routes these seats have sold so well that some operators now sell a combination of their package tours and seat-only sales.

Split Charters

Charter airlines often fly split-charters, where several tour operators book a proportion of seats, rather than filling a complete aircraft.

One charter aircraft could fly with a mixture of passengers in its cabin, including:

O Seats booked on behalf of tour operator clients.
O Seats booked by competing tour operators.
O Seat-only tickets booked by individual passengers.

Split charters can present a challenge to cabin crew: sometimes a tour operator will offer a better meal, wine with the meal, etc. and crew have to ensure that these passengers receive their extras, without alienating other passengers.

Looking over their shoulder

With the down-turn in package holidays, and the increase in people organising their own flights and hotels, many charter airlines are now entering the low cost market and aggressively selling seats on their flights, whereas before they only sold these seats if they had been released by their clients.

But both scheduled and charter airlines are worried about competition from low cost carriers. Both types of airline will have basically the same operating costs, and be aware of an article in the Daily Mail, which reported costings for an average EasyJet flight:

O Ticket sales = £6,136
O Outgoings = £5,591
O Profit   = £545

Bearing in mind that the average airline's overheads may be higher than most low cost airlines, that profit figure might be more difficult to achieve.

Although scheduled and charter airlines are copying low cost airlines by encouraging passengers to book on the web (saving airlines money), many are still tied in to paying commission to travel agents for seat sales – particularly if their parent company owns both travel agencies and a charter airline such as *Thomas Cook (JMC), Lunn Poly (Britannia)* etc. There have been angry words in the trade press recently about the way this commission is being cut down.

To pay for higher operating costs, due to commission and other factors, scheduled and charter airlines would probably be looking to gain higher revenue from ticket sales. Realising they are probably not going to be able to complete with low cost airlines on price, instead they will try to offer a value-added product:

- ○ Greater lugggage allowance.
- ○ Reserved seats.
- ○ If aircraft are delayed, they may offer refreshements.
- ○ If a long delay, they may put up passengers in hotels.
- ○ They may supply food – newspapers, etc.

It would be difficult to operate a totally low cost operation, with no frills, if the plane was also carrying package holidaymakers who had been promised a meal on board. So when it comes to fares, charter airlines offering seat-only tickets are positioning themselves mid-way between low fares and those charged by scheduled airlines.

Monarch Airlines is one charter airline now encouraging seat-only bookings by offering passengers full meals; in addition there is a complimentary bar service including wine with meals.

When passengers do their sums and compare flight costs with low cost airlines versus seat-only sales, airlines are hoping that many will think that the few extra pounds charged for flights with meals begins to seem a bargain – and they know everyone loves a bargain.

Liz Bartlett, Monarch's PR Manager, says their airline also includes in-flight entertainment as well as pre-bookable seats. This will attract many customers who have flown by low cost airlines and found their family split, as seats are not allocated.

Useful Address
www.flymonarch.com

Market research shows passengers place importance on seat comfort. In Australia, Qantas obviously thought this would impact on bookings, so when they launched their new scheduled airline, Jetstar, **Geoff Dixon**, Chief Executive Officer of Qantas, said the airline would feature leather seats and an inflight audio entertainment system. Even so, they are confident Jetstar would be the lowest cost operator in Australia.

Jetstar will operate out of Melbourne, and eventually employ about 1,000 people over the next few years. Jetstar is on www.impulse.com.au.

However, reclining seats produce a 50/50 split for/against (half of passengers like the extra comfort when they want to sleep v. the other half who dislike the way the seat in front intrudes on their space). So Ryanair has announced that they are refurbishing their cabins with non-reclining seats which are cheaper to install and save money on repairing the reclining mechanism of the many seats that are broken every year.

ROUTING

One big problem for many charter airlines is flying from A to B, if taking a direct route means going over a hostile country, or one on a war footing. So airlines are grateful to events such as the Olympic Games, which can encourage countries that were at loggerheads to co-operate and be friendly.

Athens is a good case in point. Holding the 2004 Summer Olympics there has meant that old adversaries, Turkey and Greece, are now much more amenable to allowing each other's aircraft to overfly their air space. Officials estimate that they will be able to increase the number of flights in the airspace between Athens and Istanbul by 15%, with estimated cost savings of around €40 million a year.

WHAT JOBS ARE AVAILABLE?

All airlines, whether scheduled or charter, have to abide by the same rules and regulations, and employ fully-trained cabin crew, pilots and engineering staff. Just because an airline flies inexpensive charters, doesn't mean it has any less responsibility for safety.

Similar job opportunities exist in both scheduled or charter airlines; for more information on jobs available see the chapter *Airline Jobs*.

There is a small difference in the way that sales and marketing departments work in charter airlines. Some staff concentrate on selling to tour operators, booking blocks of seats, or even complete aircraft. Most charter airlines are now offering, or thinking of offering, seat-only sales to individuals, so these will need to be sold alongside blocks.

Britannia Airways carries ten million passengers a year, and is now one of the world's biggest airlines. Initially a charter airline, it gradually started to offer a mixture of seat-only and charter bookings. Today it forms part of the giant German TUI tour operations empire, supplying seats for the different tour operations in their company, as well as seat-only sales.

Like many charter airlines, Britannia also runs an excellent engineering department, handling maintenance for their own and other airlines' planes, so there may be opportunities for engineers. These are listed on their website www.britanniaairways.com.

Charter airlines have to forecast which destinations will be popular eighteen months to two years ahead. Once it is decided that certain destinations are going to be popular, routes can be worked out for operators, and seat prices agreed, ready for brochures which have to be available in June/July for the following year. This could be a big gamble, but charter airlines employ expert analysts in this field.

Charter airlines also employ market analysts to keep an eye on oil prices. If they think there is going to be a rise in oil prices, they buy forward i.e. purchase their company's fuel stocks well in advance. Airlines can be very smug when prices do rise, if their analysts have forecast this would happen, enabling the company to make an extra profit.

Forecasting the Future

Monarch Airlines (www.monarch-airlines.com) say their Revenue Management Executives, based at London Luton Airport, have to forecast future sales to gain the maximum revenue. This involves using a mixture of manual and automated systems, setting inventory levels accordingly, taking historic trends into account, daily monitoring of seat sales as well as competitor pricing/scheduling using the GDS company systems and the internet. Other duties included producing ad-hoc reports when required.

Eurostar

With their advertising featuring 'flying' between London and Paris or Brussels, Eurostar has placed itself firmly in the airline marketing sector, and aims to attract more flyers to use its train services. The CAA says Eurostar is now the leading carrier between London and Paris with 66% of the market, and rising. On the Brussels to London route Eurostar currently caries 53%. By the year 2007 Eurostar will have the capacity to carry up to 40 million passengers a year; equivalent to around 250,000 short-haul flights.

Useful Addresses

www.eurostar.com

See also the *Useful Website Addresses* chapter..

Low Cost Airlines

Low margin high volume sales tactics are encouraging people to buy more airline tickets across the world. Southwest Airlines were first, with a low-cost operation in the USA in 1971. For years European airlines watched what was happening in North America, where new low cost airlines were challenging the big boys, and making a profit. In Britain, Freddie Laker tried challenging the system with SkyTrain, but this sadly foundered, and Europe's state-owned Airlines went back to their cosy semi-monopolostic systems until the 1990s.

European entrepreneurs, in particular those in Britain, had been analysing the costs, and realised how to make the low cost concept work in Europe. Market research showed there were plenty of customers prepared to forgo the plastic meal tray and other frills if they could get to their destination cheaply. Bankers realised that it would be possible to lend money to a low cost airline, and make a profit. So across Europe a new generation of airlines took to the air. Some went bust, some merged, but many still survive.

Watching their cosy existence being threatened by these upstarts, Europe's scheduled carriers tried to make life as difficult as possible for them. Although EU regulations allow operators within the European Community to set up in a member state, it doesn't mean the carriers from that state have to make this easy. Such tactics as encouraging environmental groups to protest about extra landings can mean local authorities slapping on landing restrictions, which won't allow extra flights.

However:

O Airlines realised passengers didn't need to fly in to an expensive major airport. Some were back-packers or low-cost travellers, happy to spend an extra hour or two getting to a city if it meant they saved money. Europe is a very crowded continent, which means there is a well-populated catchment area for most smaller airports, for leisure and business traffic.
O People buying second homes in the countryside welcomed the chance of visiting them more cheaply; areas around La Rochelle and Poitiers recorded a 20% increase in property value when the low cost carriers flew in.
O Many of the secondary airports were within easy reach of major population areas where residents welcomed the chance of a quick trip to a local airport rather than a long journey to an international or major airport.

So new companies tested the market – and when others saw bookings exceeded all predictions, the floodgates opened. It wasn't long before European airlines looked across the Channel, saw what was happening in Britain, and decided they could copy the successful formula.

> **Mike O'Leary, CEO of Ryanair, says I am not a 'cloud bunny – I don't like airplanes'**
> He got in to the airline industry when he recognised a commercial gap in the market and decided to adopt the supermarket principle: pile 'em high – sell em cheap. He reckoned tight cost management would keep overheads down, and potential passengers would be so numerous that although the profit margin was very low, high load factors would make flights profitable. He looks for every way to cut costs and doesn't even supply highlighters for office workers – deeming you can underline comments and save money by using biros which 'I tell staff not to buy – just pick them up from hotels, etc.'

SET-UP AND RUNNING COSTS

Set-up and running costs for these airlines are minimal.

○ Meals are not included, neither are drinks – but the airlines make extra money by selling sandwiches and drinks (often at inflated prices) to their captive customers.

○ Booking over the Internet means if a destination isn't selling, airlines can easily drop one loss-making destination and switch to selling another. As one major airline executive said ruefully 'it takes us months to decide to switch routes, or swop an aircraft if load factors are low – these boys do it over the morning cup of coffee'.

○ Another way is to cut luggage allowance – generally only 15 kilos as against 20-23 kilos on major carriers.

○ If you lose your luggage, surveys show some low cost carriers have few staff to deal with problem.

○ Ticketless bookings save money. Passengers booking over the internet are given a reference number as confirmation, and print out their own ticket details. This is handed to check-in staff in exchange for a ticket, so saving money and overheads for the airline.

○ Although airlines are supposed to include taxes, airport fees, security payments etc. in their prices, the no frills carriers frequently put these down as add-ons – sometimes in very small print. Gradually passengers are getting wise to this, but it is taking the scheduled carriers some time to get across the message that their prices include everything. In the airline's defence it can be confusing for them too; Manchester Airport is reputed to have more than 1,000 price bands covering runway use, aircraft parking and baggage handling.

○ Sometimes the small print allows flights to be cancelled – and all passengers might be entitled to is a refund of ticket costs. Not much compensation if you have to stay overnight at an hotel at your expense, then buy a full-fare ticket, but not paying for hotels is another way of keeping down costs.

○ They also cut back on stand-by aircraft used for back-up if there are problems.

Cost of Flights

Low cost carriers have been clever in building up the idea in the public's mind that their flights are the cheapest – so if a traveller goes on the internet to book, they will often book at whatever the current cost is on screen, without bothering to compare prices; even though they could often find a cheaper fare with a scheduled carrier. Newspaper and TV holiday programmes have found this out, but the public doesn't seem to mind.

Small airports generally have much cheaper landing fees, and many are owned by Chambers of Commerce or the local authority who are delighted when a low-cost airline opens up a route. They know this will have a tremendous knock-on effect for the local economy. Clever marketing has seen local chambers helping with subsidies when they know a low cost airline will bring in a massive increase in visitors. Also their members welcome the fact they can fly more cheaply to meet customers, and tourist industry members – hotels, restaurants, shops etc. benefit by high-spending short-stay visitors eager to try a new destination. Reportedly 'hotel reservations rose by 40% in La Rochelle' and British tourists' spending increased by £4 million in the town,after the arrival of low cost flights.

One way low-cost airlines cut costs is to point out the benefits to the local economy, then look for subsidies from airports wanting increased landings and more airport retail income. Local Chambers of Commerce representing the tourist industry can subsidise landing fees, (in one case negotiating a rate of £100 per flight as opposed to the quoted £1,000), help with advertising costs, provide free offices, crew training, check-in facilities, etc.

At Charleroi Airport (in Southern Belgium near Brussels) Ryanair negotiated a landing fee of €1 per passenger, almost half of the previous fee. However, a recent court case saw the European Union declare that Ryanair could not do this, O'Leary of course went on prime time European-wide TV to declare that this was the EU working against the individual, and got himself an enormous amount of publicity.

If Ryanair – eventually – has to repay the £3 million the EU says he should, one wonders how much the free publicity was worth.

However, the big boys took up the cudgels, went to Brussels crying unfair competition, and in many instances the no-frills carriers were forced to seek alternatives – and try even more innovative ways of obtaining subsidies.

When Ryanair flew into Strasbourg, passenger arrivals increased from 3,000 per month to 15,000. Ryanair had negotiated a subsidy from the local Chamber of Commerce. However, they had tweaked the nose of Brit Air (subsidiary of Air France), with the result there was a court case, which Ryanair lost. The French Appeals Court upheld a decision to bar subsidies, deeming them to be an improper use of public funds. So Ryanair are going back to court, but in the meantime they switched to Baden-Baden, 25 miles away in Germany.

ROUTE DEVELOPMENT MANAGERS

Most airports have now appointed a **Route Development Manager** to go out to airlines and encourage them to open routes using their airport airport. Now this department can be so busy there are several supporting staff.

Colin Oakley is Route Development Manager for Stansted Airport. He was delighted that his hard work encouraging AirPolonia to develop a route from Poland to the UK was paying off. So well are bookings going that projected sales targets have been reached far earlier than expected, which is good for Stansted.

The airport stands to benefit from airport fees levied on passengers, and from sales in retail shops. With a split 60/40 in favour of bookings from Britain, Stansted Airport will be relying on their 'buy before you fly' scheme for these passengers. Passengers can buy certain goods before they fly, and collect them on their return. The Polish passengers will probably be enticed into the duty free retail to stock up before they return home. These new passengers will keep sales tills ringing, and the airport authorities happy. If you are good at creative and strategic thinking, developing new routes could just up your street.

○ Researching the viability of flying between one airport and another.
○ You have to understand the economics of operating an airline, and work with them to discover how they can slot in as many rotations as possible in a day.
○ Promoting to potential passengers.
○ Tapping in to the ethnic market.
○ Contacting relevant embassies.
○ Liaising with Churches, religious groups and community leaders.
○ Alerting language newspapers published in Britain.
○ Contacting ethnic restaurants, shops, etc.

Profits

If a route isn't profitable, all it takes the low cost carriers is a quick negotiation with receptive airports, and a change of web pages, to switch to a more profitable destination. Bad luck if you work for the airline on the ground at this destination; you may lose your job. But the planes have to keep flying to make money, there will be an alternative destination to service and staff will be needed there. With any luck the alternative airport will be within few kilometres so you still keep your job.

LOW COST AIRLINES

Due to media overkill, people might think there was only *easyJet* and *Ryanair* slogging it out for the low cost market out of Britain. However, Wanderlust, the travel magazine, recently named *FlyBE* as the UK's most preferred low cost airline.

Wanderlust placed FlyBE's major new base, Southampton International, as the UK's top airport. Southampton has seen a phenomenal rise in the number of passengers as a result of FlyBE's extensive operations. 73.8% of readers voted for the airline, which now serves 17 UK airports and 20 international destinations. In Finland, the fastest-growing airline is *Blue1* (ex-Air Botnia), part of SAS, meaning around 50 new positions being created, mainly among cabin crew and in the technical department. It is estimated that Blue1 will have 340 employees at the end of the year, compared with 40 in 1998. In total, the SAS Group has nearly 1,000 employees in Finland.

To counter passengers' perceptions, some airlines are coming up with innovative ideas. Punctuality is very important for frequent fliers; so to reassure their passengers, *Spanair* has come up with a 'free ticket' offer. Any passenger on a Spanair flight that is delayed more than 15 minutes through a fault of the airline, receives a free ticket for their next flight. Staff go through the cabin handing out vouchers, so there is no waiting to claim.

This promotion has helped Spainair to maintain a 90% punctuality rating. However, normally delays are caused by Air Traffic Control problems outside the airline's jurisdiction, and they stipulate the delays must be their fault.

When Ryanair announced they were investing in opening two new bases: Rome Ciampino and Girona Barcelona, enabling them to reach into relatively untapped European markets, they seem well on the way to reach their target of carrying 50 million passengers a year. And to counter any adverse rulings about Ryanair using 'creative' marketing techniques at other airports, to the detriment of scheduled airlines, O'Leary has mused that he might take a stake in private airports – thereby making it more difficult for competing airlines to complain.

SkyEurope of Slovakia led the way with services from Bratislava and Budapest to London Stansted and Paris, firstly putting Slovakia on the map, then revolutionising the fare structures from Budapest and bringing much needed competition to the region. Up until that time locals had a 60 mile journey to Vienna, where fares are generally high. Needless to say, the airline is happy with passenger numbers. Recently Malev, the Hungarian airline, has countered with a £46 (ex taxes) return fare Budapest to London Stansted.

Air Berlin operates out of Berlin, and is expanding services into other European destinations (see below), but in return Ryanair and have their eyes set on Central European destinations.

Then there are *Voegol* in Brazil, *Germanwings* (part owned by Lufthansa) and *Hapag-Lloyd Express* (owned by TUI) in Germany, *Goodjet* in Sweden, *Virgin Blue* in Australia – and now QANTAS have announced they are starting a low-cost baby, *Kulula* in South Africa, *Tango* in Canada, *JetBlue* in the USA – with more start-ups every month. Even TUI, the giant German tour operator who own Britannia Airways is starting up another airline, *Thomsonfly*, to be based at Coventry. This is not a traditional airport, but ideally placed for the heavily-populated Midlands area.

What is described as the world's first backpacker airline, flying between England and Australia, and offering low fares, a full-size bar on board and in-flight catering of pies and pizzas, is about to launch. *BackpackersExpress* is scheduled to fly three times a week from Manchester to Melbourne, offering a 'one party class'.

This is only the beginning. Other carriers are lining up to enter the fray, and to counter this most of the major scheduled carriers have decided if they can't compete, they will join in. BA has been doing this, and with Austrian Airlines planning to start services to Bratislava and the Emirates starting service to Vienna as their gateway into Central Europe next year, a 25% increase in traffic is not an unrealistic forecast.

The only unhappy people are the environmentalists, who say that cheap, short-haul journeys are one of the biggest contributors to global warming. The Royal Commission on Environmental Pollution has published a report calling for a 'green tax' of £70 per passenger, saying short-haul flights have higher fuel consumption than long-haul because large amounts of fuel are consumed during take-off. But with Government proposals projecting a tripling of air travel by 2030, it looks as though the environmentalists will be thrown the sop of a small payment of £5 or £10 to compensate.

Who Flies?

The new carriers are attracting an interesting mix of business. They claim it is principally new business, increasing the overall size of the market, rather then making inroads into the existing traffic. This is all good news for the travel and tourism industry. With the low cost carriers promoting destinations and low fares rather then the airline's own product, countries and cities are getting a much needed boost to raise awareness levels and helping to place them more firmly on the shopping list of the prospective traveller.

According to Gill Wilson from the marketing consortium Visit Central Europe, these low-cost carriers are building the routes with new passengers using the internet. One good result for passengers has been that many of the major carriers have been forced to offer lower fares to try and retain customers. Savvy travellers now check with BA, Swiss and other major airlines, and are surprised to find that often these big boys can match or undercut the so-called cheap airlines.

Across the world there are people who are prepared to put up with almost anything, if the price is cheap. If they suffer horrendous delays or lack of customer care, they just shrug their shoulders and ask what can you expect from a low cost carrier? Waiting for luggage, delayed flights etc. they already know what to expect, but are prepared to take the risk as they optimistically hope for the best.

Some Low Cost Airlines

www.ryanair.com
www.easyJet.com
www.bmibaby.com
www.airpolonia.com, etc. and look in the *Website Addresses* chapter for more.
www.spanair.es
Blue1 human.resources e-mail fin@sas.se
www.mytravelairways-careers.co.uk
www.airberlin.com
www.flybe.com
www.voegol.com
www.germanwings.com
www.hapag-lloyd-express.com
www.virginblue.com
www.flytango.com
www.jetBlue.com

The Future

If you look at a map of Europe, apart from the Costas, Spain has many opportunities for a low cost carrier to make inroads. Italy receives 60-70 million tourists a year, but Alitalia made the decision some years ago to close its direct routes from other countries, leaving Milan and Rome as their only gateway airports. Visitors who wanted to visit Venice, Naples,Turin, etc. were forced to transfer at one of these gateways and wait around for a connecting flight. Now they can catch a low cost airline from a UK airport near them direct to their destination in Italy.

Tourism is opening up the Eastern European countries, but their road and train transport is very old, so the no-frills carriers will be eyeing these interesting destinations. It is no surprise that two of the most recent start-ups have been in this area: *AirPolonia* and *Sky Europe*.

Scandinavia is also opening up. SAS has already invested in the Spanish-based *Spanair*, flying between Scandinavia and the Iberian Peninsula. SAS also own a stake in the Norwegian airline *Widerøe* which has just succeeded in returning to profit following a turbulent period after September 11th. CEO Mr. Watle recently announced that 1.25 million passengers flew with Widerøe in last year, an increase of 13 percent compared with the same period last year. However, he sounded a warning, saying 'the growth in the number of passengers travelling does not reflect a growth in passenger revenue. It is exactly on the same level as last year, namely 1.1 billion Norwegian Kroner. The reason for this is that each passenger is paying gradually less per kilometre. The public is no longer willing to purchase full-fare tickets'. So Wideroe reacted by introducing a new and simpler product while at the same reducing fares by up to 25% on some routes.

Widerøe is now the largest regional airline in the Nordic countries, with 1,250 employees, flying to 34 destinations in Norway and 6 destinations abroad (including Aberdeen, Manchester and Newcastle-upon-Tyne). In 2002 Widerøe was awarded the silver medal in the competition for Europe's best regional airline.

In Poland, *AirPolonia* started out in 2001 offering cargo flights and flying lessons. With Poland's integration into the EU, the airline has recently commenced operations between Britain and Poland. Domestic flights to Szczecin and Poznań will shortly connect with these international flights, and plans are to expand to Cologne, Frankfurt Hahn, Stockholm, Brussels, Paris, Milan, Rome, Barcelona, and Madrid.

AirPolonia say 'we are able to offer low prices, because':

- Our sales and distributions costs are kept down by using a sales system based on our call centre and website.
- We do not pay commissions to travel agencies for tickets sold by them.
- Our in-flight service costs are lower as we do not offer free catering and other free in-flight services.
- We keep airport charges down by mainly using cheap airports.
- Our handling costs are lower due to the type of services we offer.
- Making fuller use of cockpit crews and cabin crews also helps us to keep costs down.
- Our carrier programme allows us more flights daily for each aeroplane.
- We only use one type of aeroplane, which also helps us to keep costs down.
- As in other low-cost airlines, our aeroplanes have a larger number of seats on board – (er, yes!).
- Efficient management systems and optimum staffing levels ensure low administrative costs and overheads.

The conditions for our airline to succeed are:

1. Integration of Poland with the European Union.
2. GDP growth expected to take place over the next few years.
3. A forecasted recovery in tourism in Poland.

One thing that may encourage passengers to return to scheduled carriers is seat pitch. Once passengers are used to flying, they may start querying the seat pitch (space between back of seat in front and the back of your seat) on low cost carriers; currently they can't expect anything more than the minimum legal distance between seats. In a case at Chester County Court, Judge Gareth Edwards, QC, called for extra leg room for passengers on long-haul flights, saying each seat should be at least 34 ins from the one in front. However, he said the court did not have the power to set guidelines, but this may set a precedent for some of the pressure groups to start backing passengers' complaints about lack of space. The award of £500 in this case could escalate, forcing airlines to take out seats and improve leg room.

If you want to know how different airlines' seat pitch compares, see the Wexas International site wwwtravelleronline.com. Currently the minimum seat pitch allowed by the CAA is 26 ins – but it is considering raising this minimum after research showed passengers in such cramped seats could be trapped in a burning plane.

Whatever the low cost airlines do to keep up the momemtum, tour operators might slow this down. Previously they were able to negotiate cheap fares direct with airlines by bulk buying. Now, easily available low fares means travellers don't have to buy operators' packages, but can arrange their own accommodation which may theoretically work out cheaper (until something goes wrong).

Many tour operators own their own airlines, and are fighting back with packages aimed at the low cost airline market: city packages, pick-and-mix packages, and anything with a low price that will encourage travellers to fly. Their own airlines are joining in; see the previous chapter.

Having ignored the package tour operators, low-cost carriers now realise that it can make sense to work with the trade, so many are looking into operating a dedicated website where tour operators can log in to reserve group bookings. Either way, the passenger will benefit, so bookings should increase.

In Asia, Tony Ryan, Ryanair's founder, is launching an Asian version of his low-cost airline, called Tiger Airways. It will be based at Singapore's Changi Airport and–in an interesting departure from the norm–is also backed by Singapore Airlines.

Whatever happens in the future, BA may regret its decision to sell off its low-cost carrier GO, albeit for a hefty profit. Recently Ray Webster, CEO of easyJet, said 'the low-cost airline market still has only 15% penetration in Europe, so there is plenty of upside'.

WHAT STAFF ARE NEEDED TO KEEP THESE AIR-LINES FLYING?

Although the low cost carriers have cut staff to the bone, they still provide employment for many people: 1,800 work for Ryanair, and 1,500 work for Flybe. Not only do they need pilots and cabin crew, but all the support staff working at check-ins, in administration and behind the scenes.

The airlines may be low cost, but **pilots** are still paid comparable salaries to traditional airlines. Ryanair say their pilots earn up to £125,000 a year plus share options.

Cabin crew may not be so well paid, but there is such demand that many apply for jobs as a way in, then go on to work for major carriers when they have experience, so freeing up more jobs.There are frequent adverts for cabin crew; most low cost carriers' websites will give more details.

Administration staff are needed too, of which sales and marketing and telesales form a vital component. Then there will be **CSAs, ramp staff, engineers,** etc. And as long as low cost carriers are around, costs will be so important that **accountants and financial analysts** will always be needed. These people are crucial to an airline operation, ensuring that costs are contained. If you are thinking of a career in this sector, financial directors, deservedly so, are generally paid extremely good salaries.

CALL CENTRES

When these airlines started up, it didn't take them long to realise that prospective passengers didn't have the time or the inclination to book with a travel agent. They were used to going online, and loved the ease with which they could book a flight from their own PC, aided by back-up from telesales agents, who could be contacted at any time. Some airlines say 94%-97% of bookings are now done over the net.

Although many airlines have moved, or are moving their call centres to India (for the cost savings), there are still jobs, especially if you speak the lesser-known languages. e.g. AirPolonia's call centre in Warsaw is open 12 hours daily from 8 a.m. to 8 p.m., 7 days a week, with the option of extending operators' work around the clock, and staff speak Polish, English and German.

easyJet's call centre is based at Luton Airport. They particularly look for French and Dutch speaking staff (A level standard or native speaker), with keyboard skills and fluent written/spoken English, to work between 20-40 hours per week. So it is possible to do part-time work.

Ben Owen, from the easyJet Call Centre says '*easyJet sells its seats direct, and our call centre team is the first point of contact that our customers have with the airline. It is our aim to provide a friendly and personalised service. We make ourselves available to our customers 24 hours a day, 7 days a week*'.

easyJet say:
- There are a variety of shifts between the hours of 7. a.m. and 11p.m., 7 days a week including Public holidays.
- Full time staff will be required to work five 8 hour shifts per week and part time staff will be required to work a minimum of 20 hours a week.
- Various combinations of shifts are available for both full and part time agents but you must be flexible in the hours you can offer and be able to work a number of evening and weekend shifts.
- We are unable to employ staff on a temporary or short-term contract.
- Salary structure is commission based and your earnings are dependent upon the number of seats you sell. Earnings average between £13,500 and £15,000 per annum for full time agents and language speakers are paid an increment of 4% for fluency in one language and 8% for fluency in two languages.

Applicants should be:

O Friendly and customer caring.
O Able to remain calm and efficient under pressure.
O An excellent communicator with people of all ages and different cultures.
O Able to take direction and accept feedback.

Minimum requirements are:

O Age 18+.
O Good general standard of education with GCSE or O levels.
O Fluent in written and spoken English.
O Knowledge of computer and keyboard skills.
O Previous experience in a customer contact role is essential.
O Ability to speak or write fluently in French, Spanish, Greek, German or Dutch.

Working for an airline Call Centre, Abby looked for an interesting job when she left college.

I did German as one of my subjects, and EasyJet were advertising for German speakers, so I thought I could practice my language skills. First I sent in an application form, which they followed up with a telephone interview to see if my voice was OK. Of course, my young kid sisters were home from school and screaming. They said I coped very well with background noise and asked me to attend an assessment day. This included a group exercise (which was rather fun), a presentation on the call centre agent's role and an individual interview. I liked the idea of flexi-hours, so I could have time off to attend interviews. About four weeks later I was sent an e-mail, followed by a letter, offering a place on a training course. Then the fun started.

Being back at work has given me a new focus, and now that I have settled in I enjoy the challenge of speaking German, so I may be here for ever! I have to work some late shifts, but not too many. We are a fun team, and although it gets frantic and you don't have a moment for yourself, every time you put the phone down after a sale you have earned more points towards your bonus.

And I get to fly – wait until I turn up at Luton with my kid sisters. That will put the cabin crew to the test!

Training courses take place Monday to Friday 9.00am to 6.00pm with the weekend off and resume the following Monday. Telesales Agents are currently based at EasyLand, headquarters at London's Luton airport.

There are jobs around the world; BA recently advertised in its house magazine for a *Telesales Agent* who must have *Australian residency and proven call centre experience with Amadeus knowledge.*

Security and Safety

PASSENGER SAFETY

Behind the scenes, and well away from the public's gaze, there are thousands of people working together to improve safety at airports and in planes around the world.

Because airports and aircraft have a high profile, they make potentially good targets for terrorist activity, especially for groups that may want to gain publicity. However, because these venues make such high-profile targets, security has improved immeasurably in recent times to counter this threat.

If you are worried you might be going to work in an insecure environment, ask insurance companies for their advice. Insurance companies carry out risk assessment as part of their work, and they will tell you that, unless you are going to work on an airfield in a war zone, or for aid flights that might be suspected of carrying arms, generally, working in aviation does not carry any extra insurance risk.

If an insurance company does not ask for a higher premium – they just don't think the risks are there. And when you think about it, the most dangerous place you can be is at home. More people have accidents here than anywhere else.

Every so often some journalist will supposedly infiltrate an airport security system to tell readers how lax this is. Today, it is more than likely that that journalist would have been under surveillance from the time they started, and the authorities have been watching them, checking to see that their systems are working. However, no one involved in this sector is complacent, and the security and safety equipment manufacturing sector constantly carries out fascinating research to improve and upgrade products.

When you go to work in an airport, you will gradually come to know about some of these highly sophisticated systems monitoring today's aviation industry. To ensure that airports and airlines are kept well guarded, so that everyone can work in a secure and stable environment, there are many jobs for people working in security. Often these are not advertised: a job will come about because a scientist invents a new surveillance system, or a company thinks of a new application for something it has developed.

In general, many security jobs in aviation can be mundane. Sky Marshals complain bitterly about the boredom of their job. But if you have an enquiring mind, if you can think laterally and when faced with a new product you ask the question 'could such and such be used for security or safety purposes?' and the answer is yes – you might have got yourself a fascinating job.

> **As the giant electronics company Siemens (www.siemens.com) say:**
> *You can set yourself a challenge. Or go looking for it. The future's full of fascinating possibilities.*
>
> *People with the ability to generate innovative ideas and the courage to implement them will be able to unlock these possibilities and turn them into realities. Siemens is looking for people like this. Team players who are ready to give more of themselves to find solutions to help make tomorrow's world a better place for all of us.*
>
> *In addition to your educational background – including basic business and PC skills – we are interested in your core competencies, your ability to succeed in different cultural environments, and naturally your language abilities. English plus another language would be ideal.*

Because the incidents attract high media attention, today passengers are likely to worry about possible terrorist activity. Recent media pictures of the forces in Britain carrying out anti-terrorism exercises at Heathrow were shown worldwide. Across the world there are very, very few incidents, but Genric, the security consultants, say that of terrorism victims :

O 69% are from business sectors
O 8% Government or Diplomatic staff
O 23% Others

Not surprisingly, **Rachel Briggs** of the Foreign Policy Centre in London says 'Companies must ensure that employees have the right information and tools to take responsibility for their own safety and well-being'.

Today, if you work for a company whose staff are potential kidnap victims, you will be trained in what to do at Airports: safest places to sit on an aeroplane and in the departure lounge, keeping baggage safe, when baggage is at its most vulnerable, avoiding mugging or kidnapping attempts, etc.

All this training emphasises that the best way to look after yourself is to be alert, watch your luggage, and ensure that you draw the attention of anyone acting out of character to the attention of the authorities. And, of course, tell them about any suspicious packages left around.

To encourage greater security for passengers, IATA has inaugurated the IATA Aviation Security Award of Excellence to be presented annually to an individual or organisation considered to have made a significant contribution to aviation security in the previous 12 months.

Gregory Khan, a Purser on Qantas Airways, was the first person to be presented with this award, in recognition of his extraordinary bravery and courage.

The citation said his actions were crucial in protecting the aircraft and safety of all passengers and crew on board Qantas flight 1737 on May 29, 2003, soon after it left Melbourne bound for Tasmania. Mr. Khan was repeatedly stabbed in the head when he confronted an attacker, who tried to storm the cockpit armed with two sharpened wooden stakes. Mr. Khan put his body between the man and the cockpit door and pushed him back down the aircraft's aisle, all the while being stabbed in the back of the head with the stakes.

If not for the actions of Mr. Khan, the man would have most likely been successful in his attempt to take control of the aircraft with catastrophic results. After his arrest and capture, during the formal police interview, it is alleged that the offender admitted that he intended to take control of the aircraft and crash it in a remote area in Tasmania. He was subsequently charged with one count of attempted hijacking of an aircraft and two counts of attempted murder.

AIRPORT SECURITY

BAA is considered a world leader in airport security, and more than one in three of their UK employees work in this sector. BAA was the first airport operator to introduce 100% hold baggage screening, and have recently recruited over 1,000 extra employees to work in this sector. They work closely with TRANSEC (Transport Security Department of the Department for Transport, or DfT) and other Government agencies to improve and innovate security measures.

TRANSEC has responsibility for ground-based security at UK airports, and the aircraft operating from them. This work comprises security policy development, issuing of secondary legislation, and monitoring and enforcing compliance with those requirements.

This covers both:

O Physical security (searching and screening of passengers, staff, cargo, catering, etc).
O Procedural security (e.g. background checks for pass holders).

Recently BAA advertised for an **Airport Security Manager** at Heathrow who would be responsible for developing and supporting the implementation of the airport's security strategy. Salary £80,000 plus car, bonus and share options.

TRANSEC are also responsible for ensuring that the staff at airports are qualified for security work; security staff must be trained to Level One using the syllabus set down by the DfT. Those undertaking the training must have attended a DfT course. In addition, staff undertaking the x-ray task at airports must pass a test set by the Department.

Useful Address
www.dft.gov.uk/training/aviation

Recent innovations have included explosive trace-detection arches for passengers: for more information see www.baa.com/security.

Security Guard

Brigette Fahy works as a Security Guard for BAA, based at Heathrow Airport

Heathrow is the world's busiest international airport and the world's second busiest cargo port. Over 90 airlines are based here, and thousands of passengers travel through Heathrow every day, each one an individual. It is our job to keep them all safe.

Allied to this is the somewhat unusual task of searching passengers' bodies and looking at their personal possessions. Even though this was very unusual initially, after a few days these barriers fall away and the importance of what we do takes over.

The best aspects of the work are that of team-working, respecting colleagues' views and opinions, but also being respected as an individual. This is very important. Also the fact that not only high standards of security are required, but there is scope for demonstrating good customer service and dealing with an unlimited variety of people and situations. In fact many passengers find travelling a stressful experience, and much satisfaction can be gained by us demonstrating a calm and professional attitude.

Self-motivation is an important part of the role, as out of necessity there is some repetition in the work. Nevertheless the rewards are there for those who are willing to maintain high standards and show first-class team-working and communication skills.

The role of a security guard is to maintain security standards and ensure the smooth transition of passengers, staff and airport users, as instructed by the Department of Transport, Local Government and the Regions (DTLR) directorate. Principal responsibilities are:

○ To screen all personnel passing through restricted areas by using both archway detectors and manual body searching, where necessary.
○ Screen all items being carried into restricted areas, using both x-ray equipment and manual search, in order to ensure that no prohibited items are taken into the restricted zone which could endanger the aircraft, passengers or crew.

○ Check identification or travel documents for all passengers, staff and airport users requiring access.

○ Resolve queries from customers and assist them with the journey through the airport.

○ Read and adhere to security notices, completing documentation clearly and concisely on any incidents which may occur.

○ Assist with emergency situations which could arise within the terminals (i.e. evacuation procedures).

○ Patrol the terminal and airside areas to ensure that the terminal is secure (i.e. any suspicious persons are identified and their presence is justified, airside/landside doors are secure, etc).

SECURITY STAFF

The security guards you see sitting at check-in, watching your luggage or hand baggage as it goes past on an X-ray screen, are the visible part of the huge workforce working today for airport security. Like an iceberg, only a small part is visible; there are many more jobs behind the scenes.

If you are in a long queue you will see guards constantly changing; they should only work 20 minutes at a time, so that they are always alert. Even so, there have been instances when a guard has missed an important item as it goes past. So to ensure guards are kept on their toes and alert, companies now build in random imprints of dangerous items on the computerised screen. The moment the guard sees the imprint, they should alert superiors. If they don't, there is an automatic alarm, and they are taken off their duties.

However, a recent letter in Skyport, the Heathrow Airport magazine, highlighted the plight of some security staff. Paid the minimum wage, they are expected to handle potential life-threatening situations as part of their everyday jobs. The writer said he was paid £5.20 per hour, for shifts that sometimes covered 12 hours, with overtime at the same rate.

SECURITY AGENCIES

Today, security is a worldwide process, with agencies consulting each other across the globe. In Britain airport and airplane security is generally under the supervision of the Department for Transport (DfT). They work closely with other agencies and exchange information constantly.

In the USA it is the US Transportation Security Administration (TSA), which is regularly in the news, often for the wrong reasons. There were many criticisms of operational procedures post September 11, and sometimes the TSA looks to introduce and upgrade security, without thinking laterally or consulting with other agencies.

By announcing that EU visitors' passports issued after October 2004 must contain biometric data – even though this is not due for introduction until later, the TSA threw the massive European tour operating industry into turmoil.

The TSA also wants to use Computer Assisted Passenger pre-screening (CAPPS II) which aims to identify potential terrorists and others who might pose a threat. However, those handling the introduction of the programme are perceived by many as being heavy handed. Civil Rights groups around the world questioned what would happen to the information on visitors once it was installed in a data bank: would this be sold to companies? They also claimed earlier systems (CAPPS) whilst in use did not prevent terrorists boarding flights on September 11.

This highlighted one of the problems of security: the need to ensure that everyone is as safe as possible, whilst being able to strike a user-friendly balance on the way this is carried out. If people are informed, they welcome security measures; installing without consultation invokes a storm of protest.

Useful Address
www.tsacareers.recruitsoft.com

Wes Carleton, writing in the respected industry publication Jane's Review says:
Overwhelmingly, US citizens have no objection to the notion of heightened airport security after September 11, and the concept of a system which would, for example, check passenger names against government databases on individuals having questionable connections with terrorists, or their sympathisers, is generally regarded as acceptable. However, CAPPS II would go much further. First it would require all passengers to provide their date of birth, home address and telephone number when purchasing an airline ticket.

Currently, when anyone purchases an airline ticket 'alert' signals should be flagged up if the purchase is:

O Last-minute.
O Cash payment.
O Long one-way trip, etc.

Eventually everyone could have a security risk category, but it remains to be seen how far civil rights campaigners will be happy for this to be adopted across the board, especially if, to recoup the costs of gathering this information, it was sold commercially.

Meanwhile, the US-VISIT program, operated by the U.S. Dept. of Homeland Security, is going forward using scanning equipment to collect biometric identifiers of incoming visitors such as fingerprints (using an inkless process) and digital photos of visitors. Pilot systems are operating successfully, because they have been introduced sympathetically with regard to passenger preference and comfort.

WHAT IS DEVELOPING?

Worldwide, passengers and Governments are crying out for more effective and faster security, forcing airlines and airports to buy equipment to speed up and improve the system. Today there are many scientists and engineers working for companies in research and development in the security technology sector, trying to come up with new and surer ways of identifying passengers.

Currently detectors designed to prevent 'dirty bombs' from being smuggled into countries and on to aircraft are being installed at Britain's airports, paid for by a £330 million security fund. A 'dirty bomb' is classed as a small amount of toxic or radiological material wrapped inside a quantity of conventional explosive, capable of contaminating large urban areas.

Once a passport was sufficient; now scientists are looking at biometric technology: using iris or facial recognition techniques, when a tiny camera takes a digital impression of our eyes, or face, and relays this information to a computer. Biometric technology can read a person's unique features, such as fingerprints, face or the iris of the eye.

Tell a friend you have never seen eyes like theirs, and you will be 100% correct. Our eyes are made up of 266 different elements, no two are the same, even if they belong to identical twins, and they never change. Handprints have 40 different elements, face scans 80.

Computers can now scan between 60 –200 points of reference, making it virtually impossible for someone to fake their identity, and can come back immediately if any points match up with a suspect.

> **Francesca Freeland of KLM thinks that biometrics are definitely the way forward for the industry:**
> *Trials of Privium (KLM's system of Iris recognition) have been very good at Schiphol, where currently KLM and Air France clients can use the service.At the moment, passengers pay €99 a year to belong to the Privium Club, and their information is stored in a computer. When they go through immigration at an airport in the Privium system, they pass through a special channel, are scanned and checked instantly by computer. This gives club members a faster route through immigration checks; worthwhile to business travellers.*
>
> *IATA have chosen iris recognition, and eventually, if adopted by all the world's airports, there will be no time advantage, so the service will be free.*

Biometric smart cards are probably the next step. Before governments will want to buy expensive machinery and set up a system to include biometric details in passports and identity cards, they will be watching how the SAS Airline biometric (iris) recognition smart cards are working, after tests at Umeå Airport in Sweden using fingerprints.

> **Charlotte Rosengren-Edgren, head of Product Innovation at Scandinavian Airlines says:**
> *We are carrying out tests using smart SAS cards, on which the travellers' fingerprints or iris images have been stored; using technology developed by Fyrplus. At the gate, the card is read without requiring contact and then the passenger puts their finger or eye in front of a scanner. Identity is verified by a comparison of the fingerprint/iris and the card content. Simple, secure and quick for the passenger.*
>
> *A smart card with stored features means that the passenger carries his own personal information. When a match is verified, SAS does not store the information, thereby resolving the issue of personal integrity. Our challenge is to raise the security level, while also simplifying the travel process. Biometry offers us this possibility.*

Looking to the future, ICAO has now adopted facial recognition as the worldwide standard for improved airport security.

FINDING JOBS

In this sector, you are more likely to be offered a job because you are interested in one aspect of security or safety, or because of some work you have done in your academic life.

You can trawl through the various websites listed under security headings; many have a recruitment page which you are asked to fill out. The company will then contact you when they have something suitable (or when they have checked you out fully).

> **The National Security Inspectorate**
>
> Jane Mottram, spokeswoman of the National Security Inspectorate, or NSI (www.nsi.org.uk) says they provide inspection and approval to companies providing a manned guarding service, or security/fire system installation service.
>
> *Companies approved by us include manned guarding companies who work in aviation security. Anyone wanting a job in this sector should approach the security companies direct for any career information, or alternatively the airlines themselves, who will have their own security advisors.*

So how do you find security companies? These companies are understandably secretive, as are the people working in them. If you are interested in working in this field:

○ Ask your lecturers.

O Go on the internet and trawl for exhibitions – security. You may find some companies are listed, so you go to their websites (if they have one) and see what they are developing. They won't have any secrets displayed, but if you like and understand what they do – contacting them could be a way in. Some will even have a Careers or Jobs tab.

O Read the financial sections of serious newspapers, especially the Financial Times. Sometimes there will be a story about a development, which could be used for security. Contact the company.

Useful Addresses
www.adt.com
www.landinst.com
www.magal-ssl.com
www.nice.com
www.novar.com
www.qinetiq.com
www.rapiscan.com

Whatever happens, more sophisticated systems are constantly being adopted, which means more work. Companies are developing increasingly innovative ways to combat crime and terrorism, keep passengers safe and handling their safety and security more efficiently. For this they will need people who look upon this as a challenge.

AIR TRAFFIC CONTROL

The safety challenge facing Air Traffic Control agencies, responsible for moving aircraft across their airspace, lies in allocating a safe distance between aircraft.

Previously, this part of the operation was controlled by paper strips containing each aircraft's information and route, handed to ATC controllers when an aircraft enters 'their' patch. Now, an agreement between Nav Canada and the U.K's NATS (National Air Traffic Services) will provide Integrated Information Display Systems to:

O Create a paperless system.
O Eliminate the need for paper flight strips.
O Allow controllers to manage electronic flight data online using touch-sensitive display screens.
O Reduce the need for voice communications among controllers and replacing the traditional paper strips.

Nav Canada (www.navcanada.ca) says the system is already in use at ten Canadian control towers, and will also provide better interface between airport systems such as gate and apron control.

Handling over 1,000 flights a day across the Atlantic (world's busiest oceanic route), the system at installed at Swanwick will help reassign airspace to make better use of what is available. With the rise in flight numbers, this will mean easier handling and potentially free up more airspace for aircraft, and eventually more jobs.

DISABLED PASSENGERS

It is not only anti-terrorism measures that concern airport security agencies. Health, safety and security of all passengers, particularly those with disabilities, is vitally important, and awareness training is built into airline and airport induction programmes.

As an example, Aer Rianta, the airport operating company, introduced a byelaw which obliged all service providers at Irish state airports to make available facilities required by passengers with disabilities, in order that they could avail themselves of all airport services. Aer Rianta continues to update and improve the facilities it provides for passengers with disabilities throughout the airport, which include:

O Set down area; specially reserved easy access car parking spaces linked to car park control by an intercom system.
O Fully accessible terminal building. Specially adapted facilities including toilets and lifts, all clearly signposted.
O New lifts with inbuilt voiceover and Braille buttons.
O A minicom telephone located at the information desk.
O Induction loops to facilitate amplification of announcements.
O A counter loop system at the information desk.
O Meet and greet system in Arrivals Halls allowing public to electronically page passengers and have messages displayed in the customs hall on a special text board.
O As wheelchair passengers have to check-in their wheelchair, along with their luggage, airports have to provide wheelchairs and trained porters to wheel these between the check-in desk and the aircraft, and again on arrival between the aircraft and the passengers' transport. This cost is either absorbed into the fee that airports charge airlines per passenger, or is passed on to the airline.

For more information about aviation medical safety issues, see the chapter *Looking After Yourself.*

VMAD

Video Motion Anomaly Detection (VMAD) is a new idea to detect thieves and help with security problems. Closed Circuit TV (CCTV) is increasingly used in the fight against terrorism, especially in large areas such as baggage halls. One problem with using CCTV to monitor an area is the difficulty of one person being constantly alert, and able to watch over a bank of screens. Boredom can set in, sending operators to sleep, however short the duty times. Roke Manor, part of the giant Siemens Group, has developed VMAD, and says this produces a monitoring system that will alert staff to a potential problem, long before they might have noticed.

Basically VMAD is a very sophisticated CCTV monitor camera, which teaches itself what is 'normal' in the area it surveys. Once set up:

O It takes time to scan its territory and learn what is normal.
O Once learnt, it constantly scans its patch, responding to any changes in movement, rather than changes in brightness and light, helping to reduce false alarms.
O Anything unusual is highlighted, alerting security staff. e.g. if someone suddenly leaves a queue and goes off at tangent, they could be someone trying to get behind the scenes or go where they are not supposed to. Their action will be followed by the computerised camera, and their screen image will be highlighted in red, quickly alerting any operator, who might not have seen what was happening, especially if it was in the middle of a large crowd.

VMAD not only helps security, but can highlight many other problems such as:

O Bags colliding or falling from a conveyor or carousel (protecting fragile cargo).
O Intruders being where they shouldn't be.
O People or bags stationary for too long in a particular area.
O Anyone jumping over a check-in desk or barrier.
O Assessing if vehicles are taking the correct route or going off-route.
O Identifying unusual behaviour around a terminal building.
O Detecting people approaching aircraft whilst on the ground.
O Detecting if a sensitive zone is approached, even at night.

Incidentally if you watch Wimbledon or Test Cricket, the same company developed the Hawk-Eye system.

Useful Address
www.roke.co.uk

Domino Effect of Flight Delays

One hold-up at the security scanners at an airport, and an aircraft's tight schedule of three rotations a day (six flights outward and back) can be thrown into disarray, causing conflict between airline financial directors and airport security advisors. Although airlines agree with security precautions – their financial directors tear out their hair whenever there are security hitches.

Security is a serious subject, but sometimes high-tech procedures can mean the wood obscures the trees. We have all read of passengers who are arrested at airports because they have joked that they have a bomb in their luggage. It is highly unlikely that a genuine terrorist would say this, but a bored, frustrated, tired and angry passenger might. However the joke is taken seriously, and the passenger enters a nightmare scenario because of a thoughtless remark.

Sadly, although the security personnel are absolutely right to treat every statement seriously, the airline ends up looking stupid – and passengers get resentful. This can be counter-productive; if a passenger suspects something isn't quite right, the sensible thing to do is report it to staff, but resentful passengers decide they don't want authority coming down heavy-handed on them, and the opportunity passes. This may have dire consequences.

Security is NOT a joke – but security staff must realise that sometimes a bit of humour or a more user-friendly approach can get the public on their side. Friendly passengers are more likely to point out something they think is strange – and thereby hangs many a discovery of potential terrorism activity.

> *London's Metropolitan Police realise their motorcycle officers must have their heads protected by helmets, but also realise that today's helmets can look frightening to the general public. They developed a helmet which could quickly have its face-guard lifted, so the public could see the officer's face – and security gained a friendlier face.*

AIRCRAFT SAFETY

One aspect of aircraft safety is the sore subject of overloading – with luggage, hand luggage and/or passenger weight. Airlines have a running battle with passengers who are determined to take on-board as much hand luggage as they can possible stagger with to the gate. But if luggage is too heavy, when the aircraft hits turbulence the locker doors fly open, and luggage flies out to hit an unsuspecting passenger on the head.

Another problem is caused by passenger weight. People are getting heavier, and the average weight per passenger, once used to calculate aircraft load weights, is probably too low for today's flyer. It is possible that inaccurate calculation of passengers' weight was party responsible for a crash in North Carolina in which 21 people died, according to the U.S. National Transportation Safety Board.

In its report on the U.S. Airways accident in January 2003 it concluded that the airline's weight estimates were unreliable, making the aircraft's rear section too heavy. When combined with the fact that mechanics had not rigged the tail flap properly, this made it impossible for the crew to control the plane.

Airlines wage a constant battle with thoughtless passengers, who, for the sake of saving time (they think – but luggage handling is so slick today that often they have no advantage over the carrousel system) will carry on board everything they possess!

Sky Marshals

Sky Marshals were probably first employed on planes in the 1960s, and came to prominence after the hijacking of TWA 847 by terrorists in 1985. El Al is known to have them on board, but will never acknowledge this. Marshals are also employed on US planes, and by some non-US airlines.

If you think this would be an interesting job, apparently it is boring, boring, boring – and although last year over 200,000 people applied to be Marshals in the US alone, none of the programmes are taking on more people. They have their undisclosed sources of recruiting people, and won't say more. This is the type of job for which you would be head-hunted – not something you apply for.

However, some people worry that if they are flying on a plane and a terrorist incident causes a marshal to fire their gun, might the bullet penetrate the cabin structure? Apparently not, according to experts. It is more than likely that Sky Marshals use specially designed ammunition, with hollow point bullets which expand on impact. These would be expected to lodge in the target, rather than emerge and cause other damage.

If a bullet should pierce the hull, according to Dr. Graham Braithwaite, of the Cranfield Safety and Accident Investigation Centre, this would cause decompression, which pilots are trained to deal with by descending very fast to 10,000 feet.

SNIFFER DOGS

More and more dogs are employed in aviation, to sniff out:

- Bombs.
- Explosives.
- Drugs.
- Banned meat and other foodstuffs.
- Tobacco smuggling.
- Currency.

These dogs are very effective, so why are they not used more? Because:

- Handlers are expensive to train.
- Suitable dogs are difficult to find and take a long time to train.

Most dog handlers are employed by agencies such as Customs and Excise, the Forces, the Police, etc. Their handlers are trained first by the agency for their normal work, then they are seconded to dog handling.

Dog handling training is long, difficult and hard work – for the dog handler. The dogs just lap it up! The handler has to learn the psychology of dog handling, where the dog's work becomes play – for the dog – and also learning about caring for the animal.

The dog will start work when it is about 12 – 18 months old, and continue working until it is around eight years of age; it can be demanding work for the dog (no-one worries about the handler!) and rummaging around boxes and vehicles, jumping up and down, can play havoc with a dog's spine.

When a dog is retired, the handler then has to be retrained with a new dog. Incidentally, although most agencies will look after dogs once they are too old to work, generally retired dogs live with their handlers' family. The handler then has the problem of going off to work with the new dog, leaving the other dog at home – when it wants to go on working.

Finding the right type of dog can be difficult. The dogs have to be focused, out-going, alert and willing to keep going all day long. When first presented with a potential puppy recruit, trainers will try them out with play-games; if the dog responds well, then they will take it on. Generally the dogs are pure-bred or crosses; nothing against mongrels, and some have been very successful working dogs, but there are certain characteristics in a breed on which trainers like to build: the agility and enthusiasm of the spaniel, the sheer determination and focus of the malinois (one of the Belgian Shepherd breed), etc.

Journalist Valerie Forster was invited to the Defence Animal Centre dog training establishment at Melton Mowbray, to watch working dogs being trained:

The first thing you notice is the number of different uniforms. Handlers come from all over the world to be trained, but as 99% work for their forces or government agencies, they are dressed in appropriate uniforms. I met Kenyan agents intent on catching smugglers dealing in elephant tusks; RAF crew who would be guarding airfields in Iraq.

The dogs were a mixed lot; most were German Shepherds or similar types, but it was easy to see those dogs who were going to work as sniffer dogs for Customs and Excise; mostly agile little spaniels, with tails like helicopter rotor blades, able to rummage inside small cavities in ships and planes – and they took me off with them.

The dogs were being trained to sniff out drugs, and this seemed to give them no problems at all. No sooner had the sachets been hidden in drainpipes, along beams, at the back of cupboards, in cisterns – or wherever, once the dog was let into the building they soon found them. First you saw the tail take off like a whirring blade, then the dog barked and sat back waiting for its toy.

People imagine that dogs are trained to hunt because they are on drugs. This is nonsense.

To get into any dog handling unit, you have to join one of the enforcement agencies first: the forces, the police, customs and excise; then apply to become a dog handler.

IATA

As an organisation, IATA is rightly concerned about safety and security, and has a large team working on these problems worldwide. IATA is broadening its focus beyond the traditional operational safety areas, into infrastructure safety comprising the safety elements of air traffic services, airports, ground handling, and the wide spectrum of regional safety initiatives. This is against the background of a number of safety threats apparent from accidents and air safety incidents.

IATA already has a well-established organisation for addressing aviation infrastructure improvements. However, a dedicated custodian of the infrastructure safety function is required to integrate and co-ordinate this function if industry leadership is to be achieved.

CAA

The CAA has a Safety Regulation Group (SRG), whose remit is to ensure that UK civil aviation standards are set and achieved in a co-operative and cost-effective manner. The SRG must satisfy itself that aircraft are properly designed, manufactured, operated and maintained; that airlines are competent; that flight crews, air traffic controllers and aircraft maintenance engineers are fit and competent; that licensed aerodromes are safe to use and that air traffic services and general aviation activities meet required safety standards.

To monitor the activities of this complex and diverse industry, SRG employs a team of specialists. They have an exceptionally wide range of skills, including pilots qualified to fly in command of current airliners; test pilots able to evaluate all aircraft types; experts in flying training, leisure and recreational aviation activities; aircraft maintenance surveyors; surveyors conversant with the latest design and manufacturing techniques; flight test examiners; aerodrome operations and air traffic control specialists; and doctors skilled in all branches of aviation medicine.

Useful Address
www.caa.co.uk

FAA

In the United States, the Federal Aviation Administration (FAA) employs, operates and oversees the largest and most complex aviation system in the world, with a safety record that is second to none. They set the regulatory and operational standards for the U.S.

Today, the FAA says it *'finds itself facing the effects of terrorism, structural change and a weak global economy.*
We are confronted with the challenges of reducing an already low commercial accident rate, building an air traffic control system capable of efficiently meeting

future demand, and modernizing our own organization'.

Way back in the 1926, President Calvin Coolidge started federal oversight of air safety in the United States by signing the Air Commerce Act, with the FAA being created in 1958.

But things need to change, and today, the FAA faces challenges demanding nothing less than transforming the system. This they intend to do with a Flight Plan system which lays out the following four goals:

1. *Increased Safety:* safety is not only a top public-interest priority; it is also an economic necessity. People will fly only if they feel safe and will return to the skies only if they trust the system.
2. *Greater Capacity:* aviation capacity is the backbone of air travel. Aviation can grow only if capacity grows. As we increase capacity, we will make sure we do so in an environmentally sound manner.
3. *International Leadership:* aviation safety is a vital national export. We will enhance America's leadership role by sharing our expertise and new technologies with our international partners.
4. *Organizational Excellence:* requiring greater fiscal responsibility, leadership, more co-operation, and performance-based management.

The FAA expects the operation to last until 2008. Their website, www.faa.gov, contains detailed explanations of the plan. With a planned increase in capacity of 31% by 2010, the aviation community needs to develop a strategy for dealing with the increase. Whilst aviation accident rates are at their lowest levels ever, the FAA understands complacency will undermine gains and prevent future progress in safety.

Required Navigation Performance (RNP)

The FAA is also committed to moving the United States from a ground-based navigation system to one located within the aircraft itself. Through the use of onboard technology, pilots will be able to navigate aircraft to any point in the world using only geographical co-ordinates.

Required Navigation Performance (RNP) is an important step in this direction. Because it can establish a high degree of precision, RNP allows for more efficient use of the airspace. In addition, RNP will assist in the development of constant angle descent approaches, increasing safety during approach and landing. Simply put, RNP will allow authorities to fly more planes, closer together, more safely than ever before.

Useful Websites
www.adt.co.uk
www.cisco.com
www.fraport.com
www.iesdigital.com

www.ish.co.uk
www.panasonic.com
www.powerforce.com
www.rapiscan.com
www.securicor.com
www.thalesgroup.com
www.vicom-cctv.com
www.viisage.com (sic)
www.yxlon.com

USA
www.galaxyscientific.com
www.honeywell.com
www.raytheon.com
www.southwestmicrowave.com

Engineering

Any pilot knows that the aircraft they fly is only as good as the maintenance that has been carried out on it by engineers. Engineering departments form the backbone of airlines, and some with large fleets employ 5-10,000 engineers. In the early days of flying, poor maintenance was a major cause of crashes. Today every airline employs qualified engineers, takes out a maintenance contract with an engineering company, or buys a maintenance package from the manufacturer when they purchase an aeroplane and/or engines.

Training has to be thorough and meticulous, as a qualified engineer is accountable in law for 'signing off' the aircraft whose maintenance they have supervised. If there is a crash due to mechanical failure they may be legally liable, and could receive a prison sentence if they had overlooked work that caused the crash.

Since September 11, engineering training has been on hold with many airlines, who have cut down on expenditure in every department, including engineering. Even British Airways has ceased its apprentice programme. So for the past three years engineering recruitment has been cut back. Now there are signs that airlines are realising that they have to address what those in the industry see as potentially a big problem: a lack of trained engineers, but they are more inclined to look for entrants who have already taken a course, and paid for it themselves. Finance directors are taking a hard look at the cost of training, especially if newly-qualified staff, in whom they have invested a great deal of time and money, go to work for another airline.

As one senior director said 'pilots have to pay for their training today – why shouldn't engineers?' Added to this, the Ministry of Education is phasing out Modern Apprenticeships for engineers, which means government funding is no longer available to contribute to costs when training staff.

To add to the problems, the Ministry is introducing a new qualification (which has not yet been finalised), which means that previous training set-ups would have to be changed, so training is being taken over by Colleges and Universities, which means students will have to pay for courses instead of being trained by an airline and receiving an allowance or wage.

However, the upturn in airline bookings is highlighting the fact that there is about to be a severe shortage of trained staff to service aircraft, so British Airways is looking to start up a PEP (professional engineering programme). You have to be aged 18-25, with A levels to take this course; look on their website for up-to-date information.

Whilst airlines halted recruitment, many qualified engineers went over to work for the railways. Their skills are transferable, and railways' engineering requirements are similar to airlines.

Some airlines still offer engineering apprenticeships, or will fund training. You have to phone employers or trawl websites for current details.

PROSPECTS

Engineers are needed by airlines, airports that provide maintenance facilities and aircraft manufacturers. The good news (for readers) is the growing shortage of suitably qualified staff worldwide. The bad news (for employers) is that they find they are battling not only with finance directors, who around the world seem to have halted in-house engineering training schemes in a cost-cutting exercise, rival companies who also want the best staff and have no in-house training, and competition from railways. Rail companies, realising that trained aviation engineers have the skills they need, are recruiting in the aviation sector – and in many cases offering more pay and better conditions.

Manufacturers now sell a package of aircraft and maintenance-for-life. Having built the plane, the aircraft company will then set up and staff an engineering base to maintain the aircraft. This means that engineers come as part of the package, rather than the airline having to find and train its own staff.

> **SEMTA (the Science, Engineering and Manufacturing Technologies Alliance) says:**
> *Demand for professional engineers is high, especially at incorporated and chartered level. This is because engineers are numerate, are used to making decisions and are able to adopt interdisciplinary approaches to problem-solving and project work. More and more, flexibility of skills and adaptability is what industry is looking for. Engineering is full of variety; there are many different careers on offer for people of all interests, backgrounds and abilities.*
>
> *Engineering depends on the skills of the engineers and other people involved. There are lots of important skills in engineering – and they're not all technical and scientific. The field needs creative people, organisers and those who are good working with others. Workers that are happy being involved in interpreting drawings and using their practical skills as well as those that enjoy team work, planning and organising people, projects and materials.*
>
> *Engineering often uses and helps to develop new technology. Engineers ensure that every product that we use is safe, reliable and can be produced and sold at a reasonable cost for the manufacturer and customers, whether it is a telephone, a skateboard or a pair of trainers. An increasing demand for products that are recyclable or are not wasteful of the earth's natural energy resources are also problems that are being tackled by many engineers and the companies that they work for.*

Useful Address
www.enginuity.org.uk.

Currently around the world heads of engineering departments are trying to convince finance directors that now is the time to recruit. However, an ex- head of an engineering department voiced the frustration felt by his colleagues around the world, saying *'There is ignorance from the Government, who are not aware what is happening at the sharp end. A select committee has warned there will be a shortage, but there is no real support for training from Government'*. He believes it is crucial to involve employers in training, and his advice to would-be engineers is: *'With 4 GCSEs at Grade C I would recommend doing a national diploma in Aerospace Studies, coupled with NVQ in Performing Engineering Operations at Level 2, which will get you 'hand skills'. That gives you several aspects of the old Modern Apprenticeship framework (now obsolete).The framework model was split between SEMTA, now responsible for the engineering maintenance side, and TRANSFED (the organisation responsible for passenger handling in transport) who are now responsible for aircraft operations and ground control, etc.'*

Useful Address
www.transfed.org

SUITABLE NVQs

EAL (SEMTA Awards Ltd) the awarding body, offers the following NVQs:

- Intermediate Cert. for IT Practitioners
- Foundation Cert. in Electronics
- Intermediate Cert. in Engineering and Technology
- Advanced Diploma in Engineering and Technology
- Mechanical Manufacturing Engineering
- Fabrication and Manufacturing Engineering
- Aeronautical Engineering
- Engineering Maintenance
- Engineering Production
- Engineering Manufacture
- Engineering Installation and Commissioning
- Engineering Design
- Engineering Systems Maintenance
- Performing Engineering Operations
- Administration
- Instrument Servicing
- Environment Effectiveness Award
- Electrical Electronics Servicing

○ Aircraft Handling Operations
○ Operations within Airports
○ Passenger/Cargo Operations
○ Aircraft Engineering Maintenance

The list is being added to constantly. Contact EAL for more details on 0870-240 6889 or www.eal.org.uk. Then you should go on to complete NVQ Level 3 in Aircraft Maintenance and do a degree in Engineering.

The Learning and Skills Council may well fund a new training centre at Heathrow's Terminal 5, and other airlines are realising they are going to have to start up training schemes again.

IT'S THE LAW

Approximately 10% of the revenue from a flight will go in engineering costs. Safety is paramount, which means maintaining each aircraft at peak operating performance by a team of highly qualified engineering staff. The aviation authorities of most countries lay down precise instructions as to how often an aircraft has to be serviced, from its engines to its airframe, even down to specifying individual parts of an airframe and how many hours they can fly before being inspected. Even if a country doesn't have such an authority, no airline would be able to fly their aeroplanes into another country's airports if these checks hadn't been carried out by qualified engineers – or if they did, the plane/s would be impounded (arrested) until the authorities were convinced that engineering maintenance had been correctly carried out.

The CAA lays down exact schedules of checks that *must* be carried out after so many flying hours, even down to individual engine components.

Each time an aircraft frame and/or engine is inspected, a suitably qualified engineer has to fill out a Mandatory Occurrences Report to confirm that this has been done. In most countries this is a legal document, and so seriously do the authorities take airline safety that mistakes by licensed engineers come under criminal law. Their professional reputation is at stake when they sign a paper to say that the aircraft has had its checks and is safe to fly. So an engineer's job is on the line if anyone discovers that he/she has 'signed off' an aircraft without doing the maintenance work, and if there should happen to be a crash the engineer responsible would be sent to jail if found guilty.

Engineers' work is so highly regarded that there have been cases of engineers checking a plane after a flight, and reporting that there has not been enough fuel on board for that aircraft to have reached its diversionary airport in the event of an emergency – and the company has been heavily fined.

So as well as being an interesting career with the chance to travel the world, engineers also hold a position of responsibility. When you go for interview, before you even start a course, you should be tested for knowledge, skills and attitude; the interviewer should be trying to ensure that you will always have a responsible attitude to your job.

Joe Desmond of Gatwick Aviation Training (GAT) is a man in love with engineering; he says he wouldn't hesitate to ground an aircraft if he found any irregularities.
Starting with the Royal Air Force as an electrician, he joined British Airways as a mechanic and never looked back. Eventually he became training manager with Saudi Arabian Airlines, until starting up GAT to provide engineering training. Joe agrees; *'The aviation world is finding that good engineers are fast disappearing to work for the train companies. Soon, there is expected to be a shortage of good, trained engineers'.*

A former colleague, Roy Drummer, was with BA Engineering for over thirty years, latterly training apprentices. He has watched the way training has developed, and is unhappy about the British Government's current NVQ (National Vocational System). *'It drives down a very narrow route, and companies tend to find NVQ paperwork is too intrusive – in fact horrendous'.*

If you want to become an engineer, both Joe and Roy recommend joining the Armed Forces: RAF, Fleet Air Arm or Army. If that is not an option, join an airline with a good training scheme, although these are getting fewer and fewer. Or take a good engineering course.

Useful Address
www.gat4training.com

Abroad
In North America demand for engineers is so great that engineering contacts say 10,000 Green Cards have been set aside for qualified engineers, while in Australia the Licensed Aircraft Engineers Association has complained that there is a severe shortage of trained engineers.

AIRLINE EMPLOYMENT

Aeroplanes make money for their airlines when they are in the air, not on the tarmac, so the only time the engineering department gets to service an aircraft is in the 'down' time – when it's not flying. Short checks can take place in between flights – longer checks have to be carried out overnight. Sometimes an aircraft has to be taken out of service, which is not popular with the financial department or operations, but it is the law.

Today, Engineers have to learn how to use incredibly sophisticated diagnostic equipment to check equipment and search for faults. There will be

X-ray machines (encased in concrete and lead-lined doors), scanners and heat detection machines with all the special handling that these entail, to scan deep inside an engine and search for faults before they become visible to the naked eye. Some of this equipment is portable, in case there is a problem away from base.

Many major airlines carry out maintenance under contract for other airlines – sometimes even rivals.

Engineering staff play an important role across the board. As well as servicing and looking after engines and the airframe, there are specialists that look after everything from electronics to seats. You may be involved with line maintenance (day-to-day servicing) or major overhauls, working on jets and propeller-driven aircraft. The average working week is 40 hours – which is often shift and overnight work.

Development engineers play an important part in an airline's plans, as they evaluate every component on an aircraft, and search for better (and of course cheaper!) equipment. For instance, aircraft seats cost anything from £1,000 in economy to upwards of £5,000 in premium class, so cost analysis is an important job to try and cut down seat costs. When British footballers trashed Cathay Pacific's new seats, not only did the airline have to replace them, but they also lost the Business Class revenue whilst the plane had to return to Hong Kong to have them fitted – an expensive business. Recently Ryanair has announced it will be phasing out reclining seats, saying this will save millions of pounds in seat repairs every year, and please those people who have had their lunch dumped in their lap when the person in front reclines their seat without warning.

Engineers have to:

○ Be able to develop their workshop computer system to integrate with the company's network.
○ Have the ability to work under extreme pressure.
○ Have good organisational skills and be able to work with the minimum of supervision.
○ Possess computer skills such as operating Excel.

What can you earn?
Recent job ads included:

○ Aircraft Structures and Stress Engineers up to £40,000 p.a.
○ Aircraft Wing anti-icing engineers at £28.05 an hour.
○ Quality Control managers at £35,000.

Useful Address
www.aviationjobsearch.com

AIRPORT EMPLOYMENT

Airports also need engineers. Maintenance managers work in a challenging environment, handling airport maintenance, taking responsibility for a team overseeing day-to-day maintenance, plus devising and implementing new ways to improve systems. You will need an appropriate engineering HNC or equivalent experience. If you understand computerised maintenance procedures that adds to your employability.

Currently many airlines have frozen recruitment in their engineering departments, preferring to contract out maintenance to companies that specialise in this. So you could be working for a service company, based at an airport, rather than the airline itself; you could miss out on perks such as flights, but pay often compensates. Opportunities may exist at a minor airport where land is cheaper: e.g. KLM do much of their servicing at Norwich Airport.

At Manchester Airport (www.manchesterairport.co.uk) they are expanding, and looking for people to work in group procurement, covering telecoms, energy, facilities management and engineering services. Salaries are up to £55,000 p.a.

The BAA are major employers, and say their maintenance managers 'work in a challenging environment, developing airport maintenance, taking responsibility for a team overseeing day-to-day maintenance, plus devising and implementing new ways to improve systems'.

You must have HNC qualification in an appropriate engineering discipline or have equivalent experience, and experience of introducing computerised maintenance procedures would be helpful.

Recently the BAA advertised for maintenance managers and technicians for Stansted Airport. The Authority was looking for skilled technicians, dealing with everything from ground lighting to X-ray equipment. Candidates needed to be HNC or ONC qualified with a high level of mechanical and electrical expertise on plant and equipment, and their associated control systems. The jobs involved shift work 365 days a year, 24 hours a day. Other BAA requirements included :

O Airport Lead Engineers at Heathrow £43,000.
O Maintenance Team Managers £32,000-£36,000 + bonus.
O Planning Engineers Gatwick £33,000.
O Resource Co-ordinators £36,000 + bonus.
O Contracts Manager £33,000 + bonus.

Useful Address
www.baa.com/Airport Jobs

QUALIFICATIONS AND TRAINING

Many of the qualifications written about in this book are also mentioned on websites or in forms as JAR (Joint Aviation Requirements), issued by JAA (Joint

Aviation Authorities). These are about to be replaced: instead of being issued by JAA in each country, across the EU these will be issued by EASA (European Safety Agency).

European Aviation will now be speaking as one voice and qualifications, for example, will be numbered EASA 66 instead of JAR 66. However, Joe Desmond of GAT (Gatwick Aviation Training) says 'most people in the industry are sticking with JAR for the moment – as everyone is familiar with the term'.

So in this book we have used the term that has been given to us by the colleges, universities or examining authorities, many of whom are keeping to the old words, knowing employers understand them. Engineers are traditionalists; they will be asking 'do you have JAR 66?' for a long time.

The issuing authority for any certificate complying with JARs or EASAs is the authority in that country, i.e. CAA, FAA, etc. so if in doubt ask this authority.

Apart from financial departments cutting down, in Britain airlines are also finding that the government, aided by EU requirements, is changing course names, qualifications and methods, so many employers have yet to catch up with the new qualification jargon. All very confusing for someone wanting to become an aviation engineer. The situation is also complicated by the fact that the government has put a tremendous effort in to changing our training system and has developed NVQs (National Vocational Qualifications). Theoretically this is an excellent idea, but as with so many Government ideas, it falls far short of what is required, principally because employers have not been consulted fully.

So in Britain, as the basis for all training, aim for 'A' levels or equivalent in Maths, Physics and English (yes, the international engineering language is English, so you have to be able to communicate in the language, and you feel a fool when someone whose native tongue is NOT English, can speak it better than you).

In Spain the picture is rosier: D. Jaime Cisneros of the *Ministerio de Educacion* recently told journalists that 80% of students on vocational courses had obtained employment in their industry within two months of completing their course aged 18. Why? 'Because we involve the employers'.

By 2007 mechanical engineers in the EU will also have to be electrical engineers, and worldwide safety demands means that pilots also have to have far more technical training than before.

Joe Desmond of GAT advises that one of the best ways of getting training is to join the army; they have the latest helicopters and you will join R.E.M.E (Royal Electrical and Mechanical Engineers), be assigned to the Army Air Corps and leave after nine years with good qualifications. If you want to do specialised work, then it is just a case of taking top-up courses to gain the required qualification.

With all engineering training, the good news is that more and more colleges and universities are offering courses tailored to particular aviation requirements, so you can start to specialise earlier. Once you are qualified as an engineer, training does not stop. As each new aircraft engine is developed, you will need to learn how to service and maintain this particular model. That is why so many websites will tell you the particular engine servicing qualification you must have.

Just because you are qualified to maintain Boeing engines, it won't mean you will be accepted to work for a company that operates Airbuses; you will have to go on a course to learn how their engines differ and how to service them.

Some airlines still offer types of apprentice scheme. To be considered for one of these, school-leavers need a good education with GCSEs or A-levels in maths, English and science. e.g. the airline Flybe asks for at least GCSE passes in Maths, English and Physics or Science. On the apprentice scheme, you train whilst you work for an employer, aiming for a vocational qualification (currently an NVQ), and may go on to take a university degree.

> **Flybe (www.flybe.com)Training Manager Donna Throgmorton says:**
> *Our training is open to the public and is also available for companies to buy into. I do have to say that our priority is ensuring our own engineers receive the training they require, but if we have any spare capacity within our scheduling we are only too happy to offer places outside of Flybe.*

Approaching a College or University for Training.

To be accepted on any course you must be:

- O Interested in practical things.
- O Want to leave school and get into a job with a real future.
- O Have 3-5 middle grade GCSEs or above.

For more information:

- O Freephone SEMTA careers hotline 0800-282167
- O Contact companies looking for entrants. Your nearest Learning Skills Council (www.lsc.gov.uk) will have details.
- O Look in local papers.
- O Ask at your careers or local Connexions office for information.
- O Go to the Engineering Employers Federation website www.apprentices.co.uk, or www.lsc.gov.uk/contractlf.cfm and www.ssda.org.uk.

WHY TRAINING LASTS SO LONG

The CAA (Civil Aviation Authority), in the USA the FAA (Federal Aviation Authority) and their equivalents in other countries, set out very exact schedules of maintenance for every type of aircraft: specifying so many maintenance checks and replacements after so many hours flying. Each aircraft has a logbook with detailed information about every check carried out, and the Engineer in charge signs off each job. Every time an aircraft goes out of the engineering base, the technicians who have lovingly serviced this machine know that if anything happens because of a fault overlooked, it will be traced back to them.

They have to be good; they have people's lives in their hands, so the training has to be thorough.

Engineers have to be aware that the regulations for the airworthiness of aircraft, engines, propellers, equipment, parts etc comprise requirements and procedures addressing the following:

1. Design standards.
2. Approval of design organisations.
3. Approval of production.
4. Maintenance standards.

These are supported by Continued Airworthiness activities such as the monitoring of accidents, incidents, and other occurrences with follow-up action.

COURSES

Foundation Aviation Degrees

Currently there are five aviation engineering foundation degrees:

○ Aircraft engineering FD at City College Bristol (awarded by Kingston University).
○ Aeronautical engineering FdSc, Farnborough College of Technology (awarded by University of Surrey).
○ Aircraft engineering FD and FdA, Kingston University (this FD is taught at a number of venues).
○ Engineering (Aerospace) FD, Macclesfield College (awarded by University of Salford).
○ Aeronautical engineering, North East Wales Institute of Higher Education.

These courses provide qualifying training for aircraft maintenance engineers. Other options are offered at the following colleges:

City College Bristol

Mechanical and electronic options for training aircraft maintenance engineers.

The course awards a Foundation Degree and the European Union recognised JAR 66 Basic Training Cert. B1 (Mechanical) or B2 (Avionic) for aircraft maintenance engineers. The course involves work on the college's aircraft and a 10-week placement at an approved aircraft maintenance engineering company.

City College Bristol, New Road, Stoke Gifford BS34 8SF; 0117-904 5000; www.cityofbristol.ac.uk.

Farnborough College
Qualification for aircraft maintenance technicians.
Farnborough College, Boundary Road, Farnborough GU14 6SB; 01252-407040; www.farn-ct.ac.uk.

Kingston University
Provided jointly by Kingston University and KLM UK Engineering Ltd. Students undertake part of the programme at KLM maintenance facility in Norwich, gaining hands-on experience of large passenger aircraft. The Kingston course offers:
Year 0: a prep year is offered to those who don't hold all the qualifications for the FD course.
Year 1: Skills and knowledge for JAR-66 A licence.
Year 2: This is an extra year enabling students to complete a BEng (Hons) Aircraft Engineering / JAR-66 C licence.
Kingston University, 53, High Street, Kingston-on-Thames KT1 1LQ; 020 8547 2000; www.kingston.ac.uk.

Macclesfield College
The European Centre for Aerospace Training (ECAT) is established at the college and it has been selected as a Centre of Vocational Excellence (CoVE) in Aerospace Engineering. ECAT facilities include a BAe Jetstream 31 commercial aircraft from Eastern Airways. It is also ideally based for work experience at Manchester Airport.
    The course covers the modules of the JAR 66 Certifying Staff Maintenance for A, B1 and B2 categories and further modules required for the award of the Foundation Degree.
Macclesfield College, Park Lane, Macclesfield SK11 8LF; 01625-410002; www.macclesfield.ac.uk.

Northbrook College
The college runs 5 Aero courses at present:
1.SEMTA NVQ Level 2 in Aircraft Maintenance
One-year course for students without any qualifications which is a foundation course leading to no. 2. (It is also used for students too young to enrol onto no.2.) It is primarily a practical course based in Northbrook's own aircraft hangar at Shoreham Airport with 3 Key Skills incorporated. Course includes Workshop Theory and Practice, Aircraft Fundamentals, Aircraft Systems, Piston Engines, Propellers, Gas Turbines. Legislation, Key Skills (Numeracy, Communication and IT).

2.EASA IR 66 Certifying Mechanic and Certifying Technician (Subject to approval)
Three-year course providing all the modules for a Certifying Mechanic after one year and Certifying Technician after 3 years, leading directly to employment in the aircraft industry. Students need to be at least 17 and have at least a 'B' grade in GCSE Maths and 3 other relevant subjects, grades 'A' to 'C' or the NVQ Level 2. Industrial experience is an integral part of the course. Main subjects studied as above, and Electrics/Instruments, Aircraft Structures, Theory of Flight, Maths/Science, etc.

3. Edexcel/BTEC National Diploma in Aerospace Engineering (Mechanical)

4. Edexcel/BTEC National Diploma in Aerospace Engineering (Avionics)

5. Edexcel/BTEC Higher National Diploma in Aerospace Engineering Northbrook College, Shoreham Airport, BN43 5FHJ; 0800 183 60 60; www.nbcol.ac.uk.

North East Wales Institute of Higher Education
Facilities include an aircraft hangar where students gain practical experience on piston and jet aircraft. FLITE static flight simulator room with simulation packages, systems and CESSNA 172 systems simulators.
Foundation Degree Aeronautical Engineering:
Level 1 – Science, Mathematics, Materials, Thermofluids, Aerodynamics, Information Technology, Industry Training and Engineering Applications – a broad introduction to the course.
Level 2 –More specific study and career-related skills. Topics include Aeronautical/Mechanical Science, Manufacturing Technology, Aircraft Structures and Aircraft Control Avionics.
North East Wales Institute of HE, Mould Road, Wrexham LL11 2AW; 01978-293050; www.new.ac.uk.
Newcastle Aviation Academy
Starting this September, the KLM Engineering and Foundation Degree is also being offered here. The course will be part funded by the Regional Development agency.
Newcastle Aviation Academy, c/ Kingston University; www.kingston.ac.uk/bridge.

KLM UK Engineering's workshops, based in Norwich, have helped develop Foundation Degrees
KLM became involved with the aircraft engineering degree when it was seeking to enhance its training provision. Requirements of the Joint Aviation Authority (JAA) dictates certain standards for the licensing of engineers – and KLM UK Engineering needed to ensure the training it offered

met these standards. As part of the degree development team KLM UK Engineering were able to ensure the course syllabus met not only industry needs and academic requirements, but also those of the JAA.

Ray Flower, KLM UK Engineering's Training Manager says that *'the foundation degree in aircraft engineering will provide the industry with engineers who possess enhanced levels of academic ability. In addition they'll be able to apply their knowledge in a more constructive way, that can only benefit the aircraft maintenance industry.*

As an active partner from the outset we've been fully involved in the course design, allowing us to ensure the course meets the needs of the industry, whilst adhering to the license requirements'.

The company's involvement goes beyond helping to design and present course modules; KLM UK Engineering also ensures that the JAA regulatory standards and requirements are met at all times.

Student Harry Enfissi says: *'this Foundation Degree is giving me and my fellow students a solid understanding of theory, coupled with the important practical skills that are essential for a career in aircraft engineering. Whilst not an easy course, it is in my opinion by far the most comprehensive anywhere in the industry and provides students with an academic and industry recognised qualification'.*

Whatever you do, you are looking at seven years training from age 16 onwards. Alternatively you can take a college course, but Ray warns that many colleges can't get funding from the Further Education Funding Council for the 'traditional' courses as they are too long. No matter that an Engineer holds a position of responsibility, if the money isn't there from government, colleges are forced to shorten training.

So it is vital to ensure that any course you take will lead to employment, or that you realise what extra training (which you may have to fund yourself) you will need to make yourself employable. You don't want to be left out on a limb at the end of your course.

Helicopter Engineers
The British Helicopter Advisory Board's website www.bhab.demon.co.uk has a training section with information: 'I want to be a Helicopter Engineer'.

Training in the United States
Laura Hopkins, Associate Dean of Aviation at South Seattle Community College (www.southseattle.edu/programs/proftech/aeronat.htm) says *'We do not exactly offer an engineering program. What we offer is a program where students come to get their Airframe and Powerplant licenses (Federal Aviation Administration license to work as a mechanic on airplanes). It is a two year program. There are not very many requirements to get in (you must be 18, have a high school diploma or equivalent, and meet with one of our counselors to determine any*

required testing). However it is an intense program. Our students go to school 5 days a week, 5 hours a day, for two years.

Useful Addresses
Arizona State University; www.asu.edu
Central Missouri State U.; www.cmsu.edu
Cloud State U.; http//stcloudstate.edu
Embry-Riddle Aeronautical U.; www.db.erau.edu
Florida Institute of Technology; www.fit.edu
Hampton U.; www.hamptonu.edu
Louisiana Tech.; www.aviation.latech.edu
Mercer County Community College; www.mccc.edu
Met. State College of Denver; www.mscd.edu
North Shore Community College; www.nscc.ma.us
Middle Tennesee State U.; www.mtsu.edu
Purdue U.; www.purdue.edu
U. Nebraska; www.unomaha.edu
U.North Dakota; www.aero.und.edu
Western Michigan U.; www.aviation.wmic.edu

Training in Canada

Canadore College; www.canadorec.on.ca
Mount Royal Coll.; www.mtroyal.ab.ca
Selkirk Coll.; www.selkirk.bc.ca
Seneca Coll.; http//senecac.on.ca
Moneton Flight Coll.; www.mfc.nb.ca
S.Alberta Inst. Tech.; www.sait.ab.ca.

Training in France

Thales (www.thalesgroup.com, or www.thales.co.uk) are a massive French and international company involved in all aspects of the aviation industry. At their branch in London, Chris, a Senior Programme Manager, says:

'Working here is an opportunity to be involved in something where you can see the impact of your work. Previously I worked for Siemens Air Traffic Management, and joined the Thales Group four years ago as a result of a joint venture merger. Currently I am a Senior Programme Manager, responsible for managing individual air traffic management systems.

The technical ability of the people I work with and their enthusiasm to do the job is very high. Those are definitely motivating factors. This business is a multi-domestic business with people distributed throughout the world. This can add complications but it also adds interest because you work with people who have slightly different cultural backgrounds.

When you fly over a country and you know that you have been directly involved in the air traffic management system that is controlling the aircraft, it is something you can really relate to. It gives me an intellectually stimulating job. Companies need development engineers/IT specialists, and sales and marketing staff – where the world's airlines and air forces are your oyster.'

CAREER PROGRESSION

Once you have obtained your Civil Aviation Authority Licence you will find this is a passport to working around the world, as many airlines in other countries want CAA licensed employees, and actively recruit those with this qualification.

Flybe say, 'as well as receiving a better than average wage as an aircraft engineer, there are plenty of opportunities to advance your position. For example, an aircraft engineer can easily move into':

O Planning
O Quality Assurance
O Design
O Management

Virgin Maintenance Planning, Engineers, says that good training gives engineers 'freedom to think outside the box'. Its team ensures all scheduled and reactive maintenance is performed to highest level of quality; short and medium term planning requirements are understood and resources available for long-term strategy. They need good communicators, especially with contractors, and work is to very stringent planning horizons.

Recently the University of Edinburgh surveyed engineering graduates. Of those who had graduated in the past year, 70% were in employment; 20% doing further study and as 10% were not available due to travelling or taking a year out, the survey reckoned 0% were looking for employment! More importantly, UMIST (beloved by employers eager to employ their engineering graduates), say 20% of engineering graduates earn above the average graduate salary within six months of graduation.

WHERE TO APPLY FOR JOBS

Engineers are expected to be computer-literate, so initially most airlines, airports and manufacturers ask you to fill in a form on-line. If your form fits, you will be invited for an assessment of classroom based tests and group exercises with working engineers. You could then be invited back for a further interview.

You must:

○ Have the right to live where the airline's engineering base is.
○ Be aged 18 – 24 for most British airlines.
○ Have or be expected to gain A level Maths and Physics or a related science subject, plus GCSEs or equivalent at Grade C in English and Maths.

Recently Skyport News announced 'Emirates signs new engine deal'
The article said the airline had signed a deal for aircraft engines, to power its latest order of 23 Airbus A380-800s. The total £2 billion investment in the 199 GP7200 engines ordered so far by Emirates makes the airline the world's largest client for this new Engine Alliance powerplant. Emirates is also the world's largest customer for the A380-800, having ordered a total of 45 of the yet-to-fly super-jumbos, or about one-third of all firm orders taken by Airbus for the new aircraft.
  The Dubai-based airline is also going to build an advanced jet engine test facility in Dubai, costing £26 million, which will expand the airline's jet engine repair and technical support capabilities.

Emirates have an apprentice scheme for UAE Nationals, but the airline does not offer work experience or internships to expatriates. Details of vacancies across the Emirates Group are found on their careers website www.emiratesgroupcaree rs.com. As they receive between 17,000-20,000 applicants a month, they physically cannot respond to everyone who applies. Apply online, and if suitable your CV goes into their database which is used by Recruitment to source candidates for current and future vacancies.

If you live near Bristol, Airbus has just announced it will need to recruit 120 new management and engineering workers to manage and assemble the composite hybrid wing of the new A400M military transport version of their aircraft.

Across the world, Airbus employs 48,000 people from over 50 nationalities. The company is proud of the fact that they instigated many innovations in modern-day commercial flight: fly-by-wire, cockpit commonality, carbon fibre usage, widebody jets – engineers will understand; if you don't, go to their website. www.airbus-careers.com.

If fighter planes are your scene, the production programme for the Eurofighter Typhoon is for 620 aircraft. For details see www.eurofighter.com.

The United States Scene

The current economic climate, and post-September 11 downturn in aviation, means budgets are tight. Some airlines are not taking on apprentices, however, the main airlines still recruit some staff, and current website information for American Airlines say they employ the following in their Maintenance and Engineering departments:

- Electricians.
- Stationary Operating Engineers.
- Industrial Electronics Mechanics.
- Millwrights.
- Plumbers.
- Welders.
- Water treatment engineers.
- Hazardous Waste Plant Maintenance Engineers.
- Heating/AC Mechanics.
- Carpenters.
- Automotive Mechanical Technicians.
- Overhaul Support Mechanics.
- Stock Clerks, etc. etc.

Useful website:
www.aacareers.com

Working in Engineering

If you have ever wondered how well aircraft systems engines are tested before being sold to airforces and airlines, it is reassuring to know that Grace Johnstone, Young Woman Engineer of the Year 2003, is one of the people working for BAE Systems, doing just that.

BAE SYSTEMS (www.baesystems.com) designs, manufactures, and supports military aircraft, surface ships, submarines, space systems, radar, avionics, C4ISR, electronic systems, guided weapons and a range of other defence products, many of these with international partners. Key skills include systems integration, complex software and hardware development and advanced manufacturing.

Currently Grace is working on the Eurofighter:
Whilst I was an Apprentice I went on an exchange to Hanover in Germany. As we flew over, there was an announcement from the Captain: I believe there is a group of apprentices from BAE. Would you like to come in to the cockpit? Once there the Captain asked me if I would like to sit in the cockpit for landing.

We test aircraft on the ground; all the systems get integrated into the aircraft, then we carry out test flights. The reason is because there are a lot of different forces acting on the aircraft, which may have an impact on their performance.

We are making sure that when it is in-flight, everything in the system works, whilst it is carrying out all its other tasks.

Engineers are used to working worldwide, and with the enlarged EU there is no bar to employment across Europe. You have to be able to speak the language of the country, but you also have to be able to speak engineering's language: English.

In Belgium, SN Brussels Airlines are looking for Aircraft Engineers to work at Zaventem Airport, Brussels. The successful candidate will be able to demonstrate:

O The capacity to perform maintenance tasks following instructions.
O Perform trouble shooting on aircraft systems.
O Properly use tools and measuring equipment.
O Read and understand instructions and technical manuals.
O Make written technical entries and any maintenance document entries.
O Communicate at such a level as to prevent any misunderstanding when exercising the privileges of authorisation.
O Comply with the quality norms in respect to cleanliness of aeroplanes.
O Reporting abnormal discrepancies to supervisors.

Requirements:

O Practical skills in line maintenance and base maintenance.
O Minimum 3 years of experience in civil aviation with similar activities or 2 years practical maintenance experience on operating aircraft after completion of a JAR 147 approved basic training course.
O Preferably licence A319 with relevant experience A319 maintenance.
O Experience with AVRO RJ85/100 maintenance is an advantage.
O Knowledge of and affinity with JAR-145.
O Have sufficient knowledge of English language.
O Be able to work in a team as well as independently.
O Willing and flexible to work in shifts.

Useful website:
www.flySN.com

Aircraft Manufacturers

Manufacturers are major employers of engineers, but so often they are overlooked. If you want to see the potential for employment, visit the Society of British Aerospace Companies' website:www.sbac.co.uk., with over 600 companies in membership, at the cutting edge of high-tech manufacture. In total these companies employ around 120,000 highly-qualified people.

Rory Galway, Equal Opportunities Manager with Bombardier Aerospace, Belfast (they took over Shorts, who made aircraft for the Wright Brothers), says:

Engineering is regarded as an old industry – people don't appreciate how high-tech it is.Bombardier have maintained trainee intake in the last 2 years with approximately 40 being recruited each year. However, we have not had a graduate intake since 2000. Future graduate requirements will be determined by operational needs.

Craft and technician engineer training positions may be available for those under 18 years of age, as are a smaller number of training positions for people aged 18 to 24.

The website www.theflightexperience.com provides useful information.

Technicians

Technicians are involved in many sides of engineering, including developing new ideas and working with other departments in your organisation. Some jobs include work for technicians as:

- Draftspeople – drafting plans and documents, often using the latest computer technology.
- Estimators – working out how much it will cost to design and make a product.
- Quality assurance technicians – making sure that the product is just right.
- Inspectors – making sure that everything is running as it should.
- Planners – scheduling everyone else's work.
- Laboratory technicians – helping with research and testing, sometimes at supervisory levels.

Useful Addresses

Alstom Transport UK; www.uk.alstom.com
Air Atlanta Europe; www.atlanta.is
Airbus; www.airbus.com
Atlas Engineering Services; www.atlas-engineering.com
AV8 Appointments; www.castle-personnel.co.uk
Airline Maintenance Resources; www.airlinemaintenance/co.uk
BAE Systems; www.baesystems.com
SR Technics; www.srtechnics.com
ARS Europe Interim; www.ars-europe-interim.com
AOES BV (Netherlands); www.aoes.nl
Jet Aviation (Germany); www.JetAviation.de
United Services GEM (Global Emergency Maintenance) has been developed to handle virtually any kind of AOG (aircraft on ground) situation; www.unitedsvcs.com

VEM (Brazil and S. America) Varig Engineering and Maintenance;
www.varigvem.com

Trains

Recently many aircraft engineers have found employment with train companies: their engineering skills transfer easily. Some companies manufacture both
planes and trains: Bombardier not only build aircraft parts, they also build those
exciting Eurostar trains, and carriages for other rail companies. Contact www.tr
ansportation.bombardier.com.

Work in the USA for Technicians and Engineers

The FAA says that to get a mechanic's licence:

O You must be at least 18 years old and able to read, write, and understand
English.
O You must get 18 months of practical experience with either power plants or
airframes, or 30 months of practical experience working on both at the same
time. As an alternative to this experience requirement, you can graduate from
an FAA-Approved Aviation Maintenance Technician School.
O You must pass a written examination, an oral test, and a practical test for both
power plants and airframes within any 24-month period.

If you are not a US Citizen, you must also meet the following requirements:

O Demonstrate you need a mechanic certificate (licence) to maintain U.S.-reg-
istered civil aircraft and you are neither a U.S. citizen nor a resident alien.
O Show the examiner your passport.
O Provide a detailed statement from your employer saying what specific types
of maintenance you performed on each aircraft, and how long you performed
it.
O Provide a letter from the foreign airworthiness authority of the country in
which you obtained your experience, or from an advisor of the International
Civil Aviation Organization (ICAO), validating your maintenance experi-
ence.
O Make sure all the documents you provide are signed and dated originals.
O Pay the fee for the document review.

Working for Boeing

Probably more than any other manufacturer, Boeing has brought air travel to the
masses, although recently the US company has forecast a rough ride until 2006.
'Orders for planes tend to lag behind general confidence', according to Tom
Pickering, senior vice-president of Boeing's international relations. Recently the
airline laid off 36,000 of its 96,000 workforce, and it has lost some of its tradi-

tional market to European rival Airbus.

However, industry analysts expect the manufacturer to come out of the doldrums when orders start to come in for the new 7E7 Dreamliner. This aircraft will please environmentalists, as it is planned to consume 20% less fuel than current planes.

New technology means that the aircraft will be built with composite parts for which humidity is not a problem, meaning the cabin will have greater humidity, thereby ensuring better conditions for passengers. This technology will enable the cabin to be pressurised to a lower level.

To work for Boeing :

o Some job applicants need to be a US citizen with security clearance due to the work involved.
o If you have a permit to work in the USA, then applicants from all over the world can apply for positions at The Boeing Company.
o All applicants must apply online and the hiring manager will screen their resume to see if they are sufficiently highly qualified.

The Boeing Research and Technology Center is in Madrid, Spain, researching environmental, safety and air traffic management technologies. Currently they are looking for university graduates with degrees in aeronautical engineering, electronics, telecommunications, computer science, economic science and psychology.

Currently Boeing are working on the following projects:

Environment: noise and emissions analysis and control.
Technologies: for a more electric airplane.
Safety and reliability of aeronautical operations.
Improvement of aerospace capacity: traffic management systems.
Cost-benefit studies: analysing aerospace technology.

Salaries for staff on these projects are up to £55,000 p.a.

Useful Addresses
www.boeing.com/employment
Intern and Grads website: www.boeing.com/employment/college

JetBlue Airways

JetBlue Airways in the USA (www.JetBlue.com) recently advertised for a Powerplant Engineer to plan, co-ordinate and/or perform engineering assignments involving specification for, and design changes or alterations to engines, engine systems, and components.

The specifications are typical for similar jobs in other airlines: to review Airworthiness Directives to ensure compliance with regulations. Review Technical Directives such as Service Bulletins, Service Letters, etc. for applicable system reliability and/or commercial benefits. Implement design changes as required. Develop customized procedures and special criteria for repairs, modifications, inspections, servicing and other maintenance actions.

Powerplant Engineers have to establish build specifications and administer configuration control for Powerplant and APU systems/components. Develop and obtain regulatory approval for technical data required for modifications/repairs of Powerplant/APU systems and components, and response for ensuring their reliability performance standards are maintained.

OTHER JOBS

If the world of satellite communications is your field, you are about to become very popular with airlines. Having spent a fortune installing in-flight phones, the world's airlines are now finding passenger's expectations have moved on. Today, business passengers want to be able to go on-line to send and receive e-mails from their laptops, whilst they are in the air.

Currently many of the world's major communications companies are involved in the race to get their equipment on board the world's airlines (except BT, who caught a cold with their telephony communication system ALICE). Watch the financial pages of the major newspapers for further announcements.

Board the aircraft, and as soon as the Captain announces you can use lap tops, your wireless machine locks on, and you can start messaging. Tenzing are currently installing the first airborne wireless hotspot on Emirates new Airbus A340-500, and their website says they are looking for engineers to develop the on-board technology. www.tenzing.com.

New systems are being developed by AIRIA to supply live TV to aircraft. Now you can see the world's news developing as it happens. As AIRIA say, new worlds of communication, entertainment and information are just over the horizon and they too are looking for technicians.

However, installing this new technology will probably produce similar problems to those when inflight telephones were first installed, and companies such as British Telecom lost a lot of money in trying to develop a system, which eventually was obsolete. One management guru likened it to plate spinning at the circus – it needed a tremendous amount of skill to keep all the plates in the air at the same time. If one fell you lost the audience – or the connection. www.airiaglobal.com.

If you speak German, SR Technics of Switzerland are expanding, and say that with the trend for airlines to outsource fleet maintenance, the future for their company looks rosy. www.srtechnics.com.

If you are thinking about working in the UK Aerospace industry, you might be heartened to know that this sector employs over 150,000 people directly, and over 350,000 indirectly.

Working with Colleagues

After every flight, pilots fill out a form called a gripe sheet, which conveys to the engineers problems encountered with the aircraft during the flight that need repair or correction. Engineers read and correct the problems, and then respond in writing on the lower half of the form what remedial action was taken, and the pilot reviews the gripe sheets before the next flight.

So engineers and pilots have to work closely together, ensuring the safety of the aircraft they service and fly.

Travel Retail

It all started at Shannon Airport in Eire. Airport authorities at their fledgling airport knew planes were flying overhead on their way to North America, and thought enviously of the landing fees they would earn if they could attract airlines to refuel at Shannon, rather than Reykjavik, Gander or elsewhere.

At the time, shopping at an airport was unthinkable. Passengers were expected to buy their goods in local shops, and wouldn't want the stress of shopping whilst waiting for a flight – or so people thought. It wasn't until some bright spark thought of offering duty free goods to entice high-spending US customers, that airport retail shopping became a viable proposition. The thinking was: if enough passengers demanded this privilege, airlines would be forced to make Shannon their refuelling stop. So with the Customs Free Airport Act of 1947, the world's first Duty Free Airport shopping was born; the forerunner of a vast worldwide industry that today employs thousands, which ACI (Airports Council International) says is responsible for 50% of airport revenue worldwide.

At first the idea was to offer transatlantic passengers the chance of buying 'the best of Ireland' such as Waterford Crystal. As more industries wanted to become involved, so spirits, tobacco and other high duty goods were added. It wasn't long before rival airports cottoned on to the money-making possibilities, and today you can buy almost anything you might need at airport shops, whose retail profits often help keep landing fees low.

LOSS OF DUTY FREE

Recently there was a glitch. Wanting to regulate everything for Europeans, Brussels bureaucrats decided to abolish duty free privileges across EU borders. Although the major suppliers such as whisky distillers and perfume manufacturers lobbied their Governments heavily, the bureaucrats were determined to harmonise tax across the EU – which of course they took to mean abolishing the little perks allowed to travellers. So instead of being able to buy goods without paying VAT (making them around 15-20% cheaper than in High Street shops), airport shops had to charge whatever local taxes were in force. VAT and other taxes are still different across the EU and harmonisation is still waiting to be introduced.

In Europe especially the prices were never wholly duty free. Operators charged what they thought the market could bear, and it was only if you were flying on a private plane and 'uplifted' your own goods from Customs bonded warehouses that you realised how very cheap genuine duty free could be. But even so, when shoppers see they can buy something cheaper – they go for it.

BAA and other operators did not want to see lucrative duty free shopping disappear, so negotiated – heavily – with manufacturers to get them to absorb the price increases. The result is that bulk buying and lower margins makes most goods slightly cheaper at airports, so although travellers are paying taxes, they can still save money.

The only way travellers can avoid paying taxes is if they are flying out of the EU; in which case they do not have to pay VAT. That is why, if you fly from EU airports, there will often be two prices – one for EU residents and one for those travelling outside the EU. Confusing, but it keeps people happy, and is the reason why airports such as Dubai have massive airport shopping malls to take advantage of the tax-free prices.

Worldwide, Travel Retail is one of the fastest-expanding industries, and in Britain, whilst high street sales are standing still or even losing ground, airport sales in the UK are expected to show 4-5% growth each year; good news for the 12,000 people who work at BAA airports in retailing.

Airport shopping is so much an accepted part of travelling that Richard Holbrooke, ex-US Ambassador to the U.N. and now shuttling around the world on diplomatic missions for the U.S. Government, interrupted his recent diplomatic efforts to tell the Tax Free World Association Conference in Cannes:

> *I understand that there are some 110 nations represented at this conference and that makes me feel as if I am back at the U.N...but a U.N. with energy! I am an enthusiastic consumer of duty-free products and later today, when I fly home, I will be using my World Points Card at Heathrow Airport. I greatly admire what your industry has done to make airports an enjoyable part of travel.*

Shortly afterwards 270 executives from 32 countries descended on Dubai to attend the annual Middle East Duty Free Conference, opened by HH Sheikh Ahmed bin Saeed Al Maktoum, President of Dubai Civil Aviation and Chairman of Emirates Group.

At the conference Abu Dhabi Duty Free Managing Director Mohammed Mounib highlighted the explosive growth of regional duty free outlets: 'Sales at Bahrain Duty Free and Abu Dhabi Duty Free grew 15% this year over last, while sales at Dubai Duty Free grew a full 17%. Sales across the Middle East region have grown an astounding 53% from their level in 1995.'

To emphasise the range of companies whose goods are found in duty free outlets, among the 135 supplier companies represented at the conference were Kraft, Nestlé, Diageo, Philip Morris, Richemont, Bacardi, Cadbury, P&G Prestige Beauté, Estée Lauder and L'Oréal – all key players in this booming retail industry.

WORLD DUTY FREE

Today, World Duty Free (WDF) the BAA's retail arm are leaders in travel retail, with sales of over £450 million p.a. WDF was set up by BAA to improve the whole duty free experience.

Mark Anderson got the idea of a career in airport retail when studying for a Master of Retail Management at Tilburg Institute in the Netherlands.
After gaining a BA Hons degree in English Language and Literature at Southampton University, Mark found himself working for the giant Netherlands owned C & A chain stores. He loved retail, and jumped at the chance when C & A offered to send him to Tilburg for a Masters Degree. However, whilst there the British arm of C & A suddenly closed, leaving Mark in the middle of his course and without a job. But course studies told him that the fastest growing retail sector was travel retail – so that's where he decided to go next. Today he is General Manager for WDF at Heathrow's Terminal 3.

For companies such as WDF and other global leaders such as Nuance (originally part of Swissair), the German company Heinemann etc. there was a hiccup recently when the EU voted to abolish duty free privileges. Airport retailing turnover was expected to diminish, but by keeping price differentials between high street and airport prices, WDF managed to claw back their turnover with intra-EU sales within a year. This still left sales to non-EU travellers being offered at lower prices, and sales staff patiently explaining the dual pricing system – which they manage to do remarkably politely and effectively.

To cut margins further, BAA made deals with gin, vodka and whisky distilleries to market their own brands, thereby reducing overheads. They hived off their retail side into World Duty Free, the company is now five years old and increasing turnover rapidly – and changing year by year.

Mark likes working in the industry, especially 'the support for us to act as Business Managers'. Some people might say there is a downside with crises such SARS, the Gulf War, etc. which can effect sales for a considerable time, but Mark accepts 'you have these impactors all the time – you almost have to expect that – although you can't plan specifically as every crisis is different. You don't know what's happening next, but have to move forward, and as retailers this is probably the most exciting part of working in this industry' which he finds exciting and challenging.

High Street stores have a cycle of trading, with highs and lows at various times of the year, 'but in WDF I can honestly say that never happens – it is much more fast-paced; you have to change, but don't always know the direction you will change! But accepting the challenge: that is really exciting. You learn from your mistakes, and try not to make the same mistake twice.'

Because of the fast pace, people working for WDF see results straight away. When we met, Mark was delighted that the latest QSM (question service monitor) had given his terminal a 4.4 rating out of a maximum 5 for staff/service. But he wasn't complacent; Southampton Airport had scored 4.8, so he was thinking of ways to match this.

One of the pluses for Mark is the variety of customers; 47 different airlines fly from Terminal 3 to destinations all over the world. Buying patterns change all the time, and currently sales techniques to Japanese buyers (some of biggest spenders) are changing. Before, the Japanese travelled in groups and their Tour Leader was the person who told them what to buy; sell to him or her, and 40 group members bought the same. Now the Japanese have been to Europe, they are branching out as individual travellers which means selling to each person, rather than relying on selling to the Tour Leader.

WDF have spent a great deal of money developing the award-winning concept of its main walk-through shop in Terminal 3, and Mark says 'brands are queuing up to come in'. Currently plans are in hand to develop a chocolate brand, plus encouraging the luxury end of the market with their World of Whiskies store – which sells bottles of whisky for up to £10,000 – yes, £10,000 for one bottle. The first mega-priced bottle of Bushmills Whisky (from the world's oldest whisky distillery in Northern Ireland) was sold to a Japanese buyer, who handed over his credit card, popped the bottle into a plastic carrier bag and strolled off. No, he said he didn't need the special wooden crate to protect it – but the salesmen reckoned they almost had a heart attack imagining what would happen if he slipped.

When he goes on a busman's holiday, which airports excite Mark? Bahrain scores highly 'it is inspirational and so completely geared around duty free'. Schiphol's 'See-Fly-Buy' logo is such a strong message which travels around the world.

What are the major problems? 'Things change fast – and the trading day has shifts spread over 17 ½ hours seven days a week'. But you get the impression Mark sees these as a plus.

Now, the latest luxury item in Mark's world is a decanter of superb Louis XIII Remy Martin Cognac with a diamond in the stopper, yours for a mere £20,000.

Ronnie (short for Veronica) Birch is another enthusiast working in Terminal 3 as Sales Consultant for Remy Martin Cognac.
She introduces passengers to the Remy Martin range of products *'which they usually know, but I am always trying to get them to upgrade. I give them a taste, and they normally like to buy to something they can't get at home; we have several bottles that aren't sold in any High Streets'.*

So what is the most popular cognac? That depends on nationality. Best purchasers are the Chinese, who favour XO, and Norwegians who go for VSOP. 'They are lovely customers and very nice to deal with'.

If you are cigar lover and know your tobaccos, you will want to linger in Terminal 3's cigar humidor – a giant air-conditioned glass 'box' kept at 15.8 C with 68% humidity – just right for the Cuban and Dominican Republic cigars that are popular with US buyers. Joe Kane presides over this mini-store, which cost £450,000 to fit out. Joe has just won a marvelous trip to the Dominican Republic presented by Davidoff, the cigar company, and if you do well there are chances to travel the world as guests of the major suppliers eager to show off their latest products.

Meanwhile, Heathrow's Terminal 4 recently opened its new Fragrance Area, devoted to perfume and 'smellies' for men as well as women, and costing a cool £750k. To make the shopping experience more exciting, a new black and white tiled floor with mirror chips and marble was installed to give a mirrored effect. This has changed the pace and feel of the area, encouraging passengers to linger – and buy. 'Accounting for 50% of World Duty Free's business, the fragrance and skin care cosmetics division attracts most of the world's finest brands,' comments Mark Riches, Managing Director for World Duty Free. In the Fragrance area is a world exclusive: the first ever Molton Brown airport store, offering 225 sq.ft. of luxurious feel-good products. This will be followed by another concession within the BA executive lounge in Terminal 1. The 350 sq.ft. Dior store represents a new partnership between Christian Dior and World Duty Free and is the first stand-alone cosmetics unit of its kind in the UK. Not surprisingly, extensive customer research went in to determining which retailers and what brands should be added to the existing airport shopping framework; the surprises were that it was the traditional, almost old-fashioned luxury brands, such as Dior and Molton Brown, that customers wanted, rather than the new heavily-advertised 'designer' perfumes bearing celebrity's names.

Harry is studying Business Admin. at a college near Stansted Airport – which means there are opportunities for part-time work locally on promotions when he can take time off from study.

I belong to several agencies, such as Angels Promotions, who supply temporary staff for promotions at airports. If I am prepared to work odd hours (which generally means working at night) I can pick up some useful fees, which help my overdraft. I started working as a 'promotion lovely'; don't laugh – it is usually girls who do this work (hence the job title), but they welcome men with open arms. We get to do the jobs like dressing up as Santa Claus at Christmas, or parading around as a parcel (luckily I was inside a box and my friends couldn't see me –but the pay was good and we were only allowed to work 30 mins in every hour). Now I am more experienced, I get much better jobs.

When a job comes up, Steve, my team leader, texts me to ask me to phone. He then gives me an outline of the job. Generally it is handing out samples of perfume, spirits or the latest cream liqueur. Luckily I have an old car, which gets me to the airport for late shifts, generally 10 pm to around 6 am. During this shift we catch holidaymakers going off on cheap charter flights. When we see a group approaching, particularly if there are older teenagers or twenties amongst them, we offer a free sample. I love hen parties; chat up the bride, get her to buy, and everyone follows. This week I am promoting a perfume that is supposedly worn by one of the TV soap actresses – she was down here at the airport to do some publicity; can't say I thought much of her close up, and, as I told my girl-friend her skin was awful! However, she received good publicity and now girls come up to me and ask 'is this the one she wears?'

When I finish my degree I may apply to work for one of the big spirit companies. I have seen the whisky centres at Heathrow and other airports, and would love to work in one, advising passengers on my favourite malts. I know there is a lot more to it than that, but a friend says you are sent on training courses to distilleries and on promotional trips around the world, so the job sounds fascinating.

Useful Addresses
Angels Promotions Agency; 0118 877 4970
Kreate Ltd;. barry@kreatepromotions.co.uk
ZOO People; www.zoopeople.co.uk

JOBS IN TRAVEL RETAIL

If the above excites you, and makes you think of opportunities, then Travel Retail can make a fascinating career that takes you around the world. There are opportunities working in retail shops both landside (newsagents, chemists, etc) and in the duty free area airside.

Operators such as BAA (British Airports Authority) and their company, World Duty Free, are mega employers worldwide, as are Nuance – once owned by Swissair, but now belonging to two Italian shareholders, Gruppo PAM and Stefanel. Then there are Gebr.Heinemann (German owned, with outlets in countries such as Turkey), etc. Air Rianta is another major player in this field, ranging far beyond their origins at Shannon, with outlets at Moscow, St Petersburg, Bahrain, Kiev, Karachi, Kuwait, Qatar, Cyprus, Birmingham, Damascus, Dusseldorf, Edmonton, Winnipeg, Ottawa, Montreal, Sofia, Beirut, Hamburg etc.

O Companies need thousands of staff, around the world. You must be prepared to work shifts; at Heathrow and Gatwick generally between 6am and 10 pm; other airports are open around the clock and generally you work an eight-hour shift.

O You have to work very fast – people are always in a hurry to catch their plane. Languages are helpful and you will be trained to identify cultural differences to help people make their choices when buying.

O If you like the work, the rewards are good. In Britain starting salaries are around £10,000 pa, but you can soon work up to £15,000-£25,000, with

managerial positions paying very well indeed.
○ Many companies have graduate entry schemes, and they look for anyone with a degree.

Benefits for all workers often include bonus schemes, subsidised meals, free life assurance and discounts.

There are also opportunities for administration and backroom staff working in sales and marketing departments, and retailers are constantly looking for ideas to keep ahead of the opposition and encourage sales. Airport retail never stands still, and themed retail outlets are the newest idea to get customers buying. The major companies have whole departments dedicated to searching and trying out new retail ideas.

The Nuance Group is the world's largest airport retailer, operating in some 400 outlets across 19 countries on four continents. Recently Nuance bought out Allders' Duty Free company, which may mean opportunities to transfer between their UK, Swiss and Hong Kong operations. Then there are opportunies to take part in special themed promotions for events such as the Olympic Games.

Nuance

Nuance has opened an 'Olympic Store' at Turin Airport, home to the Winter Olympics in 2006. Their Olympic Store is located on the departure level and has been developed in close co-operation with TOROC, the Organising Committee of the Turin Olympic Games.

The idea is not new; Nuance opened its first 'Olympic Store' in 1997 in Sydney, in the run-up to the 2000 Olympic Games. Since then, the concept is now successfully running in Athens, where the Olympic Games will be celebrated in August 2004, and in Geneva, home airport to the International Olympic Committee (IOC).

Recent job ads asked for sales staff to:

○ Identify and meet customer needs providing service in line with company standards.
○ Pro-actively inform customers of current promotions and incentives and share product knowledge when appropriate.
○ Maximise all sales opportunities through the correct use of selling skills and techniques.
○ Merchandise stock and maintain a high standard of housekeeping.
○ Follow payment handling procedures accurately and efficiently, operate tills, handle cash, cheques and credit cards and foreign currency.
○ Carry out price and code checks as necessary and assist in monthly stocktakes.

○ Safeguard company property against theft, loss or abuse and report losses to the appropriate manager.
○ Handle customer queries and complaints efficiently.
○ Work safely, carrying out personal responsibilities as stated under the Health and Safety at Work Act.

Current Rates of Pay are around £6.20 per hour plus retail bonus plus excellent company benefits, or £7.84 per hour for senior customer service assistants.

Contacts:
This is a truly global industry, and these companies (based in Switzerland, Germany, the UK and the USA) operate retail outlets all over the world. Their main addresses are listed in the *Contacts* chapter; their websites will show if they operate at your local airport.

Aer Rianta: www.aer Rianta.ie;
Alpha Retail: www.alpha-retail.com;
Dufry: www.dufry.ch
Gebr. Heinemann: www.gebr-heinemann.de
InterBaires: ☎+54 1 480 0444
Nuance (PAM Group): www.thenuancegroup.com
World Duty Free: www.baa.co.uk

USA and Canada:
Duty Free Americas: www.wdfa.com
Nuance Group: www.thenuancegroup.com

Skincare and Cosmetics

It is becoming the norm for businesswomen to buy their skincare products at the airport. When a jar of Kanebo's La Crème sells for £280 at the airport, as against £330 in a London store – well, you do save money.

Today's woman buys products that have been researched, tested and tried and found to give results. No longer is packaging important, it is what is inside that counts, provided it is seen to produce actual benefits. Have a look at the top sellers such as Clarins, La Prairie, Guerlain, etc. Their packaging is neat and attractive, but not OTT as might have been the case years ago.

When Kanebo, the very luxurious skincare range, was launched at Heathrow Airport, they invited journalists like myself to the party. Handed a goodie bag of samples to try, I was told 'use them on one side of your face only for two weeks – then tell us if you notice a difference from your normal creams'. Within one week I had discovered that there was a big difference, and since then have recommended La Crème to friends who have been suffering the side effects of cancer treatment – it has helped them overcome the dreadful eczema that comes with the typical dry skin from the drugs.

When La Prairie produced their skin caviar range (lots of little white bubbles looking like caviar, which you burst on your skin to release the lotion inside) they chose to sell it on board aircraft in the First Class section. They then found they had to train cabin crew in how to use it, as passengers often thought they should eat it rather than rub on their face – after all, it was called 'caviar'. Cabin Crew then discovered the benefits for themselves, and were delighted to be able to use a product that helped their skin overcome jet lag and dehydration caused by long flights. This is such a problem that we go in to this further in the chapter *Looking After Yourself.*

Now other cabin crew can be seen buying products when they go through airports with tax advantages. One of the perks of a job is knowing which airports give the best value for money, and flying there.

Tip

A supervisor at the Terminal 1 Beauty Centre at Heathrow bemoans the fact that most of his best workers are eventually sent by their companies to work in Terminal 3, where long-haul passengers spend more than the domestic and European fliers that fly from Terminal 1, so turnover is greater for the cosmetic houses. He says that there is a shortage of good staff, partly because they do not like shift work, and partly because 'it takes so long for Security clearance to come through'. But if you can afford to wait, 'choose which cosmetic houses you like the sound of, whose products you use, and apply to their head office, especially if you live near an airport and don't mind shift work'.

Contacts
Unlike airlines, cosmetic houses still recruit by phone or letter.
Clarins; send CV to 10, Cavendish Place, London W1G 9DN
Guerlain; 0207 563 7555
Kanebo; 01635-46362
La Prairie; 01932-827060
BAA information line; (which will get you contact numbers for other cosmetic houses) 0800 844 844

What Do Travel Retail Companies Look for?

Do you get excited by results? Are you resilient and responsible with the ability to learn from mistakes and possessing an analytical brain? WDF (World Duty Free) say they look for people able to get the best out of others, who care passionately about providing customer service. To a certain degree they must be extroverts, and WDF looks for 'sympathetic selling' and an interest in people. You have to really want to serve.

You have to get excited by seeing what the customer wants – and managers ask 'is this person going to be able to inspire and develop people?'

There are temporary jobs at Heathrow at certain peak times, and for these WDF will probably go to an agency to source these (see contacts above).

For management positions, you will need experience. Nuance recently advertised for a Retail Supervisor for Luton Airport, responsible for the smooth running of the shop floor. Minimum 12 months experience in a similar position, and flexible – as they would have to work early or late shifts, opening or closing the store.

> **When interviewing for management positions, Recruitment Consultant Anna says a degree is useful.**
> *We just need to know applicants can study, because they will constantly be sent on courses to learn new sales techniques, what are the marketing trends – anything that keeps companies ahead in this game. Degrees in Art and Design are useful as there is an art to making a tiny sales area capable of handling a massive turnover.*

Useful Addresses

Aer Rianta: Duty Free Retailing and Airport Management, Airport, Co. Clare, Ireland, plus regional offices in Bahrain and Canada; ☎+353 61 474361 and +353 1 814 4143; www.aer-rianta.ie.

ALDEASA : www.aldeasa.es.

Alpha Airports Group: Fairway House, Green Lane, Hounslow, TW4 6BU; ☎020-8707 0300; www.alpha-retail.com.

Dubai Duty Free; www.dubaidutyfree.com.

Dufy Duty Free; Hardstrasse 95, CH-4020 Basel, Switzerland; ☎+41 61 266 42 15; www.dufry.ch.

Duty Free Americas: www.worlddutyfree.com.

Gebr. Heinemann: Magdeberger Str., 320457 Hamburg; ☎+49 (40) 30 10 20; www.gebr-heinemann.de (online applications).

Nuance Group (Gruppo PAM); Unterrietstrasse 2a, 8152 Glattbrugg, Switzerland; ☎+41 1 874 39 46; www.thenuancegroup.com.

TWFA (Tax Free World Association); 63, rue de la Boétie, 75008 Paris, France; ☎+33 1 40 74 09 86; www.twfa.com.

WORLD DUTY FREE; ☎0141-585-6000; www.baa.com/Airport/Jobs wdf

Training and Qualifications

Whatever job you are going to do in aviation, you will probably need training. This can take from 4-6 weeks for Cabin Crew, up to several years for Engineers. Some training will be done by your employer; other training is organised in colleges, schools or universities to give you a qualification in order to apply for a job.

If you undertake pre-employment training, *make sure it is approved by the industry*. There are some very expensive courses that trade on the so-called glamour of aviation work, offering training that might, or might not, get you a job. You might even find comments (usually favourable!) written up on websites about these courses– which might or might not have been made by genuine students. Before investing time and money in a course, it makes sense to check it out by asking advice from :

- Friends who work in aviation.
- Careers teachers.
- Recruitment departments of companies where you might want to work: most of them will happily confirm if they know of the course and approve it, have never heard of it or – if you listen carefully – give you an indication if they don't rate it.
- If you are interested in a college course, ask the college which employers have taken on ex-trainees – then phone them.
- Or you could ask a union if they can advise you. Most unions are keen to get rid of cowboy trainers, and ensure everyone gets good training.
- Go on the internet and trawl through chat rooms to see if the course is mentioned; just make sure that those commenting don't have any connection with the course provider.
- And if your common sense tells you the course is a scam – listen to it!

VOCATIONAL QUALIFICATIONS

Vocational, or craft, courses, have been around in Europe for years; Britain woke up to them around 1987, when the Government announced it was developing NVQs (National Vocational Qualifications). It sounded a good idea, but instead of choosing one industry, setting up Vocational Training for that industry, and using the experience as a template for further courses – the government decided to roll out courses right across the board. Result – chaos.

When these courses were originally developed the idea was that there had to be in-put from employers, which meant employing teachers with industry experience. Employers thought this a good idea: students would not be able to obtain an NVQ until they had proved they could work in the relevant industry, and would be trained by someone who understood what was required. All companies were required to show an interest in the schemes.

However, some felt that they would put themselves in a vulnerable position if they gave their staff transferable qualifications, and feared that they would be spending valuable time and money in training staff who would then leave and go to other industries. Employers were reluctant to take on the burden of handling the massive amount of paperwork involved for trainees to obtain relevant NVQ. The Colleges,too, felt threatened by a qualification which could be gained in industry and not in the Colleges.

Then came GNVQs, (General National Vocational Qualificiations) which the Government stated did not need to have industry in-put (how they could be vocational without this, they couldn't explain). Colleges latched on to these qualifications, opened up new departments whose only job was to apply for funding, and many courses had no in-put from industry.

There have been so many complaints from employers that GNVQs are being phased out in 2007, and become VCEs (Vocational Certificate of Education). GCSEs and A-levels are also due to be phased out, but it is estimated this will take ten years. Keep an eye on changes in names of qualifications, and remember to ask employers what they want.

Employers complained vociferously that students coming in to industry had not been trained for what they required, so the Learning and Skills Council came up with VCEs. Fine, except the person who developed the one covering tourism (and aviation) said he was given no time to consult with the industry.

However, **Vocational Related Qualifications** (VRQ) are here to stay. They are the only Vocational qualifications which are assessed in the realistic environment, and they do have an external exam which has to be passed in order to achieve the full qualification.

So if you are thinking about taking a vocational course :

O Before you invest years of your life and sign up for a course,
O Ask an employer if they think it a good course – will you be wasting your time – can they tell you which courses are acceptable?

In Europe,NVQ courses have in-put from employers. In Spain D. Jaime Cisneros of the *Ministerio de Educacion* says 80% of students on their vocational courses obtain employment in their industry within two months of completing their NVQ courses. Why? 'Because we involve the employers'.

Back in Britain, the good news is that there are some people prepared to work all hours to develop relevant industry training. Pat Egan of Pan Aviation Training Services thought a VRQ for cabin crew made sense, so spent an enormous amount of her own time developing the VRQ for Airline Cabin Crew – now offered by colleges across Britain.

Airlines say this Air Cabin Crew Vocational Qualification gives applicants a good idea of what they want, plus teaching the basics of safety such as emergency evacuation and ditching drill. Airlines contact the colleges running courses for Pan Aviation Training Services, giving students first chance at job vacancies; some have asked for more recruits via these courses.

If you have taken a VRQ, it gives you a transferable skill which can be used to work on cruise ships, etc. If your airline ceases flying, you have a qualification that can be used in other customer care jobs. (020 7371-8731 panaviation@yahoo.com 449,Fulham Palace Road, London SW6 6SU).

Highbury College, Portsmouth is one college that offers the Airline VRQ.
The VRQ is accredited by EAL who are EMTA Awards Limited – yes, you could ask why them? – be glad they took it on as there was no other body interested in supervising the qualification.The course is operated in conjunction with Pan Aviation Training Services and lasts one year. You have to be 18 or over to enrol, and have a sound educational background, preferably including Maths and English.
Whilst on the course you will be expected to wear uniform (cost approx. £150), and pay for certain course extras (currently around £160), plus exam fees. You learn in class and in practical situations, using airlines' flight simulators. There is practical work including handling money, food service, customer care, safety and security. After successfully completing the course you receive the AVS Certificate for Airline Cabin Crew. You will also have:

○ The CIEHO (Chartered Institute Environmental Health) Basic Food Hygiene Certificate.
○ HSAW (Health and Safety at Work) Basic First Aid.
○ Welcome Host Certificate.
○ CACDP (Council for Advanced Communication with Deaf People) Deaf Awareness Certificate.
○ Rescue and Survival in Water.

No wonder airlines have taken on most of the ex-trainees!

FOUNDATION DEGREE

Don't be fooled by the name: this has nothing to do with Foundation GNVQs, but is a 'proper' degree. There is one running in conjunction with KLM (see Engineering Chapter), and trainees come out with a Foundation degree similar to an SdA or FDSc (BA for Arts).

WHY TAKE A PRE-INTERVIEW COURSE?

It will help at your interview if you have:

O Taken an approved vocational college course.
O Taken a first aid course.
O Learnt a language (including sign language).
O Taken a Welcome Host course.

And there is always the possibility that you might not be accepted to work for an airline, or there may be other reasons why you decide this work is not for you. With a good basic course you will have customer services and other skills that can be transferred to many other jobs.

Good preliminary training is not wasted. However, 'all reputable airlines provide in-house training on acceptance', according to **Gordon White, National Organiser Aviation of the Union Amicus.** He sees no need to sign up for one of the courses that charge over £1,500 for a five week course.

HELPFUL COURSES PRE-INTERVIEW

In Britain, VisitBritain (the national tourist board) offers excellent introductory courses in Customer Care. Designed for people working in the tourism industry, they are effective short one-day courses for people working with the public; their Welcome Host programme particularly will be very useful if you want to apply to work on information desks, customer check-in or as cabin crew. Their courses are:

O Welcome Host: making the right impression, remembering names and talking to customers, understanding and communicating effectively, handling complaints, etc.
O Welcome Line: dealing with telephone queries.
O Welcome All: assisting and understanding disability and special needs clients.
O Welcome Host International: basic introduction to the languages of up to six different countries and how to help non-English speaking clients.
O Welcome Management: for those in management.

These courses are now run by Tourism South East on behalf of VisitBritain. They cover a range of customer services skills, with the focus on working in the travel and tourism fields. Courses are run across the country, and you will find contact names and addresses on www.welcometoexcellence.co.uk, or phone 020 8563 3215.

First aid

Excellent first aid and save-a-life courses are run by the Red Cross or St. John's Ambulance brigade in most areas. Hospitals may also run these, particularly abroad, and there are some private courses, especially dealing with specialist training such as that needed by fire-fighters.

Although you will receive suitable training when you join a company, people interviewing you will always be impressed if you have taken a course.

CABIN CREW TRAINING

There are some cabin crew training courses offered by colleges or course providers, guaranteeing an interview with an airline when you complete the course. Yes, you will have your guaranteed interview, but this doesn't mean that you will be offered a job. These are often the courses that charge several thousand pounds or euros for a four to six week cabin crew course.

And there are college courses offering basic training for cabin crew such as the VQ course, which gives you an understanding of the industry, but broadens your training so that you can do other work if not accepted, or you decide you don't want to work in an airline. These colleges' fees are generally more modest.

If asked to pay a large sum, ask people in the industry what they think of the course; the unions are particularly helpful to anyone who wants to get the right training and asks them for advice. And as most countries' aviation authorities will insist that cabin crew are given highly specialised official training in emergency procedures, it follows that this training is carried out by the airline to ensure that rigorous standards are adhered to. So you will probably have to repeat the expensive training course, as the airline will have to sign official documents that you have carried out their approved training.

FARES AND TICKETING COURSES

Fares and Ticketing courses are generally necessary if you want to work in a travel agency, aviation call centre – or perhaps for one of the US airlines whose CSAs (Customer Service Agents)issue tickets.

ATOL (Air Transport Operators' Licences) have to be held by operators who operate package tours, so if you are taking a Fares and Ticketing course, you can get a headstart by asking the Civil Aviation Authority for a copy of their college Information Pack (free). This provides information about ATOL's travel industry role and the protection it provides. It also includes helpful facts and figures about ATOL and the travel firms licensed.

The CAA say '*with changing booking arrangements, independent travel and no-frills carriers, understanding financial protection for the travelling public can be complex and confusing without the right information. We hope this Tutor Information Pack will be a helpful resource, and we will be looking to build on this to further help support training and career development in the industry.'*

Copies are available from www.tolawareness@cpg.org.uk.

Colleges may try and sign you up to a Fares and Ticketing course if you say you want to work as cabin crew, admin. staff, etc. This sounds a good idea – until you ask around and discover that such staff will probably never ever see a passenger's ticket – let alone have to issue one. So the course could be a waste of time.

Uniform

At certain colleges you may be asked to buy a uniform. When the class goes out for a field visit it looks more professional if everyone is wearing the same uniform, rather than a combination of jeans, trainers and whatever.

Some airlines will ask you to contribute towards the cost of your company uniform which you wear during training, generally by deductions from your pay each week once you start earning. This ensures you look after your uniform.

Salary During Your Course

When on a company cabin crew training course, you may or may not be paid a wage; if you are, it is generally only a basic salary. Some companies, especially in the US, pay nothing whilst you are training; others give you a lump sum when you have completed training, to ensure you stay on the course.

WHAT HAPPENS ON CABIN CREW TRAINING COURSES?

Up-to-date information can be found on many airline websites, and also on chat rooms.

SAS's cabin crew training is highly regarded in the industry.
Their training lasts for approx. six weeks and is held at the SAS Flight Academy in either Stockholm or Copenhagen. On the course:

○ Safety routines and first aid are important factors in the part of the training involving safety. Among other things, you will experience simulated emergency situations and practice extinguishing fires.

○ Customer service, including passenger psychology is included in the service part of the training.

○ You will receive training in preparing and serving meals both in training cabins at the school as well as in the air.

○ During the training, which is free, there are no wages and after its completion you will be offered a trial employment position for six months.

Depending on the airline with which you fly, you will also be trained in their company's procedures on:

O Training in health, safety, grooming and looking after yourself.
O Understanding and completing the paperwork that needs to be filled out during and after every flight.
O Selling duty free goods, drinks and refreshments, to cash up, complete customs and excise forms.
O Giving announcements over the airline's public address system.

Most airlines carry out ongoing training for cabin crew; every year you are re-tested on emergency procedures, and first aid and medical training will be updated, particularly in using on-board medical equipment such as defibrillators, etc.

To sum up:

O Some courses are very expensive, and although 'you get what you pay for' is generally a good maxim, it has been known for certain institutions to offer highly expensive courses whose qualifications are unacceptable to the industry.
O Ask around before signing up – if you know anyone in the industry ask their opinion.
O Ask the college for names of those who have taken the course and are working in your chosen industry.
O Ask the Personnel or Human Resources Departments of companies that you might want to work for, which courses they would recommend.

WHAT OTHER TRAINING IS AVAILABLE?

For many administrative jobs, you will need to take an HND (Higher National Diploma) or degree course. This is a very small section of some suitable courses on offer:

Aviation Courses

Cranfield College of Aeronautics has been going for over 50 years, balancing the needs of industry with research in a unique way; producing people and ideas that are often quoted in today's press.

Some students arrive at Cranfield with an aviation background; others may come with more generalist backgrounds and learn about the aerospace sector. Cranfield expects to turn these students into the specialists that industry needs. The MSc programmes cover the spectrum of aeronautical related disciplines, with many courses being constructed in a modular form to allow tailoring to students' requirements.

Those arriving with work experience and basic qualifications may have to undertake a preliminary year to bring them up to degree standard. If you arrive with a degree then the Masters courses take one year from October to September. PhDs can start at any time.

Full-time courses can be residential or day-time if you live locally, and cost from £3,000 (plus accommodation) for UK students; from £15,000 (plus accommodation) for International students. Part-time courses are from £2,000 for UK and £8,200 for International students.

MSc courses are taught in small groups, and there is a good ratio of staff to students. Courses are not isolated from the real world, and many are supported by research groups working on cutting edge programmes.

The courses range from Air Transport, Engineering, Science, Business Administration, etc. through to Astro and Space Engineering. These are Masters programmes – Cranfield does not do undergraduate programmes.

The aim of all of the courses is to prepare graduates, coming either from university or from within the industry, for careers in the aerospace and related industries. Each of the taught courses involve a selection of case study work, tutorials, lectures led by college staff and senior visiting lecturers from industry, visits to airports and manufacturers, use of the extensive facilities and flights in the College of Aeronautics' own aircraft. The courses include an individual research thesis which provides an opportunity to study a problem in some detail, whilst some of the courses also include a group design project allowing the realism of industrial projects to be introduced.

At Cranfield students get the chance of seeing the work undertaken in lectures and laboratories coming to life. They may pursue the development of these new applications in engineering flight deck simulators, in one of the 12 windtunnels, in a cabin evacuation simulator or on one of the College's own research aircraft.

As well as the courses listed on their website, they have courses for Continuing Professional Development and Postgraduate Programmes. They hold Preview Days where potential students can go along and quiz lecturers and students.

Contact: www.ccoa.aero.

Engineering courses (see also the Engineering chapter)

University of Bath

Has the following Aero related engineering courses:
MSc in Aerospace Engineering en-dtps@bath.ac.uk
MEng Aerospace Engineering en-ug-addmisions@bath.ac.uk
Contact: www.bath.ac.uk/careers .

University of Bristol

Provides courses in Aerospace Engineering.
Contact: www.aer.bris.ac.uk.

City University London

City University has a number of Engineering and Aviation related course; more details on the on-line prospectus. www.city.ac.uk/ugrad and www.city.ac.uk/pgrad.

Coventry University

Is noted for training in the transport sector, and currently offers a wide range of courses for the Aviation Industry e.g. BEng Aerospace Technology/BEng Mechanical Engineering or BSc Business Management Technology.
Contact: www.coventry.ac.uk.

Middlesbrough College

Again is noted for Engineering courses.
Contact: ☎01642-296600; www.mbro.ac.uk.

Southampton Institute

The Southampton Institute offers a HND in Electrical / Electronic Engineering and a BEng (Hons) in Electronic Engineering. It also offers a BEng (Hons) Engineering with Business course.
Contact: www.solent.ac.uk/technology.

University of Sussex

For their most relevant courses for engineering see www.sussex.ac.uk/engineering/1-2-1.html

University of Ulster

Offers a BSc Hons Transport and Supply Chain Management, and, not surprisingly in an area with links to the industry, has tutors with Aviation linked interests. Short Bros. of Belfast was the world's oldest aircraft manufacturers. It is now part of the Bombardier group, who not only manufacture aircraft but also carriages for Eurostar.
Contact:www.ulst.ac.uk/prospectus/course/

Open University

The Open University gives you the chance to study for a degree at home in your own time at your own pace. Their commercial transport qualifications cover a wide range of activities within passenger transport and freight operations by road, rail, air and sea, and the storage and supply of both raw materials and finished products.

○ Logistics applies specifically to the management of the process of producing and supplying goods and services to the customer.
○ Occupations include airline pilot, air traffic controller, transportation planner

and rail operations manager.

Postgraduate qualifications are available in such subjects as international shipping and logistics, town and country planning, European Traffic and transport and logistics and supply chain management. A masters course in transport planning may be an advantage for central and local government jobs concerning airport planning.

Large companies often have graduate training programmes which are not advertised nationally, so it is worth approaching employers speculatively.

Open University Qualifications

As well as the knowledge gained from OU study, the OU says students develop many transferable skills that are highly valued by employers, such as:

O Time management.
O Self-reliance.
O Problem solving.
O Ability to understand and evaluate new concepts and prioritise effectively.

OU qualifications include:

O Certificate in Accounting.
O Professional Certificate in Management.
O Diploma in Computing.
O Diploma in Information Technology.
O Diploma in Life Sciences.
O Diploma in Mathematics.
O Diploma in Physical Sciences.
O Diploma in Statistics.
O Diploma in Systems Practice.
O BA or BSc with or without honours.
O BA (Hons) Business Studies.
O BSc (Hons) Computing.
O BA or BSc (Hons) Computing and Mathematical Sciences.
O BA or BSc (Hons) Economics and Mathematical Sciences.
O Bachelor of Engineering (Hons).
O BSc (Hons) Information and Technology and Computing.
O Bachelor of Laws (Honours).
O BSc (Hons) Natural Sciences.
O MBA.

The Open University says occupations such as airport and airline managers and other transport managers are often second careers for graduates with other management experience. Experience in export, marketing, finance, town planning, business or transport is valuable.

The analysis of data is essential in some jobs, while negotiation skills and excellent interpersonal skills are almost always required to some extent. Meeting deadlines is important and working to a tight schedule is often required. A positive attitude towards safety and responsible management practices are essential.

Before embarking on an OU course, be realistic about the time it is going to take, or might you be too old to apply for a job once you have obtained the right qualification? Airline pilots and civilian air traffic controllers do have age limits. For example British Airways age limit for certain applicants is 26, and applicants for training with the National Air traffic Services (NATS) must be under 30 when they apply, although those over 30 with relevant aviation experience may be considered.

U.S. Courses

There are so many, the best way to find them is to go on the aviation home website www.avhome.com or see the FAA's website www.faa.gov.

Avhome has links through to colleges and training establishments from Academy Education Center through to Wright State University.

Florida and the southern states are the most popular featured locations for pilot training courses, because they can almost guarantee the good weather that is needed for basic training. Some other training courses are:

O **Cornell University** offers a major in Mechanical and Aerospace Engineering.
   Contact: www.mae.cornell.edu.

O **Stratford School for Aviation Maintenance Technicians** in Connecticut, that sensibly mentions that as well as course fees you will need to buy tools; these can cost around $1,000 for aircraft maintenance courses.
   Contact: www.cttech.org.

O **Aviation Institute of Maintenance of Atlanta** offers FAA (Federal Aviation Administration) certificate courses, such as Aviation Maintenance Technical Certificate.
   Contact: www.aim-atlanta.com.

O **Povenire of Oregon** who not only offer Commercial and Airline Transport Pilot training, but also training on seaplanes.
   Contact www.kpflight.com.

And cost? Some courses start as low as $2,000 for basic engineering training, but Flight School at Palm Springs says to obtain a Professional Pilot's Licence costs from $36,000 – with the Multi-engine training package costing $48,000 plus accommodation. www.flypalmsprings.com.

Management Courses

Coventry University
Is noted for training in the transport sector, and currently offers a wide range of courses for the Aviation Industry e.g. BSc Business Management Technology.
Contact: www.coventry.ac.uk

Middlesbrough College
Is noted for Engineering courses, and also has management courses.
Contact: ☎01642-296600; www.mbro.ac.uk.

University of Bristol
Is noted for tourism degree courses.
Contact: www.aer.bris.ac.uk.

University of Strathclyde
At this university, the Scottish Hotel School offers an undergraduate module entitled Transport for Tourism, which has traditionally had a strong bias towards the Airline Industry. **Contact:** ☎0141 548 4801.

University of Surrey
Many years before Britain woke up to the fact that tourism was a thriving industry, the University of Surrey pioneered tourism degrees, and expanded these to offer training that is acknowledged around the world.
Contact: www.surrey.ac.uk.

> **Today the University of Surrey also offers courses on e-commerce for the travel industry. Course Leader, Dimitrios Buhalis, MSc in eTourism & Director, Centre for eTourism Research says:**
> *The rise in low cost airlines and the ease with which people can book on the internet, has made it very easy for people to arrange their own travel, to the degree that the Internet empowers consumers to develop and purchase their own itineraries, professionals will need to develop new communication skills and strategies. Professionalism, training and knowledge will then have to be combined with eTourism skills and understanding as well as with an adaptive and innovation friendly attitude for the successful tourism **and** travel professionals of the future.*
> Buhalis has written '*eTourism:information technology for strategic tourism management*' (published by Pearson London).

Marketing Courses

Airlines and Airports need to market themselves, otherwise they don't make money and won't stay in business. So a good marketing degree is the passport to many exciting jobs in the industry. Contact CIMTIG (Chartered Institute of Marketing) for details of suitable courses near you; see www.cimtig.org.

MBAs

One of the most significant developments recently has been the rise in popularity of the MBA course (Master of Business Administration), especially with employers in aviation companies and aircraft manufacturers. More than anything, an MBA tells prospective employers you have been through a tough course, and received internationally acknowledged top quality business training.

You take an MBA course after you have finished your degree and worked for a few years, so the average age of students on a course is 29-32 – with perhaps around 5% over 40.

MBA courses cost a lot of money – anything from £20,000 to £60,000 – or more. But employers like them, so many people think the fees a worthwhile investment, especially as MBA graduates are said to earn up to 20% higher salaries.

Are MBAs a good investment?

A recent letter in the Sunday Times asked this very question. **Chris Woodhead, the Government's ex-Chief Inspector of Schools**, gave good MBA courses a resounding thumbs up. However, he warned that some MBA courses are 'probably not worth the investment of time and money', and you should ensure you take an MBA at a college with good industry links.

There are courses all over the world, and it makes sense to think of combining study with perfecting a language. Many MBA students bravely decide to learn or improve their language skills, at the same time as they embark on the punishing MBA course work.

Woodhead says 'whichever country you choose, research the detail and reputation of the course and avoid a second-best qualification that will do little to enhance your career prospects'.

So how much will you have to invest in a good course?
Woodhead says *'the best British MBA courses, such as that run by the London Business School, are as good as any in the world. ... the School charges £41,970 for a two-year course; living expenses and course materials will add a further £16,400 a year.*

Average starting salary for graduates is £55,000 with a signing-on and end-of-year bonus of £13,000 and £7,000 respectively. So if you are prepared to invest your time and money in this qualification, companies will bend over backwards to make it worth your while.

[tnem]Comparisons with American MBAs are not straightforward, but to take that offered by Stanford University as an example, the fees are £19,675 for their nine-month course, and the average starting salary is £54,250.

Useful Addresses

London Business School; www.london.edu
Cranfield University; www.som.cranfield.ac.uk
Association of MBAs; www.mbaworld.com
Stanford University; www.stanford.edu

As Christian Mohrmann of Airbus says:

The MBA helped me acquire and substantiate a number of skills that help me in my job today. As a co-ordinator of projects I am involved in a lot of discussion in a wide range of subjects. During the MBA I have received a good general business knowledge that today helps me to think myself into specific topics.

During the MBA we were under constant time pressure. I face this problem in my daily work life as well. In addition, skills like presenting, leading discussions, moderating, etc. help me assume my responsibilities with confidence.

WHAT IS HAPPENING IN EUROPE?

Once British students headed for the US, and Americans repaid the compliment by coming over to Britain to study for an MBA. Recently Spain has become a major player on this international MBA course scene; their colleges now have well-established links with aviation companies, so British and American students are heading for the campuses and tapas bars of Madrid and Barcelona.

One reason for this rise in popularity has been the language. Although English is the most widely spoken language in the aviation industry, Spanish is now the second most important. It is spoken by all the countries in South America (except Brazil), where vast distances and high mountains make planes the preferred mode of transport, even for local people and their livestock! – so it is a rapidly expanding market.

Watching how the aviation industry has grown recently in South America, the Spanish government is now giving solid backing to the international colleges that offer top level MBA courses, drawing students from all over the world. Their Government sees training future business leaders as helping to increase Spain's influence in the developing world, so in Madrid and Barcelona superb colleges now offer tailor-made MBAs with in-put from aviation companies.

Results for ex-trainees are excellent; most students are headhunted by European, U.S. and South American companies long before the end of their course. In Britain, as Woodhead has said, our best MBA courses are recognised worldwide. If you are taking such a course in the UK, make sure it has a good reputation.

In Spain, the average cost for the International MBA programme is approx.

€34,000 for a year (plus accommodation).

> **After 5 years at Airbus, Olympios Panayiotou, having experienced two different jobs, wanted to further develop his business knowledge.**
>
> *Although I had learnt finance in my previous studies, the level of knowledge that I had was not sufficient for me to feel confident in discussions. Further, my boss at the time who had previously done an MBA was capable in the area of finance; he acted as a guiding light which fuelled my desire to do an MBA. I attended the International MBA at the Instituto de Empresa in Madrid. At the time when I was there I was one of 100 students on the course. This course was appealing because, working for an international company, I was attracted towards other international people.*
>
> *Airbus was very supportive of my decision to do an MBA and after securing a place at university they arranged a support package which included time off while still an employee of the company. Further, the company helped finance part of the course fees, on the proviso that I return for a fixed period on completion. They also paid a contribution towards living expenses over the period of the MBA. On returning to the company I was promoted to Manager Continuous Improvement and Process Integration where I am responsible for a team of staff.*
>
> *I need to be competent on various issues such as strategy and finance as well as human resource issues, particularly as I have responsibility for staff, and the MBA has helped me in these areas. Additionally, I feel comfortable in higher management circles as I can relate to business terminology which may have been a barrier previously.*

NETWORKING

An unseen but very important aspect of an MBA course is the network of contacts students build amongst themselves. This can help enormously with finding jobs, as **Christian Mohrmann says:** it was through the network of the MBA that I got into connection with Airbus in the first place. A fellow student at the Instituto de Empresa in Madrid, Olympios Panayiotou, contacted me to ask whether I would like to do a summer project for Airbus. After finishing the internship I stayed in contact with Airbus, and then received a job offer.

AVIATION-FRIENDLY MBA COLLEGES AND UNIVERSITIES

Cranfield University
With strong aviation links, their alumni directors of international companies

include many in aerospace industries. As **Shirley Jones in their Marketing Department** says 'most of our faculty have management experience with academic heads on industrial shoulders!' Their course is one-year full time.

Cranfield is noted for authoritative research, and their research programmes, especially in the aviation field, are often quoted in the press. However, being a student at Cranfield isn't all work – they set themselves some interesting tasks in their spare time, and you may have seen Jason Chaplin and his team building a replica Triplane for a BBC TV Horizon programme. This was given to them as a management problem; it had to be bought into a budget and on time: with the help of students roped in, and quite a few friends, it was.

EOI

In Madrid, EOI (Escuela de Organización Industrial)offers an MBA in Aeronautic Information commencing every October. Lecturers from EADS UK (European Aeronautic Defence and Space) deliver Aeronautic Marketing, and part of the course takes place at Toulouse Business School. Here students study International Projects management, and their two-week seminar in Toulouse includes Strategic Alliances management and Post- sales.

By June the students are ready to head off for a paid Internship lasting six months to one year; the main objective is to provide a real world connection with Aeronautic Business, and continue with the student's training.

To be accepted, students must hold a university degree and pass the selection process which consists of two personal interviews, an English exam and two general tests. Students come from Britain, Spain, France and Germany, and the course (in a combination of English and Spanish) costs €17,000.
Contact: www.eoi.es

Toulouse Aerospace MBA

The course is set in the heart of the French aviation industry, and has a high reputation, with a large in-put from the French and British Aerospace industries, and aviation professionals from over 30 countries. The business school can call on over fifty companies to supply lecturers, and most students are slightly older (average age is 35). In 2005 they are also offering a part-time Aerospace MBA.
Contact: www.esc-toulouse.com

Useful Addresses

Escuela de Administración de Empresas; www.eae.es
Escuela de Alta Dirección y Administración; www.eada.edu
ESADA (Escuela Superior de Administración y Direction de Empresas); www.esade.edu
ESIC; www.esic.es
Instituto Empresa; www.ie.edu

PILOT TRAINING

Once airlines were happy to train pilots, and paid for training. Alternatively you could go in the Air Force for national service, and be trained for free.

Today airlines are cutting costs drastically, don't have the money to invest in pilot training, and expect new pilots to fund their own courses. The Forces became fed up with people entering just to learn to fly, then leaving after the government had invested millions in their training, so now you have to sign up for a minimum of a short service commission.

Potential pilots are now faced with competing with hundreds of others for possible sponsorship, or, more likely, going to the bank manager and asking for a loan. However, salaries are so high that many consider this a worthwhile investment in their future, particularly if they have a strong desire to fly.

Jane Brookfield of European Pilot Training Academy says:
To do a commercial pilots course to gain your CPL (Commercial Pilot's Licence) you have to have:

○   Private pilots' licence (PPL)
○   Minimum 150 hours flying experience.

Then you can apply to go on our course. If accepted on the modular course, you attend ground school for six months to do JAA (Joint Aviation Airworthiness) and ATPL (Air Transport Pilots Licence) ground school exams.

Once the exams are passed, you go on to do a Commercial Pilot's Licence (CPL) which is 25 hours of flying. Then you go on to IR (Instrument Rating) tests, some in a simulator and some in multi-engined aircraft. Finally you undertake a multi-crew co-operation course. So far you have been flying on your own, but this two week course introduces you to what work will be like when you go to an airline and you have to work with other crew.

The cost is approximately £50,000 for the complete course of 12 – 18 months; contact www.eptauk.com.

Centre for Civil Aviation at London Metropolitan University. They have been running ground based studies for pilot qualifications for over 30 years, and recently launched two new degree courses – a Foundation Degree in Aviation Management & Operations and a BSc Degree in Aviation Management. Both of these courses provide students with a broad range of career opportunities in aviation management and operations related industries.
Contact: www.londonmet.ac.uk/ca

Cabair College of Aviation at Cranfield is noted for its training, but makes the very practical suggestion that you should have an aviation medical *before* you sign up for any course. Otherwise you may find that you have paid out a lot of money, but for some medical reason you cannot obtain a pilot's licence – and your course fees go down the drain.

]em]They have an extremely informative website, are very practical in their approach, and helpful if you are looking for ways of funding training.

In Europe
Lufthansa has a very good training course (and an excellent website) as does Cirrus Flight Training, part of the German-based Cirrus Airlines, where, if you would like to know more about flight training, Ms Anke Rupp is extremely helpful.

For Cirrus contact info@cirrus-flighttraining.de; for Lufthansa see www.lnfl ighttraining.com.

In the USA
Flight schools are listed on FAA's website, from A & M Aviation to Wright Flyers Academy.
Contact: www.faa.gov

Cost
The cost of training depends on many factors. If you have managed to gain entry into the local air cadet force, you will probably already have received some training. However, you are still looking at anything from £30,000-£80,000 or more. The European Pilot Training Academy charges approx. £50,000 for a course of 12-18 months.

Europeans can cut costs by taking a training course in the US. There are excellent schools in many locations, and the southern US states have the advantage of good weather, so it is rare to have to suspend a day's training because of wind, snow, fog, etc.

Sponsored Cadet Scheme Entry
Many companies once funded cadet entry schemes, but with cutbacks this happens less and less. However, some airlines such as Thomas Cook's airline still run schemes.

There are other schemes sometimes offered by airlines, perhaps in conjunction with a college, depending on which airline needs to recruit a large number of pilots at any one time. There is no central place to find out information; you have to keep on looking and asking.

Some schemes are tied in with finance packages where you pay back the airline from your salary. **Remember to check with your bank to see if you can obtain a better deal.** Also, competition for places is fierce.

The Thomas Cook scheme is aimed at young people wishing to become airline pilots, who do not have a professional pilot's licence. *In association with our training partner CTC McAlpine, we are providing an innovative new sponsorship scheme that will enable four applicants achieve their dreams. For more details see the Cadet Scheme pages and CTC McAlpine's website.*

Applications for this scheme should be made through CTC McAlpine's website and not directly to Thomas Cook, but visit thomascookpilots.com for background information about working as a pilot at Thomas Cook. www.ctc-mcalpine.com.

Simulator Training

This will happen more and more on your training course. Once pilots were trained by going up in the air in a plane to do 'circuits and bumps' – over and over again, until they got it right. If you didn't – tough. This was an expensive way to train, particularly if a trainee pilot crashed – so someone had the bright idea of inventing a simulator. This is a small enclosed cabin set out like an aircraft cockpit, with an incredibly sophisticated computerised visual display and audio unit. The instructor can pre-set almost any weather conditions, tune in to the most difficult airport at which to land – then throw in a few wobblies like an engine cutting out. When trainees come out of some sessions they are lucky if they can still stand upright.

Using simulators has cut costs, but it is still an expensive course. If you aren't sure if this is for you, or you want to know more, you can fly 'tasters' at local flying schools. In Britain www.flyingzone.co.uk has a list of local clubs.

Combat Training

A recent copy of Aerospace International had an interview by Richard Gardner with a battle-hardened pilot, talking about the new RAF Lossiemouth simulator training.
'Simulation possibilities are truly awesome – we've never had anything like this before, with the degree of total realism. You can carry out a complete sortie, throwing all sorts of technical failures and new threats along the way, and it is just like being there. You get completely immersed as you deal with sorting the problems and the completion of the mission, and sometimes it is quite a shock at the end of the session when you have 'landed' and realise you have not in fact left the ground!'

Simulator technology is getting smarter; the latest model is a Link Simulation and Training F-16 simulator for the US Air Force, which allows crew of different aircraft types to train in virtual formations for combined missions. In the Iraq war pilots were able to rehearse their missions until they were as perfect as possible, before setting foot in their planes.

At a Royal Aeronautical Society (RaeS) Conference, figures were quoted showing the difference in costs for simulator training v. real planes:

- Commercial Aircraft   1 : 10
- Blackhawk/Seahawk Helicopters   1 : 15
- Boeing 747   1 : 42

So not only are these simulators used more and more to keep costs down and introduce different types of operation for pilot training, but there is employment with the companies that manufacture these simulators.

Useful Addresses
www.embryriddle.edu
www.und.edu
www.delta.com
www.landings.com
www.panamacedemy.com
www.flight.schools.raajobs.com
www.tabexpress.com
www.jetcareers.com
www.pilotmarket.com
Cabair College of Air Training; www.ccat.org.uk
Cirrus Flight Training; www.cirrus-flighttraining.de

For fun, go on to www.FlightSim.com for a site devoted to simulators with what a geek says has 'all sorts of cool add-ons'.

OBTAINING FUNDING

Most trainee pilots will borrow money from the bank to fund their CPL training. Your local bank manager is the first person you should approach. They won't show you the door – in fact you will probably get to talk to an advisor who has already handled several pilot loans.

NatWest Bank has formed links with the Association of MBAs, and will look favourably on anyone applying for a loan to do an MBA course; call 0800-200 400. HSBC also has a sympathetic approach towards loans: contact your local branch, even if you are not a customer.

Many commercial pilot training colleges will arrange loans, especially in the United States. However, before accepting a loan, it makes sense to take their offer to your bank and ask if they can offer better terms.

It might be possible to obtain a grant. For more information:

○ Look up the funding section on the website of the college you are interested in.
○ See the 'Directory of Grant-making Trusts' published by the Charities Aid Foundation. It costs £80 so ask your local library or college if they have a copy. www.dsc.org.uk.
○ In the US ask your library or college if they have a copy of 'Grants Register' (costs $200) published by Palgrave Macmillan Press.

Career Development Loans
These are Government funded loans to pay for training. Sadly, unless you have some funding already they will probably be of limited use for pilot or MBA training, as the current limit is £8,000. But they can be useful to pay for other training – especially for short courses. If you do receive a loan, these have to be repaid, but at favourable rates, and often not until you have started earning. More information from 0800-585 505.

OTHER TRAINING

Air Traffic Control
National Air Traffic Control. To work in ATC, you need at least five GCSE/SCEs at Grade C or above or equivalent, including Maths and English, have studied to A level standard (2 A levels/3 Highers), be aged 18 – 29 and speak good English. Cadets are selected by tests and interviews. There is also a Direct Entrant Graduate scheme for Systems Engineers, Software Engineers and Operations Research.

NATS' training facility is at Bournemouth Airport, where you are trained on a simulator and also with practical experience. Eventually you will be able to handle air traffic control across Britain, possibly the most complex airspace in the world. Contact www. nats.co.uk.

Air traffic control elsewhere in Europe. With the increase in EU member countries, the European Commission intends to harmonise air traffic controller training throughout Europe by the end of 2005. Their intention is to improve standards and safety, and reduce the long- standing shortage of controllers, estimated to be the biggest single cause of air traffic delays in Europe, and a bone of contention between airlines and their passengers.

The most recent estimate is there is a shortage of ATCs of 10-12% in the 38 Eurocontrol member states (EU plus surrounding countries). Integra, the Danish consultancy company, reports that widely different ATCO training standards interfere with job mobility between EU countries.

In Switzerland, Skyguide Training courses accept trainees for its free courses starting in October for Air Traffic Controllers, and in November for Air Navigation Service Employees. www.skyguide.ch

Passenger Handling
Customer service agents and passenger service agents will generally receive a minimum 3 weeks training, paid for by the company, when you start work. Progressing up the career ladder, your company will expect you to take further training (in company time and at their expense) e.g. to become a Ramp Handling Agent you will go on a one week course.

Safety and Security
In France they are very keen on nationally recognised diplomas, and Servair has set up the Aéroform vocational training centre at Villepinte, Paris, dedicated to training in airport assistance and catering. The course covers safety, security, runway assistance, cleaning, cabin, catering logistics, etc. The security course has a diploma, making it recognised across France. www.servaircatering.com.

> **Some companies' in-house training is so good it receives awards.**
> Emirates Group won a gold 'Excellence in E-Learning Award' from brandon-hall.com, a leading US eLearning research and consulting firm. The Emirates 'eLearning Route Map' achieved gold in the Best Practices category for the quality of the business case, overall eLearning strategy and financial model. 'We are particularly proud of this achievement in the first year of operation of the eLearning team,' said **Mark Daldorf, Emirates' Vice President Human Resources Development**. 175 entries underwent rigorous review by 188 independent judges with expertise in instructional design, online learning and organisational change.

CONTACTS FOR TRAINING AND COURSES

These are some of the many thousands of addresses for qualifications authorities, courses and training. More are listed in the chapter on training.

It would be impossible to list all the courses and training available in the aviation world, but the majority of the contacts listed on these pages are included because they have been particularly helpful, run by enthusiasts keen to help new entrants, and are often willing to point you in the right direction even if you are not sure exactly which course it is you wish to follow.

Aviation is a global industry, and often the colleges listed have contacts with training courses in other countries. This enables you to mix-and-match training, taking part of a course in one country, then finishing the course in another.

AGCAS: (Assn. Graduate Careers Advisory Services) ☎0870 770 3310; www.agcas.org.uk.
Association to Advance Collegiate Schools: (US) www.aacsb.edu.
Association of Licensed Aircraft Engineers: www.lae.mcmail.com.
Association of MBAs: ☎020 7246 2686; 25 Hosier Lane, London EC1A 9LQ;

www.mbaworld.com.
Aviation Safety and Airworthiness Training: www.bainessimmons.com.
Aviation Security Training: www.dft.gsi.gov.uk.
Aviation Training Directory: www.icao.int.

University of Bath: Careers Advisory Service; ☎01225 386009; www.bath.ac.uk/careers; Aerospace Engineering: en-ug-admissions@bath.ac.uk.
University of Bristol: ☎0117-928-8221; 11 Priory Road, Clifton, Bristol, BS8 1TU; www.aer.bris.ac.uk; careers-gen@bristol.ac.uk.

CABAIR College of Air Training: ☎01234-751243; Cranfield Airport, Bedford MK43 OJR; www.ccat.org.uk.
Career Development Loans: ☎0800 585 505.
Cirrus Flight Training: ☎+49 (0) 6332 99 36 29; Flughafen Saarbrucken, D-66131 Saarbrucken, Germany; www.cirrus-flighttraining.de or info@cirrus-flighttraining.de.
City University London: www.city.ac.uk/ugrad/ and www.city.ac.uk/pgrad.
Coventry University: www.coventry.ac.uk.
Cranfield College of Aeronautics: ☎01234-751243; www.ccoa.aero.
Cranfield School of Management: ☎01234-751243; Cranfield, Bedfordshire, MK43 0AL; www.som.cranfield.ac.uk.

EADA (Escuela de Alta Dirección y Administración – MBA college): ☎+34 934 520 844 C/AragÃ³, 204, 08011 Barcelona; www.eada.edu.
EAE (Escuela de Administración de Empresas): ☎+34 902 18 06 33; Avda. Catedral 6, 08002 Barcelona; www.eae.es.
EAL (Emta Awards Ltd): ☎0870 240 6889; 14, Upton Road, Watford WD18 OJT; www.eal.org.uk.
Embry-Riddle Aeronautical University: www.erau.edu.
EOI (Escuela de Organización Industrial – MBA college): ☎+34 91 349 56 45; Gregorio del Amoro, Cuidad Universaria, 28040 Madrid; www.eoi.es.
ESADA (Escuela Superior de Administration y Direction de Empresas – MBA college): ☎+34 934 952 099; Av. Pedralbes 60, E-08034 Barcelona; www.esade.edu.
ESIC (mba college): ☎+34 914 524 100; Av. Valdenigrales s/n, Pozuelo de AlcorcÃ³n 28223 Madrid; www.esic.es.
European Association of Aerospace Students: www.euroavia.net.
Institute of Air Navigation training services: www.eurocontrol.int.
European Pilot Training Academy: ☎01202-581122; Aviation Park West, Bournemouth International Airport, BH23 6NW; www.eptauk.com.

Flybe Training Centre: Hangar 21, Exeter Airport; ☎01392-266925;
Engineering: engineering.personnel@flybe.com.
Cabin Crew: cabincrew.personnel@flybe.com.

Pilots: pilots.personnel@flybe.com.
Administration: administration.personnel@flybe.com; www.flybe.com
Foundation Degrees: Information ☎0800 917 6699.

Gatwick Aviation Training: ☎01753-535783; www.gat4training.com.
Global Engineering Educational Exchange: www.iie.org.

de Havilland Museum: Just off Junction 22 of the M25 lie the grounds of Salisbury Hall, now home to the de Havilland Heritage Centre. They have Comets (world's first jet airliner), Chipmunk trainers, Vampire and Sea Vixens, and Mosquitos – all built by this famous factory. You can watch teams of enthusiasts restoring these planes, and even volunteer to get engineering work experience; Sunday is best day for this. www.dehavillandmuseum.co.uk.
Helicopter Training: www.alanmann.co.uk.

IE (Instituto Empresa): ☎+34 91 568 96 42; Maria de Molina, 11, 28006 Madrid; www.ie.edu.
IFCA: In-flight Catering Association: works with University of Surrey for training in-flight caterers; www.ifcanet.com.
International Fire Training Centre: www.iftc.co.uk.

Learn Direct: to discuss career options with a learning advisor at their advice line, call ☎0800- 100 900 or email enquiries@learndirect.net; www.learndirect-advice.co.uk.
London Business School: ☎020 7262 5050 Regent's Park, London NW1 4SA; www.london.edu.
Loughborough University: www.lboro.ac.uk.

Macclesfield College: www.macclesfield.ac.uk.
Middlesbrough College: ☎01642-296600; www.mbro.ac.uk.
Northbrook College: ☎0800 183 60 60Cecil Pashley Way, Shoreham Airport, Shoreham-by-Sea, BN43 5FF www.northbrook.ac.uk.
National Air Traffic Services College : www.nats.co.uk.

Open University: ☎0870 9000 301 PO Box 625, Milton Keynes, MK7 6YG; www.open.ac.uk.
Orlando Flight Training: ☎1-800 259 2100 606 N.Dyer Blvd., Kissimmee, FL 34741; www.flyoft.com.

Pan Aviation Training Services: ☎020-7371-8731; panaviation@yahoo.com.

Qualifications and Curriculum Authority: ☎020 7509 5555; www.qca.org.uk.

Red Cross: Find training contact in local phone book.
Redhill Helicopter Training Centre: ☎01737-823282.
Royal Aeronautical Society: www.raes.org.uk.

Smallpiece Trust : promotes courses and careers in engineering; www.smallpiecetrust.org.uk.
Stanford University: www.stanford.edu.
Southampton Institute: ☎023-8031 9975; Faculty of Technology, Southampton Institute, East Park Terrace, Southampton S14 0YN; www.solent.ac.uk.
South Seattle Community College: ☎206-768-6629; www.southseattle.edu/programs/proftech.aeronat.htm.
St. John's Ambulance: First Aid training - see local phone book for nearest centre. **www.studentpilot.net:** website if you want information about pilot training in the U.S.

Transport Security Directorate: www.dft.gsi.gov.uk.

University of Surrey: ☎01483-300800 Guildford GU2 7XH www.surrey.ac.uk.
University of Sussex: Career Development and Employment Centre, Falmer House, University of Sussex; www.sussex.ac.uk/engineering.
www.technopolis.be: ☎+32 (0)15 34 20 20.
www.thomascookpilots.com: for details about becoming a pilot under Thomas Cook sponsorship scheme.

Tourism Training Organisation: Helpline for general info on jobs and training; ☎0906 553 2056 (calls cost £1 per minute); www.tourismtraining.biz.
TTC (Travel Training Company): ☎01483-727321; www.ttctraining.co.uk.

UCAS (Universities & Colleges Admissions Service): with information on over 1,250 tourism courses; ☎0870 11222211; PO Box 28, Cheltenham GL52 3LZ; www.ucas.ac.uk.
University of Ulster: www.ulst.ac.uk For info on BSc Hons Transport and Supply Chain Management with Aviation linked interest.

Welcome Host Courses: ☎023-8062 5436; www.welcometoexcellence.com.

FURTHER CONTACTS

www.aerosociety.com/careers
www.aviationcourses.com
www.bestaviationschools.com
www.cabincrewdirect.com
www.cabinfevercrew.com

www.careerintravel.co.uk
www.iaot.net
www.travelvocation.com
www.worldwidetraveltraining.com
www.wicat.com

Institute of Logistics and Transport; www.iolt.org.uk
QCA (Qualifications and Curriculum Authority); www.qca.org.uk
Red Cross; find training contact in local phone book.

Association of Graduate Careers Advice Services
You can go to www.open.ac.uk/courses for a full list of courses and qualifications.

AgCAS Sector Briefings provide information on the current state of different industries and advice on entry plus case studies, reading suggestions and Internet links. Available at www.prospects.ac.uk/links/SectorBs

AgCAS Job Profiles are at www.prospects.ac.uk/links/occupations. You can search types of jobs alphabetically such as Air Traffic Controller or through categories of jobs such as Transport and Distribution.

AgCAS Signpost Leaflets provide information about opportunities available with a given degree. They are available at www.prospects.ac.uk/links/signposts Relevant subjects include Business, Economics, Geography, and IT.

You may also find relevant information on the following sites:

Royal Town Planning Institute; www.rtpi.org.
British International Freight Association (includes the Institute of Freight Forwarders) ; www.BIFA.org.
The Chartered Institute of Purchasing and Supply; www.cips.org.
Institute of Export; www.export.org.uk.
Supply Chain Knowledge Centre; www.sckc.info.

Go Skills
Go Skills is the new sector skills council looking after passenger transport, including aviation. (Used to be TRANSFED). Currently they are setting up a number of sector skills councils in cohesive groups of industry for the passenger transport industry, which includes the non-engineering section of aviation.

Go Skills can give you information on the Aviation Modern Apprenticeship scheme – contact your local Learning and Skills Council who will know which local employers are involved. Contact GoSkills at Concorde House, Trinity Park, Solihull, B37 7UQ; ☎0121-635- 5520 www.goskills.org.

Work Worldwide

Aviation is a global industry, providing job opportunities around the world. In this chapter we mention some of the sectors where work is available, and highlight unusual opportunities. The airline world is expanding, and jobs are increasing because:

O Passengers are becoming more adventurous and flying to lesser known airports.
O Business travellers think nothing of hopping on a plane to talk to a contact face-to-face. A decade ago telephone video conferencing was supposed to put an end to business meetings; instead, it has made them more popular as people talk on a conference telephone link, and then decide they need to get face-to-face to iron out a contract.
O With the rise in holiday entitlement, and more leisure time, added to a better standard of living, travellers have the opportunity and the money to travel more.

Even when an event such as September 11 virtually halted trans-Atlantic travel overnight, leisure travellers just switched to short-haul flights. They travelled, but in different directions. Banks are still prepared to finance the many airlines currently starting up; they have seen the worst scenario, and realise that the industry recovers.

We tend to think of airline companies as being relatively new, but KLM has been going for over 84 years, closely followed by Finnair (www.finnair.com) which celebrated its 80th birthday in 2003. Today Finnair is proud to have carried over 150 million passengers: 'a clear vote of trust from our customers', according to President & CEO Keijo Suila. .

As the European Union expands, employment barriers are coming down. To work in administrative or engineering jobs you have to be able to speak the language of the country in which the company or airline is based, but provided you speak that language, generally there are no barriers to working if you are a resident in another EU country, or of a country whose residents are allowed to work in the EU.

Outside the EU, employment rules vary. Generally in North America you will find it impossible to find a job unless you have the appropriate work permits, yet in the Gulf most airlines recruit some of their staff, especially cabin crew, from around the world: e.g. Gulf Air currently has 64 nationalities working for the airline.

AIRPORTS

One of the best places to find 'static' jobs is at airports. Log on to your local airport's website and you will be surprised at the variety. Information staff, security, town planning graduates, engineers, and many others are wanted. A tiny sample of recent adverts for BAA staff include

- ○ Heathrow/Stansted – Airport Lead Engineers providing people management skills and 'minding' airport infrastructure from runway lights to access roads (Heathrow £43,000, Stansted £32,000 p.a.)
- ○ Glasgow – Maintenance Team Managers to head operational teams of shift technicians (£33,000 + bonus)
- ○ Gatwick – Planning Engineers from all disciplines to maximise the lifespan and safety of assets, and who are familiar with benchmark standards, maintenance strategies and asset inspection legislation (£33,000 + bonus),
- ○ Heathrow – Resource co-ordinators to manage day-to-day relationships and performance assessment of specific contracts (£36.000 + bonus)
- ○ Stansted – Contracts Manager to review, analyse and monitor contracted maintenance services, and to provide a strategic overview and set standards (£33,000 + bonus)
- ○ All Airports – Engineering Duty Manager to organise resources and balance the competing needs of customers and stakeholders (£26,000-£33,000)

For more details, go to www.baa.com., phone 0141-585 6000 (they have a central recruiting office for all airports) or e-mail people – management – admin@baa.com.

Useful Addresses
For a sample of current jobs available around the world, try:
www.flightinternationaljobs.com; www.workthing.com
www.aviationjobsearch.com

CATERING

One good source of jobs is in the catering sector, where staff are needed for:

- ○ On-board airline catering suppliers.
- ○ Airport fast food outlets.
- ○ Upmarket restaurant outlets (often themed) appearing at airports around the world.

Even with the rise of low cost airlines and their minimal catering, most airlines still offer meals. Low cost airlines tried to do away with catering, then realised that passengers start walking around the aisles if they weren't tied down by trays, looking for something to chew on. So now they make money by selling snacks, and everyone is happy.

Simulated Aircraft Cabin
So important is airline catering that a recent development introduced the world's first Simulated Aircraft Cabin, designed to test meal quality by simulating cabin conditions at 30,000 feet. Up there cabin pressure, humidity and temperature changes can play havoc with taste buds – not to mention oven performance. Until this came along airlines regularly had to take aircraft aloft to test new meals.

When Herman Wolke, CEO of Lufthansa SkyChefs (one of world's largest airline catering companies) was asked what his biggest catering problem was, his rueful reply was 'designing an oven that will cook bread rolls at 35,000ft'.

IN-FLIGHT CATERING

With a worldwide turnover currently estimated at $14 billion a year, this section is expanding rapidly. For logistical reasons, most airline caterers are based on or near an airport. The market is split roughly 30% Europe, 35% Asia/Pacific region and 26% in North America.

If you are interested in administration, logistics, catering cost analysis etc., airlines will almost certainly want your expertise in their catering section.

O The largest employers are LGS Sky Chefs, and Gate Gourmet.
O There are over 600 flight kitchens worldwide.
O An average airline kitchen employs 150 people preparing 6-7,000 airline meals a day.
O Meals are designed for easy-assembly. Full colour photos of the plated meal are placed in front of staff on assembly line – all they have to do is copy the picture exactly.

Many airline caterers belong to **IFCA (the In-flight Catering Association)** who have a very informative website www.ifcanet.com, giving details of members. These range from food preparation companies to recycling organisations (today airlines are being forced to become more eco-friendly). Their website tells you what is happening globally in this sector, and there are very helpful research forms and student fact sheets.

Every year IFCA hosts the Mercury Awards, the 'Oscars' of the airline catering industry. Airlines have won the coveted statuette for:

O Meal plans for those on special diets.
O Unusual solutions to mass catering for cheap charters.
O Chefs in the air.

Every year produces more exciting and innovative ideas.

Flying bmi from London to Scotland, we imagined that on-board catering would be almost non-existent – until we were handed a Bento box; these Japanese-style boxes were made out of recyclable packaging, so food keeps fresh. Being handed food in an attractive box, rather than plonked on a tray, meant passengers had the excitement of opening the box – and inside was a small amount of food imaginatively presented. No wonder bmi won a Mercury award for these Bento boxes.

The airline catering sector is such an important jobs-provider that the University of Surrey now has an IFCA Professor, and has published the Flight Catering Book.

Useful Addresses
www.ifcanet.com
www.alpha-flight-services.com
www.cara.com
www.lsg-skychefs.com

Meals on Board

Today, very few airlines cook and package their own food. Hygiene laws have made it too expensive for companies to support their own kitchens; it makes more sense to contract the work out to a specialist caterer.

However, the palmy days of airline catering, when the big companies gained contracts to supply millions of pre-packaged meals every year, looked to be over. Post September 11, airlines searched for every way possible to cut costs, trying to equate two well-known facts:

O Passengers say they don't like airline food.
O Passengers complain vociferously if food isn't offered to them once they are on board, and looking for something to occupy their time.

So airlines are using every imaginative trick in the book to persuade passengers to pay for the food, whilst still offering it on board. The low cost carriers have persuaded passengers that they are going to have to pay for food from a trolley, and on the whole, although the cost is about double what it is on the ground (sandwiches cost £4-£6), the quality is good – and passengers appreciate this.

Some years ago Lufthansa pioneered the concept of selecting your own sandwiches and snacks in the departure lounge, prior to boarding the aircraft, and carrying them on board with you. This saved time and money. Recently the idea surfaced again in the States, and this option is also being offered by Swiss Airlines.

The idea has merit, with more variety and fresher food, but passengers are perverse and it is taking them time to accept the idea of choosing their meal on the ground, rather than on board.

At New York's John F. Kennedy Airport, BA is successfully pioneering the concept of dining at the airport before you catch your flight. Instead of wandering aimlessly around before boarding, if you are a First or Business Class passenger you can go to the BA Lounge, sit down in their restaurant and eat a three course meal whilst waiting. Once on board, you settle down to sleep.

Time-poor cash-rich business passengers accept and appreciate this – it remains to be seen if leisure travellers could be persuaded to follow the same concept.

Many people have forecast that with low cost airlines abandoning in-flight catering, the days of the meal on your lap are over. However, never underestimate the fickleness of the travelling public. Having been shown that by getting rid of in-flight catering, airlines can offer very low fares – they are now starting to think that perhaps they do like a meal on board after all. Airlines employ very sophisticated marketing analysis – and currently airlines such as Monarch are emphasising in their adverts that their fares are low – yet they still provide a meal.

Whilst other airlines started withdrawing their in-flight meals or charging for them, SN Brussels Airlines announced it has improved its in-flight catering service in economy class; introducing a 'Brussels Bistro' menu on all flights. Healthy breakfasts, hot meals, snacks and salads, are all presented in boxes, for ease of stowing on aircraft and handing out to passengers.

> *'While the trend in the aviation world is to offer less and less service, we have decided to go against the flow,'* says **Philip Saunders, Executive Vice President Commercial of SN Brussels Airlines,** *'customer research tells us that our passengers are highly appreciative of complimentary quality meals and high levels of cabin crew service.'*

CATERING ADMINISTRATION

Financial and logistics training can be useful, and profitable. Airlines no longer uplift food from their home airport; on flights between Britain and Australia, for instance, they may take on food in Bahrain from a huge local kitchen complex, or in Los Angeles, depending on which route they are flying. One major reason is cost of fuel: every pound of weight on board an aircraft uses expensive aviation fuel to fly it through the air.

So kitchens along the way have the staff and equipment to provide and cook the food; where your administrative expertise comes in is:

O Sourcing food from around the world, making sure it is edible, free from health risks, and familiar to passengers.

O Ensuring it is cooked to passengers' tastes.

O Training the multi-lingual kitchen staff to plate it so it will look attractive, even when knocked about on trolleys between the kitchen and aircraft.

O Ensuring it can be easily heated by cabin staff coping with ovens that will not perform at 35,000 feet (if you have ever tried to boil water on a ski-ing holiday up a mountain – you get the picture).

○ And finally, it has to be to your ethnic passengers' tastes – they have nothing else to do for 18 hours than wait for food – and complain if it isn't what they are used to.

However, the traditional concept of 'dining in the sky' has been turned on its head by airline bosses such as Stelios Haji-Ioannou of easyJet, who says 'if you want to eat, go to a restaurant'. easyJet offer snacks on board, and load up their in-flight trolleys with snacks once a day, rather than at the beginning of every flight (saves time, and the airline money).

To hit back at this, Monarch's website has a large banner 'Do other low cost airlines leave you with an empty feeling? We won't'. And go on to say they offer 'Good food and specially selected wine' for their lead-in fare of £28 one way to various European destinations.

If catering logistics, administration and delivery interest you, a recent press release from BAA will show the potential for administration jobs in airport catering. Once a job in catering at an airport meant handing out sandwiches and burgers; now it can mean running a multi-million pound operation, catering for different people's needs 24 hours a day.

New Catering Balcony at Heathrow Terminal 1

The Opening of a new landside catering mezzanine level at Heathrow's Terminal 1 includes outlets such as Wetherspoons, Costa Coffee, Caffé Italia and Café Rouge. This balcony is just part of a £30 million recent investment on catering developments across BAA's 7 UK airports. At the opening, Catherine Loveridge, Head of Catering at BAA said:

We are committed to changing the face of airport catering, and this redevelopment is part of a UK airport-wide programme of improvements. We've already completed catering revamps at Glasgow, Aberdeen, Southampton, Stansted and Gatwick landside with further developments due at Gatwick Airside. From talking to our customers we know that they want quality, value for money and recognised high street brands and this is what we are working to deliver. Across our UK airports more than 90% of the eateries are high street brands and customers can be sure of getting good value with all prices benchmarked against the local high street.

BAA Retail hosts over 130 bars and restaurants at its seven UK Airports, including **Pizza Express, Frankie and Benny's, Est Est Est, Café Uno Presto, Pret A Manger,** the upmarket **Caviar House Seafood Bar** and **Chez Gerard.** So, if you are looking for a summer job – or a career – it's worth checking out the outlets at an airport near you.

CHARTERING

Because of security scares, the urge to get somewhere quicker, the loss of Concorde, and just because some people are rich enough to avoid the herd – private aircraft charters are on the increase; all needing pilots and usually cabin crew.

In the United States the President has Airforce One (and a back-up) to fly himself and his staff around the world. Crew come from the U.S. Airforce.

In Britain, there is the Royal Flight, used by H.M. The Queen and members of the Royal Family, the Prime Minister and certain Government Ministers on official business. Once the Queen's Flight aircraft were part of the RAF, but today they are chartered from Air Partners, who have recently been awarded the Royal Warrant. They have announced they looking for additional airline and air charter executives – but not cabin crew.

To work as an air charter executive, you have to have a good understanding of the local charter market, and appreciate the potential in this sector. Clients can range from Chief Executives of companies with a high-risk kidnapping factor, to footballers and pop stars trying to avoid the fans. Currently Air Partners have 125 executives working for them around the world.

LOUNGES

If you don't want to fly, or work as a PSA, you could try working in a VIP Airport Lounge. Once these were exclusively for First and Business Class passengers; now airlines are finding it is profitable to open them up to all passengers, and charge an entrance fee. Today passengers have to arrive earlier for security checks, but find sitting around in the departure lounge is boring, and there is a limit to how much time they want to spend in shops.

Francesca Freeland of KLM analysed their needs, and suggested making more use of Holideck (their VIP Lounge at Heathrow's Terminal 4).
One of the best areas of profitability is the business class lounge. This was provided for First and Business Class passengers; we felt we should open this up to people who can pay on the door to come in. Now it is a very popular service. Passengers have a choice of different areas: the Music Zone where you can down-load your own choice of music for the flight; a Smoking Room, a children's area with playstations, a sports bar, and two quiet zones, or Havens, where mobile phones and TVs are banned. Upstairs is the Flight Deck, where visitors can see Windsor Castle in one direction, and Canary Wharf in the other. Charts show what Ramp Handling staff are doing with their bats, and in the background you hear the ATC controllers' voices talking down the planes on their approach.

Other airlines across the world are copying KLM's formula, from Europe to

Australia. Virgin has found that many customers for Virgin Blue, their low cost Australian airline, are happy to pay extra for their lounge.

CARGO

Keep an eye on cargo airlines – they are bigger than you might think, and expanding rapidly. Every major international airline has a cargo division; some belonging wholly to the airline, others have become so profitable they are hived off into a separate company.

> **SAS (Scandinavian Airlines System) now has SAS Cargo, where revenue is around 3 billion Swedish Kroner a year (£230 million).**
> The group is 100% owned by SAS, employs 1400 people and operates to 105 destinations on three continents. As a result of opening up routes between Copenhagen and Shanghai in China, they have increased cargo capacity, adding about 100 tons of capacity per week between the two countries.
>
> SAS believe Shanghai is situated in a very fast growing market. Globalisation has made more businesses move their production to China, and this is where they see the fastest growing market in airfreight. The route will be flown with the biggest aircraft in the SAS fleet; Airbus 340, which can lift about 18 tons of cargo each way.

Useful Addresses
www.airfoyle.co.uk
www.capitolcargo.com
www.klmcargo.com
www.lhcargo.com
www.nippon-cargo.com
www.unitedcargo.com
www.sascargo.com.

You don't have to work as a pilot or in the sales department – there are many, many jobs in administration and handling the logistics of moving valuable cargo from one venue to another.

AIRLINE MARKETING WORLDWIDE

Other chapters deal with the effects of low cost carriers, but marketing departments worldwide are currently carrying out survey after survey hoping to predict what the travelling public will want.

If anyone owns a reliable crystal ball, they could make a mega-fortune in predicting what it is they will want – and more importantly, what they will actually pay for.

By far the most profitable sector (per mile of seat revenue) is up the front in

Business and First Class. One or both of these classes will produce between 12 and 20 times the revenue obtained from an Economy Class seat. It doesn't take long to work out that, even with better seats, more expensive food and drink, and a higher ratio of cabin staff, the person up front is contributing a larger profit per seat. The trouble is, it costs a lot more in advertising and promotion to get people to sit in that seat.

It is only a couple of decades since airlines had the revolutionary idea of introducing separate classes on board, and charging passengers more to sit up front. Now, with the volatile market fluctuating up and down overnight, airlines are just not able to predict in advance how bookings will split between classes.

First Class is quietly disappearing on certain British Airways routes, principally because they seem to have decided to amalgamate the two classes, and thereby save overheads.

After vast improvements in their Business Class product, whose reclining seats are only 6 inches shorter than First Class for up to a 50% less fare, the airline has removed the front cabin from some routes, is concentrating its advertising on its Business Class Club World and Club Europe branding, and is looking at other routes to see if this is a viable option on these.

In Germany, Lufthansa has been so successful in its trials with dedicated Business Class only flights to the United States, they are looking at increasing the destinations.

Post September 11 many financial departments in companies questioned the added cost for their executives to sit up front, and low cost carriers like Flybe and easyJet suddenly found they were very popular with company finance directors (who don't usually get to travel, so can be slightly envious!) However, the market is gradually getting back to normal, executives are missing their leg room, and managing to persuade the accountants that it is worthwhile paying extra to keep them comfortable. It only needs these executives to murmur 'such and such a company always flies their executives First Class' to get twitchy Human Resources directors worried about resignations, and urging finance directors to authorise the extra seat cost.

However, post September 11 marketing departments are having to come up with flexible solutions, changing dinosaurs into modern, lean, efficient airline operating systems. Travel Agent implants (agency staff working in a client's offices) and business travel agents are becoming adept at finding less expensive ways of flying up front: keying Heathrow to Moscow into several search engines, I came up with flight costs of £1,600 return by BA Business Class, but if I wanted to spend an hour in the duty free shops at Zurich Airport, I could fly Heathrow – Zurich – Moscow for £650; it didn't take me long to start planning how I could spend that money in the shops – pity this was only an exercise!

The Momberger Survey (the airline's trade newsletter) highlights current trends for major airlines to dispense with Economy class in some aircraft cabins, and make the seating Business Class only. This is a big commitment; it costs money to take out seats and change the cabin seating configuration (seating plan). However, it is proving extremely popular; not least with Cabin Crew, who have more time to serve passengers as there is a higher staff ratio to customers.

Valued added services
These services are one of the areas that will expand; even low cost carriers, traditional enemies of frills and extras, are now offering supplementary services.

Virgin Blue has experimented with pay-per-use lounges at Brisbane and Sydney, where users pay a nominal fee of USD $3 to enter. This has been a success, and is bound to be copied.

Catering is also about to be changed on low cost carriers; Virgin Express is launching Alpha D'Lish (sic) which enables passengers to pre-book their meals, instead of hoping there will be something they like on the aircraft trolley.

In-Flight Chefs
Gulf Air has introduced an innovative in-flight Chef service and are now looking to recruit and train more qualified chefs to develop this service on their international routes. They want *'motivated customer-orientated professionals'* to provide passengers with a modern contemporary in-flight service.

To become an In-flight Chef you will require:

o A trade certificate in commercial cookery and substantial post-apprenticeship experience as a chef, preferably gained within a 5-star establishment.
o Culinary skills combined with a very strong commitment to customer service, while communication skills and personal presentation will need to be of the highest standard.
o Personal qualities including warmth, diplomacy and professionalism.
o Ability to liase directly with catering suppliers to ensure optimum product integrity.
o Able to prepare, plate and present meals to premium customers.
o Ability to conduct quality assurance audits.

Gulf Air say chefs:

o Will be based in the Kingdom of Bahrain, and fly to any one of 49 international destinations.
o Have a tax-free salary and generous allowances.
o A free, fully furnished shared apartment.

On the transatlantic route bmi airlines are also experimenting with supplying chefs on board.

Useful Addresses
www.gulfairco.com, www.flybmi.com.

Interviews

There is plenty of good advice in books and on the internet about interviews in general. So in this chapter we concentrate on interviews for cabin crew.

Cabin crew interviews generally take longer, and go into more depth, than interviews for many other jobs. Not only do airlines have a large number of applicants to choose from, but they have to ensure that those whom they pick will be capable of handling any emergency that might arise. For those of you who haven't been to an airline interview before, those for cabin crew generally last all-day.

○ Some airlines have helpful advice about their interview procedures on their websites: BA's website is particularly informative.
○ As airlines are in the enviable position of having numerous candidates for most positions, many airline staff will tell you they had to apply to several airlines before they were accepted by one.
○ It is helpful to think of each airline interview as a step in a training course; take note of what happens, and use this as the foundation for your next interview. Eventually you will have enough experience, and be accepted!

WHEN DO AIRLINES RECRUIT?

Airline recruitment is almost continuous, with most airlines having personnel departments (also known as human resources) or agencies handling interviewing on a year-round basis. Interviewing, selection and training can take up to six months or more. There is usually an airline somewhere that is currently recruiting.

Look for details of forthcoming interviews on airline websites. If a large amount of staff are required, particularly for cabin crew at the beginning of the summer season, you may see adverts in local or national newspapers.

WHAT WILL HAPPEN ONCE I HAVE APPLIED?

Airline selection processes may involve three or more stages, depending on the position for which you are applying.

1. First fill out and send off an application form.
2. If you meet the airline's first set of criteria, you will be invited to attend an assessment, which will generally last the whole day.
3. For some jobs you may be required to sit tests and take part in other exercises before progressing to the final stage.
4. You may be called back for further assessment.

Most airlines expect you to apply using their online application form; only a few airlines still ask for the traditional CV and letter. As soon as the airline receives your application, they will look at your experience and qualifications, and check whether you have submitted all the information they require. Leave anything out, and it's into the waste paper bin with your application – so make sure you check, check and check again before you send off any form.

If you haven't access to the internet, ask a friend, or go to your local library. Failing that, there are internet cafés you can use.

MyTravel Airways has introduced telephone interviews; it won't be long before other airlines copy this idea.
If your online application is successful, we give you a telephone interview (don't worry – you don't have to wait by the phone – you will be called back if you are out!). The telephone interviewer will ask you questions relating to the position you applied for, and will answer your questions about the airline and the work.If successful, you will be invited in writing to an assessment day.

WHAT HAPPENS AT THE INTERVIEW STAGE?

This really depends on the airline, but normally at this stage up to 80% of applicants will have received a 'no' on the basis of their written application. It isn't anything against you – just that airlines have so many applicants they cannot interview every one. Most airlines operate a group interview, where they give all candidates an insight into the company and discuss conditions of employment. You might be asked to attend up to three interviews, each one could last all day.

During your main interview day you will be given a general knowledge test. The best preparation for this is to start reading a good quality newspaper such as the *Daily Telegraph, The Independent* or *The Times* every day. In the test you will be asked general knowledge questions. Sample questions from a recent interview:

O What are the capital cities of European countries?
O Which countries are in the European Union?
O How do you spell Edinburgh?
O What is the name of the chairman of the airline for whom you wish to work?

○ Who is the Minister responsible for Aviation?
○ Where does our airline fly to?

And watch out – there is always a numeracy test, and an old trick is to ask you to give equivalent costings for £2 *not* £1, so do find out how much a Euro is worth.

Dress smartly. This means a suit or jacket and trousers if you are male, and a tie (this can be colourful but not from food stains). Not too much jewellery; if in doubt leave it off.

Women should wear a suit, jacket and skirt or smart dress. If you are happier wearing a trouser suit, that is all right, but it must look business-like. Wear make-up, but nothing glittery. Nails must be clean and well groomed (you will have to serve food, so many interviewers make a point of looking at nails). You can have discreet nail polish but again nothing too flash; interviewers say blue nail polish puts them off – makes you look as if you are cold.

Read the airline's website or interview instructions carefully for restrictions on tattoos, piercings, etc. *Always* make sure your shoes are clean and polished. Airline interviewers love polished shoes. If you have to wear a coat and/or carry an umbrella, leave this outside the interview room. Clutter drops around you and makes you feel ill at ease.

Lukie Hield works for a large tourism recruitment company, and says

You are going to feel nervous and the interview panel will be expecting this. They don't like cocky know-it-all applicants, but will make allowances for nervousness. If you think you are making a bad impression, take a deep breath and start again.

Do watch out for the nice lady who gives you an amusing and interesting account of the history of her airline or company. If you think this interlude is to give you a chance to gather your thoughts, you are wrong. At the end of a tiring day you will be given a test asking you questions about what she told you

---

If you are not successful, build on your interview experience; apply to other airlines, and you may well be successful with the next company.

Beware – one well-known airline will ask you at the end of a long interview day to try on their uniform. If you are female you will also receive a complete make-up. You think all this attention means you have passed the interviews? Sorry. It is solely to see if you look good in the uniform.

CABIN CREW REQUIREMENTS

During your interview day, you may be checked on any of the following:

○ Health and eye sight (contact lenses usually accepted).

- Height – generally from 5ft2ins-6ft2ins (1.57m-1.87m) with weight in proportion.
- Languages, including sign language.
- Some airlines will require specific languages.
- They may ask you to bring your passport.

Mission Statement for Cabin Crew
Lisa Ulberg from Scandinavian Airlines System sent us this 'mission statement' for their cabin crew. Read this before an interview; think about it and decide what you can give to the airline.

- We view each customer as an individual with personal needs and desires, which it is our task to fulfil.
- Our service must be characterised by simplicity, freedom of choice and consideration. We must be the equals of our passengers and have them feel that they are being well cared for, while at the same time we stand for absolute safety and punctuality.
- SAS is a Scandinavian company working in an international environment. We view cultural/ethnic diversity as an asset and strive for a working environment which is characterised by knowledge, respect and tolerance towards other cultures.
- The vision of SAS is to make Scandinavians proud of their airline and as an employee you are an important and self-evident part of that process.
- We fly about 20 million customers per year and each customer has on the average ten contacts with some of us during their journey. It is on these occasions that the customer's good impression of SAS can be reinforced and hence where you as an employee become our greatest competitive advantage.
- Exciting job with demanding requirements. As an employee onboard, you need to possess qualities which at times can seem to be the direct opposites of each other. For example, this means that along with having to be sensitive and service-minded you must also be an authoritative leader in an emergency situation.
- You must also like intensive contact with people, while at the same time being able to manage things on your own when you find yourself in a different place, often in a different country.
- The working hours vary widely. We fly around the clock, all days of the week and Christmas Eve as well as New Year's Eve too. Your schedule is given to you roughly 14 days in advance and it includes standby obligations. Standby means that you are on-call and can be called upon to work at short notice.
- The work is characterised by a large degree of irregularity and a fast pace. It involves contact with many people and new colleagues each

and every day. And of course, you find yourself continually on the road: in Scandinavia, in Europe and in Asia and the US.

APPROACHING AN INTERVIEW

British Airways recruitment department say good preparation is by far the best way to eliminate interview nerves. They want to see what you are capable of and whether you would be suited to the position. Of all the airlines around the world, their website currently gives the most helpful advice about interviews, and how to handle them. So read it, even if you don't live in one of their catchment areas. www.britishairwaysjobs.com

BA say following these simple guidelines will help you give the best possible account of yourself on the day:

O Make sure you can talk confidently about everything on your CV or application form.
O Research the position and list the skills and experiences being sought. Review your own background and think of specific examples that match them.
O Learn as much as you can about the company. Corporate websites often have good background information. Keep an eye on national newspapers and the business press.
O Prepare a list of questions to ask your interview panel. When they ask 'is there anything you want to ask us', they expect you to have bothered to have found some questions you want answered.
O Remember to engage with the interviewer. Take your time if needed to answer questions fully and pay attention throughout.
O Don't avoid talking about a period in your life where you encountered difficulties or felt your performance wasn't as you might have liked. Instead, talk about what you learnt from the experience and how it helped you move forward.
O Practise your responses to specific questions. It will give you confidence and make you feel more at ease.
O Airlines take recruitment and selection very seriously. While it's clearly in your interests to be treated fairly and with respect, it's also essential that airlines select people with the qualities essential to offer passengers the best service.

British Airways recruitment team says:
Our team is comprised of experienced recruitment professionals with diverse backgrounds gained in blue chip businesses and from within British Airways itself. When recruiting, we ensure we take an objective view and follow best practice guidelines laid down by The British Psychological Society (BPS) and the Chartered Institute of Personnel and

Development (CIPD). We also carefully adhere to Equal Opportunities legislation.

Our recruitment methodology is based on looking at capabilities – also known as competencies. These capabilities are sets of behaviours, skills and knowledge that can be determinants of job success and focus on what the role for which you've applied involves. They're a valuable tool in ensuring consistency and accuracy in assessments and increase the reliability of the selection process.

WHAT WILL MY ASSESSMENT CONSIST OF?

Most airlines will contact you to inform you what you will be doing on the day. During the day group exercises will look at how you work with other people, in particular examining your influencing, communication and teamwork skills.

Assessment methods used may include group exercises, interviews, psychometric tests, presentations, fact-finding exercises and one-to-one role-play.

You will have a one-to-one interview, where you will be asked about yourself and your experience. You may be asked for examples of how you behaved in different situations drawing on examples from work, university, school, a club or home.

You will almost certainly be asked to complete psychometric tests. These are timed exercises that look at your ability and potential, and you can look up sample tests on the internet. Don't worry if you don't finish them – that doesn't matter. Tests used most often focus on verbal and numeracy skills, and also include a personality assessment, another tool designed to find out more about you.

Presentations

Generally you will be asked to give a presentation in front of a panel – some-times in front of the others being interviewed. This presentation is a chance to show your ability to communicate to a group of people. You will be given the topic on the day and will have time to prepare. On some occasions you may be sent information prior to the assessment day.

You may also take part in a fact-finding exercise, looking at your ability to interact with someone else and obtain information from them. You will be given all the relevant information on the day and will have preparation time prior to the exercise.

Role-plays usually involve an assessor acting as your client or customer in a simulation of a negotiation exercise, interview or performance appraisal, for example. You will be given a briefing before the exercise starts.

How Do I Prepare for My Assessment Day?

Reflect on what you have done at work, university, school, in a club and even at home. Think about examples of when you have interacted with people, the problems you may have encountered, the outcomes and what you learned from these situations. Think about why you want the position and what skills would be required for the role. Concentrate on what you do well and what you need to do to improve. You could seek feedback from sources such as colleagues, friends, tutors, customers or clients.

Prior to your assessment try to have a good night's sleep. Get to the assessment in good time. Remember it's your day and it's about you. The company's aim is to assess you fairly and give you the best opportunity to demonstrate your potential – and to assess whether the company is right for you.

Finally, be yourself. It's the surest way to succeed!

WHAT HAPPENS IF I AM SUCCESSFUL AT INTERVIEW?

You may be taken on just for the season, or offered a full-time job, subject to certain conditions. Depending on the job you have applied for, you will probably be sent for a medical examination, at the company's expense. If you pass this, you then go on to the appropriate training course. If accepted as cabin crew this is paid for by the company. Cabin crew receive the most comprehensive training, including studying various aircraft and where the emergency exits are positioned, safety procedures, customer service etc. If you are taking a position elsewhere within the airline you may receive training on their reservation systems and procedures, the routes the airline flies etc.

UNDER EIGHTEEN?

You can still prepare for aviation work by taking courses that will be useful, and look good on your CV.

- Take a First Aid Course. These are run by the Red Cross or Red Crescent, St. John's Ambulance or your local general hospital.
- Take the four-day course in Health and Safety offered by many Environmental Health Departments of Town Halls.
- Start reading a quality newspaper. You will be asked questions on general knowledge at your interview, and reading a newspaper is the best preparation.
- If you are taking a GNVQ make sure you take the Travel Geography option.
- Help out with a local charity looking after people.
- Phone the Tourism Helpline on 0906 553 2056 (calls cost £1 per minute and you must have the consent of a parent or guardian) and ask them for hints, tips and how to prepare.

THE FUTURE

As airlines are going over to online applications, and some airlines will only accept applications in this form, the next interview technique might well involve advertising yourself on your own website. For fun, have a look at Rob Lawrence's site. When he wanted a job, he hired St. Luke's, the leading advertising agency famous for its Ikea adverts, to help him produce his own website to advertise himself. www.givebobajob.co.uk.

Recently, at interviews, some applicants have given their web addresses. If you have your own website, it is well worth including it on your CV. But for the moment, until the aviation industry is ready – keep on sending applications online or by snailmail – whichever they ask for.

Useful Websites
www.airlinecrew.net
www.Aviationinterviewscom
www.crewstart.com
www.pilotmarket.com
www.SAS.se
www.willflyfor food.cc

The following Occupational Psychology companies' websites contain tests that are often used in assessments:

www.shldirect.com/shldirect-homepage/SHLDirect-1.asp
www.ase-solutions.co.uk/support.asp?id=62

Regulations & Regulatory Bodies

WHY THEY ARE IMPORTANT TO YOU

When the Wright Brothers took off on their historic flights, no one asked if they had a certificate of airworthiness for their plane, if they had been trained to fly, or if they had filed a flight plan. No one had even thought about the problems this new form of transport would produce, or how to ensure the safety of the people who took to the skies.

In the early days of flight, anyone who wanted to fly took their life in their hands. But gradually, as companies started to make money out of offering flights to an eager public, authorities, quite rightly, started to question safety aspects. They wanted to know if aircraft had been maintained and serviced, whether the pilots were competent to fly, etc.

So regulations designed to protect the flying public came into force, and today no one would think of flying with any company ignoring these rules. Across the world regulations are constantly being up-dated, and after any crash, investigators will share their knowledge with their colleagues in other regulatory bodies, to try and learn from mistakes, and so improve safety.

Every country in the world with an international airport will have some form of air regulatory body, and some, such as Britain's CAA and the U.S's FAA, will have influence worldwide. In order to carry passengers, cargo or mail for payment, air operators based in the European Economic Area (EEA) must:

o Hold an Operating Licence granted by the Member State in which they have their principal place of business. For UK airlines, licensing is undertaken by the CAA.
o In order to qualify for an Operating Licence, an operator must meet a number of requirements, including those in respect of its safety and insurance arrangements, and its nationality of control.
o For operators of aircraft with 20 or more seats, there are also financial criteria to be met.
o Operators who hold operating licences are able to operate within the European Economic Area (EEA) without the need to hold further licences. For operations beyond the EEA, they will normally need to hold one or more Route Licences, which are also granted by the CAA, etc. The legal frame-

work for licensing is contained in a number of separate pieces of legislation, regulations and other sources.

It is thanks to regulations that air travel has progressed so far and so fast, and insurance companies say you are safer up in the air than in your own home. These are some of the regulatory aviation bodies that look after the world's airlines: sometimes there is duplication in their roles, but gradually they are defining their own areas of expertise.

CIVIL AVIATION AUTHORITY (CAA)

The CAA says it has recorded a drop in fatalities of 97% during the past 30 years. According to them, the UK aviation safety record is almost four times better than the world average, while carrying more than 100 million passengers each year.

However, neither the aviation industry nor the CAA are complacent about this hard-won UK safety performance. The CAA says 'a systematic approach to managing risk is at the heart of our combined efforts to uphold and, where possible, improve the continued safe operation of public air transport systems'.

ATOL

As well as monitoring safety, one major role of the CAA is providing financial protection for holidaymakers under its ATOL (Air Travel Organisers' Licensing) scheme.

ATOL exists to protect the public from losing money, or being stranded abroad, because of the failure of air travel firms. First introduced in 1972, it gives comprehensive consumer protection to the 28 million people in the UK who buy flights or air holidays each year on ATOL affiliated airlines.

The CAA monitor carefully which way the industry is going, and has recently published a new ATOL leaflet 'Don't Take a Sporting Chance', warning sports enthusiasts planning a trip abroad to check that they are ATOL protected, or they could lose their money. The leaflet gives advice and tips about financial protection to those travelling to or organising a sports event, and highlights the risks they may be taking in putting together their own travel packages. If an operator is a member of the ATOL scheme, from the moment you book to when you arrive home, the money you have paid for your travel and other services is protected.

Air Rage

The public may hear about the CAA when there is an incident of air rage. International regulations formed by the CAA and similar authorities back-up the airline captain's authority; which is just as well, because sadly air rage seems to be on the increase. Footballers in particular seem to cause a tremendous amount of well-documented problems, from Paul Gascoigne to Vinnie Jones.

No wonder the England Rugby team were such favourites with BA. Apparently they decided to go to sleep on their return flight from the World Cup in Australia, rather than spend the night celebrating in the bar on board.

Working at the CAA

The CAA is an extremely complex organisation, and each of its business areas is responsible for recruiting the people with the particular skills and knowledge it requires. Job opportunities arise across the whole organisation, but will broadly fall into the following areas:

O Air Safety.
O Economic Regulation.
O Airspace Regulation.
O Consumer Protection.
O Environmental Research and Consultancy.
O Corporate which includes Finance, Human Resources and Legal.

As well as recruiting new entrants, particularly to work in Consumer Protection (see website below), within Air Safety Regulation there are specific roles where there is an ongoing need for experienced and qualified people. These are:

O Flight Operations Inspectors (Heavy and Helicopters) – holding a current UK or JAA ATPL with extensive experience as a commander on large public transport aeroplanes/public transport twin-engine equipped helicopters (minimum of 2,000 hrs in command).

O Airworthiness Surveyors – 10 years experience in aircraft maintenance, with an HNC and appropriate BCAR Section L or JAR-66 Licence.

O Air Traffic Control Inspectors – extensive ATC experience with a civil ATCO licence with current or recent competence in aerodrome/approach/approach radar ratings and a current medical certificate.

Useful Address
www.caa.co.uk

FEDERAL AVIATION ADMINISTRATION (FAA)

The FAA is an agency of the US Department of Transportation, working very closely with the CAA and colleagues in other regulatory bodies. They are the aviation industry's governing body in the U.S., and in the States are the foremost point of contact for current and future pilots. The FAA has a comprehensive list of aviation-related publications and organisations.

Useful Address

www.faa.gov.

TRANSPORT CANADA

In Canada, Transport Canada is the authority that licenses pilots and registers aircraft.

NavCanada is a not-for-profit organisation monitored by Transport Canada, and is responsible for developing and administering aviation-related policies, regulations, and services set by Transport Canada. However, unlike the FAA, NavCanada neither licenses pilots nor registers aircraft.

Useful Address

www.tc.gc.ca

INTERNATIONAL AIR TRANSPORT ASSOCIATION (IATA)

IATA is an airline trade association, not a regulator, although its international standing means it is consulted by governments and regulatory bodies. Its mission is to represent and serve the airline industry, and it could be said that the organisation is the web that knits together the worldwide aviation industry. According to IATA, '*International air transport is one of the most dynamic and fastest-changing industries in the world. It needs a responsive, forward-looking and universal trade association, operating at the highest professional standards*'.

Founded in 1919, IATA brings together approximately 280 airlines, whose flights comprise more than 95 percent of all international scheduled air traffic. Not every airline belongs to IATA (some for very good reasons), but if their name is not shown amongst the list of members, it is as well to ask why. 1,700 people in 80 different countries work for IATA, whose head office is in Geneva; with a sub-head office in Montreal, Canada.

In a changing world, airlines must co-operate in order to offer a seamless service of the highest possible standard to passengers and cargo shippers, and much of that co-operation is channelled through IATA. Some of the services it organises are:

- ⦿ Airlines knit their individual networks into a worldwide system through IATA, despite differences in language, currencies, laws and national customs.
- ⦿ Thanks to IATA, individual passengers can make one telephone call to reserve a ticket, pay in one currency and then use the ticket on several airlines in several countries – or even return it for a cash refund.
- ⦿ It is a useful means for governments to work with airlines and draw on their

experience and expertise.
- Working standards within the aviation industry are developed within IATA. In fostering safe and efficient air transport, IATA serves the stated policies of most of the world's governments.
- The organisation ensures people, freight and mail can move around the world as easily as if they were on a single airline in a single country.
- IATA also ensures members' aircraft can operate safely, securely, efficiently and economically under clearly defined and understood rules.
- By helping to control airline costs, IATA contributes to cheaper tickets and shipping costs.
- IATA is a collective link between third parties and the airlines.
- Passenger and cargo agents are able to make representations to the industry through IATA, and derive the benefit of neutrally applied agency service standards and levels of professional skill.
- Equipment manufacturers and third party service providers are able to join in the airline meetings which define the way air transport goes about its business.
- IATA offers joint means – beyond the resources of any single company – of exploiting opportunities, reducing costs and solving many aviation problems.

Cabin Crew

If you work as cabin crew, you probably owe your job to IATA safety regulations. Cabin crew are on board, officially, to ensure that as many passengers as possible are helped to escape in the event of the plane ditching or crashing.

It is debatable which airline first employed air stewardesses; at first the majority were trained nurses, and it soon became evident that they could be used to supervise passengers in the event of an accident. Later on it was pragmatically decided that they might as well do something useful on board like serving food. Companies thought they shouldn't be standing (or sitting) idle whilst the plane was flying.

The number of flight attendants is determined by the regulator and is based on the type of aircraft and the number of passengers carried. This is why low cost airlines could do away with the food and drinks, but not with the cabin crew.

Billing and settlement plans

Global aviation has to have a simple way of transferring money from one airline to another. No matter if this is a multi-national carrier flying the world, or a tiny little airline with a couple of planes; if they belong to IATA, it takes one simple transaction to make payments across the world.

Around the world, there are travel agents who have taken IATA-approved courses to handle airline travel. Generally they will belong to IATA's billing and settlement plans: the clearing house system allows airlines and agents to settle their many complex transactions with one simple transaction at the end of each month.

Working for IATA

If you want to work for IATA, its website www.iata.org has a recruitment section, with jobs advertised all over the world, particularly in its dual HQ centres: Geneva and Montreal.

Switzerland: 33, Route de L'Aeroport, 1215 Geneva; ☎+41 22 770 2525.

Canada: 600, Place Victoria, Montreal, Quebec, Canada 4Z 1M1; ☎+1 514 8 74 02 02.

UK: Central House, Lampton Road, Hounslow TW3 1HY; ☎+44 20 8607 6200

As well as entrants, IATA constantly requires specialists for positions such as the one featured below.

Product Manager, Airline Training

Location: Montreal. Reporting to the Assistant Director, Airlines Training, responsible for the on-going development of existing and customised training products and tasked with the research, identification and development of new, innovative training products.

Develop detailed proposals for creating new classroom courses, featuring course outlines, objectives and intended learning outcome, and research with reference to published information, in-house IATA experts, outside academics and airline industry experts. Proposing business and implementation plans to support the development of new courses, specifying budgets, marketing plans, as well as details regarding course material, the course leaders (instructors/consultants) involvement and delivery logistics.

Management level jobs at IATA require:

○ University degree preferably in Education or an air transport related field.
○ Minimum 5 to 7 years experience in the air transport industry with international exposure.
○ Proven strong analytical and organisational skills with the ability to manage multiple projects simultaneously whilst maintaining high attention to detail and meeting deadlines.
○ Excellent communication, negotiation, and interpersonal skills, including the ability to deal professionally with, and gain the co-operation of, customers, suppliers and contacts at a senior level.
○ Excellent oral and written communication skills in English with developed editing and proof reading skills.
○ Knowledge of other languages (French, Spanish) would be an asset.
○ Excellent PC skills particularly with MS Office programmes (Word, Excel, PowerPoint and Outlook).
○ Availability to travel.

EUROPEAN JOINT AVIATION AUTHORITIES (JAA)

The Joint Aviation Authorities (JAA) is an associated body of the European Civil Aviation Conference (ECAC). It represents the civil aviation regulatory authorities of a number of European States, who have agreed to co-operate in developing and implementing common safety regulatory standards and procedures, intended to provide high and consistent standards of safety and a level playing-field for competition in Europe. Emphasis is also placed on harmonising the JAA regulations with those of the USA.

JAA's work started in 1970 (when it was known as the Joint Airworthiness Authorities). Originally its objectives were only to produce common certification codes for large aeroplanes and for engines. This was to meet the needs of European industry, particularly for products manufactured by international consortia (e.g. Airbus). Since 1987 its work has been extended to operations, maintenance, licensing and certification/design standards for all classes of aircraft. Common procedures and the approval of design, production and maintenance organisations are also covered.

A single Joint Certification team, working on behalf of all the JAA countries, is used for certification of new aircraft and engines. After the successful completion of the evaluations, Type Certificates are issued simultaneously, and on a common basis, by all member states.

Currently there are five divisions :

1. Certification.
2. Regulation.
3. Maintenance.
4. Operations.
5. Licensing, and the Secretariat of the Chief Executive.

The 'largest' countries (France, Germany, and the United Kingdom) each pay around 16% of operation costs, and the smallest around 0.6% of the total contribution income.

The international promotion of the JAA system and its regulations has a two-fold aim, namely improvements of the safety level of aircraft flying into the pan-European airspace, and that of the European public travelling in other parts of the world. At present, Central JAA is widening the scope of its activities and – under financing of various sponsors including the European Union – provides information and advice for major international co-operation programmes through participation in Advisory Panels and Steering Committees, as well as Workshops in the interested countries.

JAA and the FAA have made a commitment to harmonise their standards of design, safety and airworthiness where appropriate.

INTERNATIONAL CIVIL AVIATION ORGANIZATION (ICAO)

In Nov. 1944 the US government extended an invitation to 55 States or authorities to attend an International Civil Aviation Conference in Chicago. 32 States which attended set up the permanent International Civil Aviation Organization (ICAO) as a means to secure international co-operation, and the highest possible degree of uniformity in regulations and standards, procedures and organisation regarding civil aviation matters.

The most important work accomplished by the Chicago Conference was in the technical field, because the conference laid the foundation for a set of rules and regulations regarding air navigation as a whole, bringing aviation safety a great step forward, and paving the way for a common air navigation system throughout the world. Eventually they were also to cover:

O Generally applicable rules and regulations concerning training and licensing of aeronautical personnel both in the air and on the ground.
O Communication systems and procedures.
O Rules for the air and air traffic control systems and practices.
O Airworthiness requirements for aircraft engaged in international air navigation as well as their registration and identification, aeronautical meteorology and maps and charts.

For obvious reasons, these aspects required uniformity on a worldwide scale if truly international air navigation was to become a possibility. Activities in these fields had therefore to be handled by a central agency, i.e. ICAO headquarters, if local deviations or separate developments were to be avoided.

Useful Address
www.icao.int

EUROCONTROL

Eurocontrol is the European Organisation for the Safety of Air Navigation. This civil and military Organisation which currently numbers 32 Member States, has as its primary objective the development of a seamless, pan-European Air Traffic Management (ATM) system to cope with the forecast growth in air traffic, while maintaining a high level of safety, reducing costs, and respecting the environment.

Useful Address
www.eurocontrol.int

PASSPORTS AND VISAS

Aircrew are subject to the same regulations as passengers, and have to hold visas, if required by a country. It is up to you to provide your original passport, and pay for this. If an airline wants you to fly into a country where it is considered more acceptable to have a duplicate passport (perhaps to include a visa from one country that may not get on with another country) then generally the airline will pay for this duplicate. Unless it is a condition of employment that you have to be in possession of certain visas, it is generally the airline that will apply for and pay for these.

BRITISH AIRLINE PILOTS ASSOCIATION (BALPA)

Founded over 50 years ago, BALPA is the most advanced specialist aviation association in Europe. Services include:

O Pilots' Advisory Group.
O Experienced representatives.
O Legal support.

BALPA works hard to improve pay and conditions for members, lobbying the UK Government, etc. Their Technical Department provides up-to-the-minute expertise on all areas of flight-deck life, including medical, safety and security.

Full Members have to hold a Commercial or Airline Transport Pilot Licence, or equivalents, or a Flight Engineer Licence and be engaged in UK commercial flying. Other categories of membership include:

O Trainee Associate.
O Unemployed.
O British members working overseas for non-UK companies.
O Class B pilots not required to hold a current CPL or ATPL e.g. ground instructors, helicopter winchmen or service contract pilots.

Membership Fees for full membership are 1% of gross pensionable annual salary.

Useful Address
www.balpa.org

AMERICAN AIRLINE PILOTS' ASSOCIATION (ALPA)

ALPA promotes and champions all aspects of aviation safety throughout all sections of the aviation community, both in the U.S. and liasing with similar associations abroad. It represents, in both specific and general aspects, the collective interests of all pilots in commercial aviation; assists in collective bargaining activities on behalf of all pilots represented by the Association; promotes the health and welfare of the members of the Association before all governmental agencies; is a strong, forceful advocate of the airline piloting profession, through all forms of media, and with the public at large; and is the ultimate guardian and defender of the rights and privileges of the professional pilots who are members of the Association.

Founded in 1931, ALPA is a combination of a professional association and a union representing around 70,000 airline pilots in the USA and Canada.

Code of Ethics

The ALPA website has an interesting Code of Ethics, which lays down a pilot's responsibility. Pilots have hundreds of lives in their hands, and the code makes it very clear that for these people the highest standards are vital. The code says :

○ Airline pilots will keep uppermost in their mind that the safety, comfort and well being of the passengers who entrust their lives to them are their first and greatest responsibility.
○ Airline pilots will faithfully discharge the duty they owe the airline, which employs them and whose salary makes possible their way of life.
○ An airline pilot will accept the responsibilities as well as the rewards of command, and will at all times so conduct him/herself both on duty and off as to instil and merit the confidence and respect of his/her crew, fellow employees, and associates within the profession.
○ Airline pilots will conduct their affairs with other members of the profession and with the association in such a manner as to bring credit to the profession.
○ To an airline pilot, the honor of his/her profession is dear and he/she will remember that each pilot's own character and conduct reflect honor or dishonor upon the profession.

EUROPEAN UNION

One of the impacts of European Union legislation on the travel industry has been the production of the Package Travel Regulations. Up until ten years ago, one of the major problems facing holidaymakers was what happened if they booked a holiday, and this didn't deliver what the clients had paid for. Regulations, which became law in 1992, now gave clear guidelines on what tour operators and others selling packages were responsible for.

A package was defined as including two out of three of the following elements:

1. Travel.
2. Accommodation.
3. Services (car hire, ferry tickets, etc).

The Regulations said anyone booking a package with a EU-based travel agent and/or tour operator had the right to expect that they would receive what they had paid for, or be fully compensated if something went wrong. The Department of Trade and Industry publishes a free guide to The Package Travel Regulations; phone 0870-1502500 for a copy.

ENVIRONMENTAL GROUPS

Today, ecological lobbies are so powerful that no airport can even consider expansion without consultation with interested groups. Whenever there are plans to expand an airport, the environmental groups are there to protect local residents and try to get 'friendlier' plans approved.

Airlines, realising they have to satisfy today's eco-consumer, employ consultants to come up with ideas and solutions for ecological problems, from helping mitigate the effects of aircraft emissions, to providing healthier food on board.

The CAA's Environmental Research and Consultancy Department (ERCD) is helping to minimise the impact of aviation on the environment, by carrying out a range of activities in the field of aviation and the environment, including noise monitoring, noise contour modelling and research into the health effects of noise. Although noise issues tend to be of most concern around airports, the impacts of aircraft emissions on local air quality are also becoming increasingly important.

If you want to see what this involves, you can go onto the CAA'S Noise Monitoring pages, where you learn about the noise monitoring work they do around the London airports (some typical aircraft sound clips can be downloaded). They are experts on the effects of aircraft noise on people (see Noise Effects), having assisted government with many research studies, and also take a keen interest in the environmental impact of aircraft emissions (see Air Pollution).

There is also a useful variety of web links to other organisations involved with aviation and the environment, including links to many UK airports, plus you can order a free CD-ROM: Introductory Presentation and Technical Resource, introducing ERCD's main areas of work, as well as an archive of ERCD's recent documents.

Useful Address
www.caa.co.uk.

The Armed Forces

Some people will enter the armed forces because they have a vocation; others will consider joining up as an inexpensive way to be trained as a pilot or engineer. But beware, the forces are aware that their excellent free training is a major incentive, and you will have to prove you intend to stay for the minimum period of a service contract.

The Forces offer a good life, with a chance to travel, and many people say one of the biggest pluses of working in this sector – although not often mentioned – is the sense of family. Every member of the forces belongs to a unit, squadron, regiment or ship, where support comes from the top, and also from your peers. These peers operate a 'buddy' system, looking after you in good times and bad.

Conditions
Although theoretically you are on duty 38 hours a week, in practice you are on call at all times. During exercises and operations, hours may be long and irregular. You must be prepared to go wherever you are needed around the world, and may spend long periods away from home.

Skills and Interests
If you hope to join as a pilot officer, you should be:

○ A resilient, resourceful leader, able to inspire and motivate your unit.
○ Self-disciplined, confident and determined.
○ Able to assess the strengths and weaknesses of the people in your command.
○ Able to think and react quickly.
○ Ready to accept responsibility and make decisions.
○ Able to communicate with people at all levels.
○ Physically very fit with a good level of stamina.
○ Prepared to operate in dangerous combat situations.

Entry
You do not necessarily need any higher educational qualifications; it is more important that you have the right qualities. However, a good general education is essential because the training is demanding and you will have to pass a selection test, interview and medical examination. The test is based on reasoning, numeracy, literacy and mechanical comprehension.

Depending on the service you want to join (RAF, Army, Navy or Marines), the basic minimum entry requirements are five GCSEs (A-C)/S grades (1-3) including English language and mathematics and two A levels/H grades.The management system is based on different ranks within three groups of personnel:

O Trade technicians.
O Non-commissioned ranks.
O Officers.

In addition, for a commission, you will generally require a minimum of 140 UCAS Tariff points at A/AS Level, or the equivalent, and 5 GCSEs, or equivalent, including Maths, English and either a Science or foreign language. You should have the potential to study for a degree (although a degree is not always a requirement).

You can join the services either as non-commissioned personnel, or as an officer. All entrants carry out the same initial training, before specialising in a technical field, or opting for trade training.

You need to be aged between 16 and 26. For some jobs you can be accepted up to 33 (e.g. for specialist trades, such as Firefighter, if you've worked in the Fire Service, or in a driving job, the higher age limit applies because you will already have basic experience).

Non-commissioned and commissioned officers
If you enter the forces as aircrew, technician, specialist artificer, etc. you earn promotion in most trades from junior ranks to non-commissioned personnel, taking on management and instructing roles through experience, performance and development. If you have the right qualities, you will be in line to apply for a commission as an officer.

Applicants offering alternative qualifications are considered on their individual merits for commissions as officers. Direct graduate entrants must have a UK degree or equivalent, and English and maths at GCSE (A-C)/S grades (1-3). They should be under 26 on the first day of the month of their entry.

University cadetship entrants must be under 22 on the first day of the month of their entry. University bursary entrants must be under 22 when they get the bursary and under 26 on actual entry. Exact details of scholarships and bursaries are available from armed forces careers officers, as are nationality and residence requirements. Generally you join the services on an initial commission which will last eight to twelve years, depending on the service. Direct entrants should be between 17 and 26-33 (depending on the branch of the service) on the first day of the month of entry. Late entry is rare.

Other requirements
The minimum height requirement is 151.5 centimetres (approximately four feet

eleven and three quarters), and the minimum weight requirement is 60 kilos (approximately nine stones six pounds). Weight must be in proportion to height. You must be a British, Irish or Commonwealth citizen and all entrants must pass a medical test and a three-stage selection procedure. For details of qualification equivalents see either the Qualifications and Curriculum Authority (England, Wales and Northern Ireland) or the Scottish Qualifications Authority.

Sponsorship

A bonus for joining the forces is the help given for funding your training. For instance, the RAF says 'we can invest in your future by funding your studies until you're ready to start training as a pilot. You can apply for an RAF Pilot Scholarship of £1,000 during the Sixth Form if you do not intend to go to university. Alternatively, you can apply for a Sixth Form Scholarship of £1,000, followed by a University Bursary of £1,000 a year if you do a degree. In return, they ask you to become a member of the University Air Squadron (or Air Training Corps while you are at school) and join the RAF once you finish your studies.

As well as financial support, the RAF say it's an opportunity to get first-hand experience of the challenges you'll face working with people, technology and aircraft – and 'we'll also give you free flying lessons!' To find out more, contact an RAF Senior Careers Liaison Officer via the careers staff at your school or college – or visit your local recruitment office.

ROYAL AIR FORCE

Currently Britain's Royal Air Force employs 53,000 full time and reserve members in jobs ranging from Aerospace Systems Operators, Cabin Crew (known as Steward/esses), Air Traffic Controllers, Avionics and Mechanical Aircraft Technicians – through to Pilots.

The RAF is organised into three commands: Strike Command, Logistics Command and Personnel and Training Command (which obviously concerns itself with training).

Strike Command is directly concerned with flying and operating missile systems. Its units are based in the UK and overseas.

Logistics Command supplies and maintains RAF operations worldwide, and also runs ground-based systems and international satellite communications for all the UK Armed Forces.

Pilots

Pilots play a varied role in the RAF; you could be a combat pilot flying fast-jets, fly a multi-engined transport aircraft or a rotary wing aircraft.

○ Fast-jet aircraft such as Tornados are used for combat, and also to patrol the skies. As the pilot of a Tornado, your primary role will be air-to-air combat or ground attack.

○ Multi-engine aircraft such as Hercules are used to ferry troops and supplies, and also for humanitarian aid in war and emergencies. In a Hercules transport aircraft, you could be sent anywhere in the world on military support or humanitarian aid missions.

○ Rotary-wing helicopters are used for Search and Rescue, ferrying troops, combat missions, etc. In a helicopter your duties might include anything from search and rescue flights to ferrying troops and equipment into combat zones.

Once you've completed initial training, you'll be selected for fast-jet, multi-engine or rotary-wing streams. You'll then receive further training on the aircraft type you've been assigned to, before becoming 'combat ready'.

Female Pilots
The RAF has male and female pilots. If you are good enough, you will get selected; there is no gender barrier to flying the different types of aircraft. **Flt. Lt. Michele Tompkins** flies Harrier Jump Jets from RAF Cottesmore Airfield. She says *'Although all jet fighters are challenging, the Harrier is the ultimate test because it can hover as well as fly conventionally'*.

Engineers and Technicians
Engineers are stationed around the world wherever there is an RAF base. Currently there are bases in the UK, on Cyprus, Ascension Island, Goose Bay Canada and the Falkland Islands, plus temporary bases wherever there may be an emergency.

Other RAF Jobs
Administrative Officer; accountant, personnel officer, estates manager or public relations, etc.

Aerospace Systems Operator; defending the air, tracking aircraft by radar and using computers to identify them and to plot their speed and position.

Air Cartographer; create and update maps, charts and books used in the planning and completion of flying missions.

Air Steward/Steward; runs dining rooms, bars in Officers' and Sergeants' Messes, and is responsible for in-flight meals and safety.

Air Traffic Controller: controls some of the world's most modern radar and communications equipment.

Aircraft Technician (Avionics); maintains all photographic, electrical and electronic equipment on aircraft.

Aircraft Technician (Mechanical); maintains an aircraft's mechanically operated systems, including the engine.

Dog Handler: whenever an airfield is established, in a war zone or elsewhere, it has to be guarded, and the most effective way is by using dogs. Radar can pick up most things, but a dog knows everything that goes on in its territory – and woe betide an intruder who falls foul of a RAF Police Dog. Handlers generally start working in the Police.

Getting in

Even if you aren't applying for university funding, it helps if you become a member of the Air Training Corps at school, or join the University Air Squadron when at university. When you are 17 ½-23 years old you can apply to join the RAF; if chosen, you have to sign up for a minimum length of 12 years service. Pay is from £28,500-£83,000. You must be British from birth, or hold dual British/other nationality.

Useful Address

www.rafcareers.com

ROYAL NAVY

The Fleet Air Arm produced some of the first combat pilots in the world; during World War I many pilots formed part of the RNAS (Royal Naval Air Service) until it was decided to form a separate force, and the Royal Air Force came into being.

Today's Royal Navy is not only about warships. The Fleet Air Arm has a range of high-tech, fixed-wing and rotary-wing aircraft currently in service, and the service needs highly trained men and women to keep things running smoothly.

Pilot training

The Fleet Air Arm is the Royal Navy's airborne force. Pilots can be based on board an aircraft carrier, or ashore.

Paul had always wanted to be a naval fighter pilot, and applied to join the Royal Navy at school

I'd dreamt of being a naval fighter pilot for some time. However, I decided to study for a degree before commencing officer training at Dartmouth. I thought I was giving myself a safety net should things go awry. Now the thought that I could have been flying the Sea Harrier three years earlier is very appealing.

At the moment I am working to progress to the front line squadrons, learning to fly, operate and ultimately fight in the Sea Harrier. The Sea Harrier is a very capable air-to-air fighter. It can be flown conventionally, but it can also hover as well as launch and land vertically. I recently became the 187th person to hover a Sea Harrier.

The training is demanding but it has been built up over a couple of years. I recently finished my advanced flying training on the Hawk in Anglesey – it's a fantastic jet aircraft. Before that I was based near York training on the Tucano, a turbo prop aircraft. Initially I learnt the ropes on light aircraft and spent a brief spell flying helicopters. I am one of the very few people I know doing a job they truly love. I've fought other aircraft at 20,000 feet, broken the sound barrier, and led low-level strike formations. Every day I do and see things I can't begin to describe to my friends from school or university. When I hear them describe their job as challenging, dynamic and fun I feel really smug!

Helicopter Pilots

Helicopter pilots may be based on an aircraft carrier, or at a shore base such as RNAS Yeovilton or RNAS Culdrose, where their purpose is to meet the operational requirements of the Fleet Air Arm's front line squadrons. At Culdrose their principal role is to support the Anti-Submarine Warfare and Airborne Early Warning helicopter squadrons, in meeting the operational requirements of that task group command by providing 24 hour, 365 days-a-year military and civilian search and rescue for the South West region.

The Sea King helicopters of the search and rescue squadron are ready to go whenever the need arises. Often operating in extreme weather conditions, thousands of people owe their lives to the outstanding feats of bravery performed as routine events by the duty crews. Culdrose is also responsible for the Operational and Advanced Flying Training of helicopter pilots, observers and aircrewmen, in subjects as diverse as search and rescue, weather forecasting, aircraft handling and other aviation specialist subjects. All members of the Fleet Air Arm will, at some time in their career, train or serve at RNAS Culdrose.

Aircraft Handler

Many of the Royal Navy's aircraft and helicopters are flown from aircraft carriers, with teams of Aircraft Handlers doing everything from preparing the flight deck and moving the aircraft, to firefighting and rescue work.

When landing on the tiny area of a carrier's flight deck, when the ship could be difficult to find due to weather and other conditions, the deck pitching as the carrier meets the waves, and the shortness of the strip leaving no room for error, the job of the Aircraft Handler is essential for safety, and fire fighting techniques for various operational duties will form a major part of your training course.

It is the Aircraft Handlers' job to make certain that the preparations for flying run as smoothly – and safely – as possible, ensuring each aircraft is in the right place at the right time, from leaving the hangar down below to the moment of launch at the start of a mission, and to landing at the end of it. This work is so essential that you'll find Aircraft Handlers wherever and whenever the Navy is flying. On land, that means at Naval Air Stations up and down the country. At sea, it means in ships that may have just one helicopter, as well as in carriers with a squadron or more of aircraft.

Firefighters with previous fire fighting experience can apply to join up to the age of 33.

Air Engineering Technician (AET)

As an AET you will receive one of the best technical and management training courses to qualify you as a highly skilled engineering technician. Modern Naval aircraft are extremely complex and contain a great many systems and sophisticated equipment. These all have to function correctly or the aircraft will not be able to operate effectively. As a technician, you will be trained to carry out flight servicing, routine servicing and defect rectification to ensure the aircraft are kept safe to fly and in constant operational readiness.

AET Training

You need to be between 16 and 33 years old. All entrants are required to pass a series of selection tests, an interview, medical examination and fitness tests, designed to assess whether you have sufficient ability, practical aptitude, determination and personal qualities to embark on intensive engineering training and to meet the challenge of a Naval career. The interview gives you the chance to see if life in the Royal Navy is for you, just as much as it gives the Navy a chance to see if you have the right qualities for the job.

During training you will be supervised at all stages, but when you are judged capable you will gain the essential 'Qualified to Maintain' (QM) and the 'Qualified to Sign' (QS) awards, meaning you will be fully qualified to undertake aircraft servicing work yourself and sign for carrying it out. Once you've completed this training, after about 12 months in the Navy, you will be advanced to AET 1st Class. The next step up is Leading Air Engineering Technician (LAET). This will involve specialist training in one of two trades: Mechanical (M) or Avionics (Av). At this level you will be expected to take charge of small groups of AETs to carry out maintenance of complex aircraft systems within your specialist trade. As a potential LAET (M) you will undertake an extensive technical training package. This will include aircraft design, flying controls and propulsion systems, hydraulic and fuel systems, logical faultfinding, craft training and supervisory practices.

As a potential LAET (Av) your training package will include electronic principles, guided and air launched underwater weapons, aircraft navigation systems, power supplies, radar and electronic warfare sensor systems, digital techniques and communication principles. Logical fault finding, supervisory practices and craft training are also included. On being selected for Petty Officer Air Engineering Technician, you can expect to be given extensive further training, making you the systems expert in your field. You will be trained to diagnose complex faults in state-of-the-art aircraft systems and use all your engineering skills and judgement to make what could be complex and difficult repairs – and in fast-changing and often inhospitable conditions. You may even be required to fulfil other specialist Air Engineering roles such as Flight Test Engineer where you will diagnose faults in the air alongside the pilot; this will also attract extra pay. On successful completion of initial professional training you will be awarded a City and Guilds qualification in General Engineering, and on completion of the Petty Officer AET Qualifying Course, you will gain a Foundation Degree in Aeronautical Engineering.

Promotion

If you're selected for Fast Track promotion you can expect to reach the rank of Petty Officer by your early twenties, having gained a Foundation Degree in the process. For those not selected for Fast Track, providing you show determination, ambition and have the personal qualities the Navy looks for, you can expect to reach the rank of Petty Officer by your mid-twenties. Indeed, the best of those not selected could be promoted to Petty Officer only some 6 months behind the Fast Track with subsequent promotion on merit. Outstanding ratings that demonstrate a high potential for leadership and advanced training can be selected for a commission as an officer.

Useful Address

www.royal-navy.mod.uk

ROYAL MARINES

There are about 700 officers in the Royal Marines. Recruitment varies each year. However, competition is fierce and you will also be expected to prove a good level of physical fitness.

Royal Marines officers lead teams of commando-trained soldiers in combat situations, at sea or on shore. After training as an officer, you can specialise in one of ten roles, including helicopter pilots – flying the full range of helicopters used by the Royal Navy and Royal Marines. Today Royal Marine officers are more and more involved in leading peacekeeping and humanitarian missions.

Training

The first 12 months are based at Commando Training Centre Royal Marines (CTCRM), Lympstone, Devon. There are five phases of training:

○ Initial training – general fitness, drill and weapon handling, and the role and history of the Royal Marines.
○ Military training – gym and assault course work and advanced weapon train-

ing, military law, current affairs, IT, and nuclear, biological and chemical defence.

○ Amphibious training – practical exercises on raiding and landing craft and familiarisation with the Special Boat Service.

○ Commando course – four weeks' increased physical training, amphibious and patrolling exercises and education in survival techniques, leads to Commando Test Week. On completion, trainees are awarded the commando Green Beret and will then be allowed to take part in the passing out parade.

○ Advanced military training – includes instructional and supervisory techniques, live firing and a ten-day final exercise testing management technique and leadership skills.

You then go on to command a troop or other sub-unit consisting of up to 28 men. Officers are fully qualified after 12 months working in one of the specialist activity areas of the Royal Marines.

Opportunities

After three years' development as a lieutenant, you can expect promotion to captain. Subsequent promotion is by selection based on your performance record, qualifications and aptitude. It is possible to become a major by the age of 30, a lieutenant colonel by your late 30s, and there are opportunities to achieve the rank of colonel and higher.

Annual Income

As a guideline:

University cadet entrants are paid between £10,074 and £14,177 a year while at university.

Lieutenants earn £13,944 on entry at age 18, and up to £20,173 on entry at age 21.

Captains earn between £31,069 and £36,951.

Colonels can earn up to £70,312.

Extra allowances are paid for family separation, special service and flying duties. Where accommodation is provided, deductions may be made from the annual income.

Free leaflets and advice are available from all local armed forces careers offices. The addresses of these can be found in telephone directories listed under Naval Establishment. The Royal Navy web site contains a wide range of careers information, including details of Royal Marines' careers: www.royalnavy.mod.uk.

THE ARMY

The AAC (Army Air Corps) operates and flies all the Army's helicopters. Its primary function is to destroy enemy armour using attack helicopters. It has a variety of other roles, including reconnaissance, the provision of airborne command posts and the direction of artillery fire. In addition to flying military helicopters, AAC pilots take on the same management responsibilities as every other Army officer, leading their ground crew, signallers and trainee pilots.

You can go in as a school leaver, undergraduate or graduate. The Army recruits all year round and has vacancies in IT/Communications, engineering, logistics, admin and finance. You can be male or female; minimum age 17 Years 9 Months, and sign on for a minimum service of seven years (including one year of training).

Education Standard

For a Commission you will require a minimum of 140 UCAS Tariff points at A/ AS Level, or equivalent, and 5 GCSEs, or equivalent, including Maths, English and either a Science or foreign language. You should have the potential to study for a degree (although a degree is not a requirement).

Personal Qualities

An ability to remain cool, confident and clear headed under stress is required, together with intelligence, determination and a sense of responsibility and urgency. An interest in and an ability to get on well with people, an awareness of the world around you, and cheerfulness are also needed.

Training

One year of initial training at Sandhurst in leadership, army organisation and battle skills is required by all. You then attend a 16-month fixed wing and heli-copter pilots course, carried out jointly with Royal Navy and Royal Air Force Officers and Army NCOs. Following the award of wings you will be trained to fly an army helicopter before being posted to an Army Air Corps Regiment.

Conditions of work

You can be posted throughout the world either on a permanent posting or on temporary training. As a single officer, your home will be in the Officers Mess; if married you and your family will normally be allocated an officer family quarter. There will be times when you are required to live under field conditions. Sport and adventure training offer a great opportunity to take part in your favourite sports, and get paid for it in the process!

Career Structure

Your initial appointment will be as an officer pilot before, within your first tour, taking command of a Flight. Your promotion is within the Army's 'Stepping Stone' career structure based on time of service. You can expect to spend some time away from flying – for example using your aviation knowledge working in headquarters. As you progress up the career path you will return to flying at various stages in your career.

Follow-on trades

Dependent on qualifications and service you can be selected for postgraduate degrees in technical and managerial disciplines. There are also opportunities for training and employment as a flying instructor or test pilot, or to become professionally qualified through various civilian institutes.

Rates of pay are very competitive, with graduates starting on £18,798, rising to £22,587 for Lieutenant, £28,813 for Captain, £51,191 for Lieutenant Colonel and £71,106 for Brigadier.

Useful Addresses (UK)

www.army.mod.uk
www.armyofficer.co.uk

Useful Addresses (United States)

U.S. Air Force; www.airforce.com
U.S. Army; www.army.mil
U.S. Navy: www.navy.com

Useful Addresses (Canada)

Canadian Navy; www.navy.forces.gc.ca
Royal Canadian Air Force; www.rcaf.com

Internet Advice

The forces around the world are past masters at recruiting. Their standards have to be high; they cannot waste valuable time and funds training the wrong people, so their selection processes are organised to be fun, challenging, and encourage those people who can think for themselves and perhaps have hidden leadership qualities.

Go on forces' websites, and have fun playing Top Gun; finding out about service life (including the lows), and browse some of the best designed websites around.

If you decide on a career in the forces, as a technician, engineer or pilot, you will receive some of the best training for a top civilian job in aviation, although this should not be your prime motivation – you will be found out in preliminary testing.

Looking After Yourself

This chapter is mainly for those of you who will be flying – especially cabin crew. You are going into an industry that has an aura of glamour, but don't think this comes about easily. You have to look after yourself, and pay particular attention to your health, otherwise you could find yourself grounded by the company doctor. You will receive regular medical check-ups, but there is a lot you can do to make sure you stay fully fit, able to fly and looking good.

HEALTH

Exercise is vital for good health, and one of the easiest ways of exercising is cycling; perhaps cycle to work? It's good for the heart, and strengthens your legs; you are going to need strong legs for the miles you will do walking up and down aisles.

Eating and drinking
Again and again you will be told 'drink lots of plain water'; not coffee, tea or fizzy drinks. Caffeine is now regarded as a no-no, and fizzy drinks are also suspect, especially when flying.

Watch what you eat, particularly when it is an airline meal. Turkish Airlines recently counted up the calories in an airline breakfast, and it came out to a massive 750 – 1250, so be warned! Today, crew are often given different meals, and fresh fruit, supplied just for them, to ensure they eat healthily. Eat plenty of fruit, salads and vegetables (remember the advice is to eat five portions a day), and watch what you buy when at home. Buy and eat organic, wherever and whenever possible.

Taking sensible precautions
You may be completely unfazed by recent reports in the media about cancer scares amongst cabin crew, in which case skip the following paragraphs. But if you are worried, what has currently been discovered might help clear muddied waters, and provide some ideas for sensible precautions.

At ground level the atmosphere acts as a natural shield, but at high altitudes air thins out, and provides less of a shield for the sun's rays: hence cosmic radiation (the collective name for radiation from the sun and the wider universe) which can potentially be a problem. At the Northern and Southern poles the Earth's magnetic field is less effective at deflecting particles, which might pose a slightly greater risk for long haul flights across the Arctic to Japan.

Although people say there is no proven link between cancer in flight crews and cosmic radiation, according to the National Radiological Protection Board, a transatlantic flight is equivalent to receiving at least one chest X-ray. So the Board recommends taking sensible precautions. Anything that disrupts the body clock is bound to cause stress, and stress is one factor that can increase risks.

Having said that, the majority of cabin crew seem to be very healthy! Probably because they are more aware of the risks, and pay attention to wearing skin protection when out in the sun, drink lots of water, eat healthily, and rest whenever possible.

HEALTH HAZARDS

Jan Fairfax is an award-winning journalist who has written extensively on all aspects of health and medicine for over 20 years, and has given permission for us to quote from an article she wrote for *Medicine Today Magazine*. This magazine goes to health professionals, who know there are millions of nasty bacteria and bugs floating around – most of which won't harm us – and the article is discussing their patients.

Since this article was written, many airlines have taken measures to improve air quality, and remove water containers from possible contamination – but this takes time.

The Health Hazards of Flying by Jan Fairfax ©

So there you all are, impatiently queuing at the airport check-in desk, raring to be off. You mentally tick the list again: Passports, currency, tickets, hotel voucher, insect repellent, first-aid kit, flip-flops... You've thought of everything.

Or have you?

You've probably read about the dangers of deep-vein thrombosis when flying. But have you really considered exactly what else happens to the human body when it's crammed with 400 others in a pressurised cabin, sealed in a thin metal covering, hurtling through the troposphere over 30,000 feet high at so many miles a minute?

Infections

It's common knowledge that people frequently develop colds and chest infections shortly after flying. Here's why. Once the aircraft doors are sealed, dry, cold air is imported from outside at high altitude. Older planes still import 100% of their air but most new planes re-circulate 50% of cabin air to save fuel. *Best A.S. Pan American World Airways Air-conditioning Tests During Revenue Flights, Aviation Space and Environmental Medicine 1980 (2) p 170.* All airlines use HEPA, the High Efficiency Particle Air filter to remove dust, bacteria and viruses from the air. But around a quarter of the passengers will be carrying cold or influenza viruses that they breathe or cough out into the air around them. These viruses circulate through many pairs of lungs spreading infection in the stale air before it gets filtered again. *Mar J. Risk of Respiratory Tract Infections During Air Travel JAMA* 1987 (258) p2764. And if you are travelling to and from a Third World country there's the added risk of catching pulmonary tuberculosis.

The reason why passengers find themselves in a yawning, semi-zombified state so quickly in aircraft is because CO_2 levels are higher now than ever permitted before and oxygen levels are lower. This is why it's worth trying to get a seat as near the nose of the plane as possible. Fresh air enters at the front of the plane and it moves through the body of the plane before being extracted into the HEPA air conditioning system at the rear. As well as being thin, the air is also exceptionally dry, causing dry eyes, sore throats, parched skin, itchy nose and headaches. The reason it can't be humidified is blamed on the weight of water and the perceived cost. The pilots have a separate ventilation system in the cockpit.

The economy of weight and space governs so much in aircraft. Full water containers are very heavy, which is why the water supply to the fountains in the lavatories is limited. Unfortunately the containers are stored close to the septic tanks and have a high likelihood of being contaminated. Research by the Public Health laboratory found that 15% of the water in aircraft contained *E.coli* and human excrement so drinking it or brushing your teeth is not recommended.

Air pressure, alcohol and food
You might gain comfort from the free alcoholic drinks and food, or you could if I wasn't going to explain that your poor liver swells by up to a third in flight which makes it much harder to metabolise alcohol and to digest fatty food. Most airlines serve food with a high fat content because smaller quantities satisfy the appetite. It's the importance of weight and space again. The food is pre-cooked and reheated in the galley so there is always the danger of Clostridium perf-ringens, a nasty bacillus which causes food poisoning. Apart from the stressed liver's retarded digestion of alcohol, booze seriously depletes the body of water. It takes twice the number of water molecules to flush the alcohol molecules from the body. And it's wise to avoid all caffeine (a diuretic or kidney stimulant) contained in drinks like coffee, tea and colas. The prudent take a two-litre bottle of still water on board.

The air pressure in the cabin drops as the plane ascends while the gas inside your body expands causing all the internal organs to swell which is why it is important to wear loose, comfortable clothes when flying. The fluctuating air pressure (and changing time zones) also disrupts all the hormonal cycles, particularly the sex hormones, which is why air stewardesses frequently have irregular periods and have to be grounded if they want to conceive. *Preston F.S. et al Effects of flying... on menstrual length...airline stewardesses Aerospace Medicine 1973 (44) pp438-43.Desir D. et al, Effects of jetlag on hormonal patterns, Jnl.of Clinical and Endocrinal Metabolism, 1981 (52), p.628-41.*

Radiation

Meanwhile, as the plane cruises through the upper air, radiation from the sun easily penetrates through the thin metal casing. The radiation levels during flights are higher now than they have ever been because planes fly higher (where the air is thinner) to save fuel. The estimated exposure to cosmic radiation per passenger crossing the Atlantic once is equivalent to one and a half chest X-rays. No one knows if such levels of exposure, or higher cumulative levels, are potentially harmful to pregnant women, infants or pre-pubescent children but the Society of Radiographers advise this vulnerable group to avoid X-rays unless absolutely necessary.

If flying is hazardous for passengers, what about the health of pilots? Despite their superior level of mental and physical fitness, they may suffer high incidences of certain cancers and an increased mortality. *Davies I.D. et al, The mortality of British Airways pilots 1966-89, a proportional mortality study, Aviation Space & Environmental Medicine 1992 (63), p 276-9. Band P.R. et al, Cohort study of Air Canada pilots: mortality, cancer incidence and leukaemia risk, Amer. Jnl. of Epidemiology, 1996, (143-2), pp.137-43.* In December 1999 *The Lancet* published a Danish research paper that reported that pilots who had flown more than 5000 hours had an increased risk of myeloid leukaemia and cancer, and Lufthansa is conducting a large, retrospective study of all its flight personnel.

Jet lag

There's been lots of research on the physiological and psychological effects of jet lag. Humans are biologically programmed by their body clock to sleep when it's dark and be awake and alert in daylight. These sleep-wake patterns are called circadian rhythms. *Horne J.A. et al Human Circadian Rhythms Biological Psychiatry 1977 (5) pp179-90.* Flying through time changes severely disrupts these rhythms causing mental and physical fatigue. This has been shown by poor performances in psychological tests of intelligence and logic and physical tests of co-ordination and reaction times up to five days after arrival. *Wright J.E. et al Aviation Space and Environmental Medicine 1983 (54) pp 132-7. Preston F.S. Temporal Discord Jnl. of Psychosomatic Research 1978 (22) pp377-83.*

DEEP VEIN THROMBOSIS (DVT)

The most widely publicised hazard of flying is the threat of DVT, also known as economy class or coach syndrome. Human beings are not designed to sit in cramped conditions for prolonged periods of time. Regularly worked leg muscles pump the blood up through the deep veins in the calves into the femoral veins in the thighs and thence up to the heart and lungs. The narrow aircraft seats and the short seat pitch (the space measured from the back of the actual sitting area to the back of the seat in front) make it difficult to move and, with the knees bent, the blood pools in the deep veins in the calves forming long clots in the susceptible. The periods of immobility are much worse on long-haul flights when passengers drift off to sleep in cramped conditions. *James P.B., Jet lag, pulmonary embolism and hypoxia, Lancet, 1996 (347), p.1697.* The danger is that clots can break off and travel to the lungs as pulmonary emboli, causing death, or they can block the leg veins causing severe problems in the circulation which may necessitate amputation.

No one knows how many people have a deep vein thrombosis caused by flying as most develop the condition some weeks after flying and don't make the connection. Professor Vijay Kakkar, the Director of the Thrombosis Research Institute in London, estimates the risk of a DVT at one in 12,000 but there have been no studies to substantiate this and some blood and circulation experts feel the problem may be much more common, causing perhaps as many as 2000 deaths a year. *Johnson R. Economy class syndrome – a false economy? Royal Aeronautical Society conference on passenger health in the air, London 12 April 2000.*

People aged over 40, or with any circulatory disorders, or who have recently had surgery, are especially vulnerable to DVT as are pregnant women and women taking the contraceptive pill or hormone replacement therapy. You will now realise how important it is to move around as much as possible and to regularly and rhythmically flex your feet and rotate your ankles to pump blood through the vessels in your calves. Cabin crew who are always on the move are much less likely to be affected.

So the hazards of flying include catching a cold or a chest infection, getting something nasty from the water, upsetting your liver by eating airline food or drinking alcohol, food poisoning, radiation exposure, being dehydrated, becoming severely disorientated and fatigued and, of course, getting a potentially fatal deep vein thrombosis. *Bon voyage!*

If you want to look up more information Jan suggests the following websites:
www.tri-london.ac.uk (the Thrombosis Research Institute)
www.aviation-health.org (the Aviation Health Institute)
www.asma.org/html/publicat.htm (articles from NASA on flying health)
www.flyana.com (compiled by a former air stewardess now consumer activist)
www.hughes-syndrome.org (info on sticky blood research at St. Thomas's).

FACE, SKIN AND FEET

Looking on the bright side
Today, flight crew's health is very carefully monitored by company doctors, as well as the unions, who work together to ensure that you stay healthy. No one knows if there are more cancers reported in crew simply because their health

undergoes regular check-ups.

You will be weighed, and woe betide you if your weight increases too much – it's off roster until it comes down. Companies realise your skin can't look good all the time, but too many late nights and you could be called in and told your face doesn't fit the company image.

Looking After Yourself: Tips From Cabin Crew

Don't skip this – particularly if you are a male reader. It is essential that you start looking seriously at what you put on your face and body. I am not talking about cosmetics, but skincare. Cabin crew are particularly susceptible to skin problems caused by dehydration, jet lag, stress, thin air, etc. Dry skin can make you feel tired and irritable; at worst it might make you prone to skin cancer. Your face feels dry and taut, your skin itches, your nails flake and your feet feel horrible.

There are three steps to looking after your facial skin:

1. Cleanse at least twice a day – morning and night.
2. Tone.
3. Protect.

1. By cleansing, I don't mean soap and water. Ordinary soap can't get rid of all the grime our skins pick up daily; leave some of the grime, and this can cause spots. If you want to test this, wash with your ordinary soap, then go over your skin with a cleanser and clean cotton wool pad; it is frightening how much grime the pad will pick up, but shows you need a properly formulated cleanser to keep your face scrupulously clean. Companies such as Clarins and Clinique now make cleansers specially formulated for men, or you can buy special face-cleanser soaps. Men are reputed to be lazy, so their products are often two-in-one, but girls, don't think you can switch, as men's skin is different, with a sub-layer of thicker skin.
2. Toning lotion gets rid of any vestiges of residue cleanser. It is vital to protect your skin with either moisturiser and SPF factor cream, or a combination product (for men and women).
3. At night use a specially formulated cream.

> ### Daniel Cooke, British Airways Purser, says
> *I was advised by my trainers 18 years ago that all men should use a skin conditioner when flying, even if not already doing so. I have used one ever since on or off the aircraft. We were advised that:*
>
> O *Sun protector should always be used whenever outside – those rays are more harmful than we can imagine. There are a wide range of men's products; or use products made for both sexes.*
> O *One should always drink – sipping preferably- plenty of pure water*

> *during flying hours and afterwards. Add a little lemon or other natural flavour if water is not to your taste.*
>
> O   *Avoid fizzy drinks and too much tea or coffee. There are legal restrictions on alcohol – sometimes as much as 24 hours before a flight. That is for safety, but also a great asset for well-being too, even when travelling as a passenger!*

As you get older, you will need to change your skin care routine to more powerful products. There is no need to use these when you are young – the expense is probably wasted on young skin – instead ask the major companies to recommend suitable products.

You now have a chance to buy the world's best products; airport shops have a bewildering amount of products on display, but look for the companies that spend their money on research, rather than on the latest designer-perfume. To launch a perfume costs millions; companies cream off the sales from those customers who must have the latest, then a year later the product is quietly dropped, seen off by the world's best-selling perfume, Chanel No. 5. No one has been able to develop another scent that suits so many women.

All the companies I mention in this chapter have been around for a long time, spend a great deal on research, and don't depend on expensive packaging to sell their products. Instead, they train their staff to genuinely help you, and won't sell you a product if they don't think it right for you.

If you are worried about E-numbers, preservatives, etc. look for names such as Avene and Avalon, who make organic and/or plant based products. However, there are preservatives and preservatives, and without 'good' preservatives many products would not be able to be sold, as they would go bad before they reached the shops. If you are worried, ask the advice of an advisor or chemist.

Useful Addresses

www.avalonorganics.com;
www.clarins.com;
www.clinique.com
www.chanel.com;
www.esteelauder.co.uk;
www.kanebo.com;
www.pashley.co.uk

Sun protection (SPF)

For daytime your skin needs the protection of a minimum SPF (sun protection factor) of 15. Note that two lots of SPF 8 cream, one layer on top of another, still only add up to SPF 8, not 16. For skin protection in very sunny climates you ideally need an SPF of 25-30. And don't forget that SPFs also protect against pollution, so it is sensible to wear them all year round.

When you go to buy products, why not spoil yourself and buy the best – not just the cheapest? Most airports sell the major products at tax-free or duty free prices; one of the perks of the job. Colleagues will tell you which airports have the best bargains, and even if your roster is only domestic or EU trips, BAA makes your life easier by offering staff discounts at their airport shops. This makes it easier to buy good skincare inexpensively: men's as well as women's.

Your body's skin

Like your face, your body skin needs protection from sun and pollution. Always use a product with minimum SPF 15 factor on exposed parts, such as hands and neck, even in winter. Boots, Malibu and Ombra at Aldi make inexpensive creams that give good sun protection. Otherwise try La Prairie, Clarins, Decléor or Clinique.

Don't forget to guard against insects. Even if you take anti-malaria tablets, you can still get this dread disease; the only way to avoid it 100% is to make sure you don't get bitten. A firm called Jungle Formula make products to keep insects at bay, and say their sprays can be used on clothing as well. They warn that their products last up to 6 hours in Europe, but only 2-3 hours in a tropical climate, so they make small spray bottles you can carry around.

And don't forget that the nastier insects come out at night. Clarins make a sweet-smelling moisturiser to be used at night, which contains an anti-mosquito formula.

Nails and hands

The skin on hands needs protecting from sun and washing up (yes, you will have to do this on board); hands are constantly under the tap. Dry air causes flaky nails and nasty (sometimes painful) splits at the end of your fingers. Manicare suggests you use nail treatment oils on the tips of your fingers as well as on the nail. If you have badly flaking nails, they make a nail mask which works on the same principle as a facemask, giving nails an extra boost. And their products are colourless, so men can use them too.

Useful Addresses

www.kanebo.com;
www.manicare.com.

Legs and Feet

'My poor aching legs and feet' is the constant cry of cabin crew – sadly this goes with the territory. Just to make you feel even better, your ankles are more than likely to swell – look behind the curtains on a long haul flight and you often see crew with their legs high up on the wall – trying to reduce fluid. Another tried and tested remedy to avoid swollen ankles is DVT socks (Scholl make these) or, for women, maternity tights.

Bliss is the name of a company who make blissful products to pamper feet. Cabin crew used to make a beeline for their store in New York; now their products are sold everywhere. Major cities have their treatment salons, which are very popular with cabin crew off duty.

There are spray products that are helpful, which can be sprayed on through tights, but sadly not through socks! Decléor make Circulaspray, Clarins make Lait Jambes Lourdes; both work miracles (beware, there are copy products at half price – which don't produce any benefit).

Useful Addresses
www.drscholls.com
www.blissworld.com

ALCOHOL

For the moment there is no worldwide benchmark for alcohol consumption; it is up to individual countries and their airlines as to what is considered acceptable. However, two recent cases where pilots were taken off flights in Denmark and the USA look like being the catalyst that might tighten up regulations.

Currently the airline industry often relies on self-policing, and in Britain the CAA says 'annually, on average, we have 12 to 15 British pilots referred to us on alcohol-related issues.' They do state reassuringly that 'we have no evidence of a growing problem', but recently the Department of Transport issued guidelines stating that flight deck crew, cabin crew and air traffic controllers are now subject to a limit of 20 milligrams of alcohol in 100 milligrams of blood; engineers are subject to a limit of 80 milligrams in 100 milligrams of blood. These guidelines give the police powers to test suspected offenders. However, many airlines have a zero tolerance limit, with no alcohol allowed to be present in the blood.

In the US, pilots are subject to random breath tests, and the *Daily Telegraph* said there had been a dramatic rise in the number of pilots found to be intoxicated prior to flying, with last year 22 US airline pilots found to be over the limit.

OTHER MATTERS

Work For The Disabled

There are reasons why you can't do some jobs if you have disabilities such as deafness, limited vision or mobility. That said, you will find most airlines are approachable; they deal with disabled passengers every day, so know what is possible for people who want to work for them. The Government website is www.disability.gov.uk.

Clothes

Most of the time you will be wearing uniform. You may wonder why, as you are quite convinced it makes you look horrible. However, it identifies you to passengers. Wearing uniform also saves having to spend money on working clothes, so you can splash out on casual clothes.

Before packing your suitcase, think of where you are going to stay on stop-overs. In certain countries, casual clothes can cause offence, so take advice from your teachers and older crew; they know what to wear in which countries.

Finances

You are going into an industry that sometimes suffers from a down-turn. Post September 11 many airlines folded; others soon took their place, but it was a worrying time for personnel. It makes sense therefore to start a savings plan to tide you over if the worst happens. Take advice from the tremendous amount of help available; from your company, the financial pages of newspapers, the internet, etc.

Think of a way you want to save, and then split your savings between competing companies. e.g. if you decide to take out a pension with your company, at the same time take out a pension with an independent company; split the payments between them – then if one scheme fails, you have something to fall back on.

Inoculations

The company doctor will ensure that you get your jabs; you won't be admitted to certain countries if you don't possess up-to-date inoculations, so guard your record card carefully. Sadly, although modern day medicine has eradicated many scourges, when the Iron Curtain fell, tuberculosis (TB) came over the wall and is now a big hazard. Your company doctor will probably insist you have the TB inoculation – but even if they don't, working in a confined space you would be silly not to have it, unless there is a valid reason.

Have fun!

Having read this chapter, keep the information you need in your head, and go out and enjoy yourself. As I said, most cabin crew are very healthy; they wouldn't enjoy themselves so much on stop-overs (swimming, eating good food, dancing, etc) if they weren't in the best of health. So enjoy!

Looking to the Future

In the past twenty years the public worldwide has become used to low cost flights. Whatever threats there are from terrorism and other security scares, being able to fly has become such a part of many people's normal routine, it looks as if the increase in airline passengers will continue to rise.

With so many airlines starting up to take advantage of this trend, it is inevitable that some of these airlines will fold. However, the public's desire for travel will almost certainly ensure that the competitor airlines will still be flying and expanding.

Airports

Although Ryanair announced it would be looking at buying airports as a way of controlling landing fees and costs, it was Thomson (part of the TUI tour operating empire) which became the first low cost airline to take control of an airport, adding Coventry Airport to its group. In the teeth of fierce local opposition, it announced it will use the airport as its base for its new low cost airline,Thomsonfly.

Currently Ryanair has come up with a proposal to resolve the impasse with the EU over Charleroi Airport; it remains to be seen if competitors will want to copy their idea as a way of reducing their own costs, or if they want to ensure that Ryanair are made to pay a competitive rate to fly into this airport.

EU Regulations

As from 2005, EU regulations will give passengers new rights to compensation (plus meals, refreshments and overnight accommodation where appropriate) for flights that are cancelled or delayed for at least five hours.

Currently, if there are delays or flight cancellations, the low cost airlines don't offer much in the way of food or accommodation – passengers are usually left to fend for themselves, being told this is the price they pay for having a low fare in the first place.

In the days when ABTA (Association of British Travel Agents) was first founded, some industry members were appalled that 'their' trade association went all out to champion the consumer. ABTA realised that no-one would have confidence in its members, if they could hide behind a trade association when something went wrong. Thanks to this championing of the consumer, the

ABTA logo is one of the most recognised and respected across the UK, and holidaymakers are confident that if they book with an ABTA member their holiday is protected. Eventually low cost airlines will probably have to come up with an equivalent organisation to satisfy consumer groups.

Almost certainly low cost airlines will increase their fares, to take in expected extra costs from EU regulations. It remains to be seen how much they will absorb in the interests of being able to attract passengers with low fares, how much they think the public will pay, and if they learn from ABTA's example.

If these airlines play their cards right, the new regulations will come just at the right time to restore confidence in their operations. There are signs that the public's love affair with ultra cheap flights is waning, as they count up the cost of returning from abroad when their £1 flight is cancelled, and the airline hides behind the small print and says it is not liable to get them home.

If the EU Regulations make airlines do their costings to spread repatriation costs across the board, by putting up passengers overnight when there are delays, etc. they will ensure public confidence returns.

Whatever happens, major scheduled airlines that are now offering low fares to compete, may find more passengers switching to their flights.

Landing Slots

A landing/take-off slot is the time and space allocated to an airline to land or take-off at an airport. These are crucial to its profitability if it wants to attract high-spending business travellers who want early morning and late afternoon flights as being the best option to fly in for business meetings, and return home the same day.

Generally, most profitable slot times are:

- 6-9 am
- 2-3 pm (for meetings concluded in a morning)
- 6-8pm (for meetings finished late afternoon)

Times with less demand are:

- 10pm-6am (almost negative demand from short-haul business travellers)
- 10am-2pm (only limited appeal for longer short-haul flights)
- 4-6pm (lull before business travellers return home)

The potential profit for a good slot at Heathrow Airport is so enormous, it is said Qantas paid nearly £20 million for two return flight slots per day. The previous high was probably set when American Airlines and United Airlines are said to have bought their way into Heathrow in a reported £18 million per slot deal with Pan Am Airlines.

These slots are never sold on the open market, and selling them could be contrary to Brussels' law. Airlines use a device called slot exchange to get round this: exchanging a valuable peak time slot for one late at night - and money is possibly paid quietly on the side.

Ownership of these slots seldom appear in the balance sheets. Airlines such as BA, with 40% of the landing slots at Heathrow, potentially own slots worth over £2 billion; its latest annual report valued these at £72 million. Bmi is another large beneficiary, and people worried less when the airline declared a £20 million loss; its slots could be worth over £800 million at Heathrow alone.

To put the potential for business travel profits into context, Sunday Times analysis said if BA had a short-haul service out of Gatwick that was just breaking even, it would make a profit of £2 million a year if shifted to Heathrow.

If an airline wants to increase landings at the world's major airports, it has two options:

O Move to another airport
O Buy slots from another airline

Many small airlines will sell their slots if they need to raise cash; the problem is, the world's major airlines are running out of small carriers willing to do this.

So this is why BAA is making enormous waves to get another runway at Heathrow, whilst Schiphol, Frankfurt and Paris wait in the wings, eager to snap up long-haul business traffic that might get frustrated if it can't expand at Heathrow, and moves elsewhere.

Up-market Flights

With all the talk of low cost flights, the other end of the spectrum is quietly thriving.

The new airline **flyblu** aims to bridge the gap between economy and business class, by offering new levels of comfort for those travelling on a budget. Flyblu claims it is not a low-fares airline, but a best value service, offering the largest economy class seat pitch in the skies today with a massive 6 inches more legroom than most carriers, and 70 less seats than average scheduled airlines.

Other key innovations include hand-held personal in-flight entertainment, enabling every passenger to stop and start films and other entertainment to suit them.

The flyblu vision has been made a reality by midlands businessman Aden Murcutt who decided to establish an airline that would bring back the pleasure of flying. '*The flyblu proposition is simple,*' explains Aden, '*we aim to give all of our passengers the flight experience they so long for, at a price they can afford. Unlike travelling in the lowest-priced cabins of other airlines, we aim to make the experience of travelling with flyblu an enjoyable part of the holiday.*'

Useful Address
www.flyblu.com.

Private Club Flights

Some airlines even charge passengers for the privilege of flying with them, on top of the fare: there is a reason for this.

> **One airline that makes these charges is Geneva-based Club Airways**
> Realising there was a gap in the market between scheduled flights, with possible security and terrorist risks, and the high cost of chartering a private aircraft, Club Airways has been launched to provide all the benefits of private hire, at a lower cost, but with a guarantee of members' fees to offset running costs.
>
> Members pay a subscription of €1500 a year, and can then fly to selected destinations at a price equivalent to business class; currently flights only operate in Europe. Members have the benefits of private hire, with no waiting time, getting straight on to the aircraft, car parking near the runway, etc.
>
> One benefit that has come from this club is the tremendous networking possibilities, as business passengers meet up frequently on flights. For many people, the subscription is worth every penny (or euro) as they get to sit next to potential customers in a relaxed club-like atmosphere.
>
> Currently only about ten people work for Club Airways in administration. All their aeroplanes are hired in – but there is employment for the crews that work for private charter companies.

Trains

Trains can provide similar jobs to airlines, and in Europe post September 11 many airline staff found work in this sector. Now the airlines are having to compete with the high wages offered by the rail companies to engineers and to stewards and stewardesses. According to senior engineers, good training enables you to make the switch easily, and ex-cabin crew enjoy the working conditions.

In some cases airlines now work directly with train services. Air France has a franchise with the Thalys rail line from Paris to Brussels, bringing in passengers from the heavily-populated Belgian catchment area to fly around the world from Charles de Gaulle Airport. Brussels airport is too small to serve this traffic, so catching a train to catch a plane makes sense. Special carriages and dedicated staff serve and look after their airline passengers on the luxury Thalys trains.

US airlines have also found this system saves money and makes sense, so they fly in to Charles de Gaulle as well, where passengers for Belgium disembark and take the Thalys intercity express directly from the airport into the centre of Brussels.

Eurostar employs many ex-cabin crew for their on-board meal service. They like the work, appreciate freedom from jet lag, and the fact that salaries are relatively high. The one barrier to the work is that staff must speak French and English; Dutch, German and other European languages are a bonus, but many cabin crew don't have language skills.

Where Else?

South America is opening up rapidly; as mentioned in the training chapter. The Spanish Government are watching this market, hoping to regain their influence, remembering how much South America contributed to Spain's coffers in previous centuries.

Insiders believe the next market to expand will be China. The Olympics in Beijing in 2008 will focus the world's attention on this country; if it can address worldwide concerns voiced on its human rights programme, the market is enormous.

Currently a joint-venture team of Dutch airport planners NACO, British architects Foster and Partners (designers of Stansted Airport) and engineers ARUP (Sydney Opera House) is working with the Beijing Institute of Architectural Design on a proposed $2 billion expansion of Beijing's airport.

So it looks as if there will be jobs working in aviation for many years to come.

USEFUL WEB ADDRESSES

More and more airlines will ONLY accept online job applications, saying they do not have enough staff to open envelopes: Emirates say they receive well over 10,000 applications a month. So if you don't have access to the internet, ask your local library (many of whom offer free internet access training courses), try college careers offices, or visit an internet café.

These sites have been checked as the book went to press, but you may have to use a search engine if the address has changed recently. We have included the name of the company if it isn't easy to read from the web address.

We haven't listed companies by country, as today so many are multinationals, offering employment in many different countries. On websites there is usually a section you can click on bringing up specific career information for your area.

We have included telephone numbers if companies conduct telephone interviews, and addresses where companies accept written applications.

AIRLINES

www.aacareers.com
www.adria-airways.com
www.aerarann.ie
www.aerlingus.ie
www.aerann.com
www.aerolineas.com
www.aerolloyd.de
www.air-berlin.com
www.aircanada.ca
www.air-dolomiti.it
www.aireuopa.com
www.airfrance.com
www.airindia.com
www.airjamaica.com
www.air-liberte.fr
www.airlinair.com
www.airluxor.com
www.airmalta.com
www.alaskair.com
www.aldeasa.es
www.alitalia.com
Air New Zealand: www.airnz.com; London based flight attendants phone 0207 939 9947

www.AirPolonia.com
www.air-scotland.com
www.airsouthwest.com
www.airtransat.com
www.air-transit.com
www.airwales.co.uk
www.airplus.com
www.airsouthwest.com
www.airlineApps.com
American Airlines: ☎001 963 1110; www.myAAjob.com; for jobs at Heathrow. Send CV with covering letter to Human Resources, American Airlines, 23-59 Staines Road Hounslow, TW3 3HE.
www.aurigny.com
www.aua.com
www.avianca.net

www.basiqair.com
www.braathens.no
Blue 1: human.resources-fin@sas.se
www.bluefoxairlines.com
Britannia: ☎01582-428295; www.britanniairways.com
British Airways Recruitment: ☎0870 608 0747; www.britishairwaysjobs.com; www.britishairways.com/travel/home/public/en – gb
Bmi: 0208 990 7854 www.flybmi.com
Bmibaby: www.flybmi.com e-cabincrew.recruitment@flybmi.com
BWIA International: www.bwee.com

www.canadian-affair.com
www.cathaypacific.com
www.cirrus-airlines.de
www.cityairline.com
www.clubairways.com
Continental Airlines: www.continental.com
www.cyprusairways.com

DBA (formerly Deutsche BA): www.flydba.com
Delta Airlines: U.S. employment hotline 800-659-2580; www.delta.com/inside/employment/index.jsp
www.denimair.nl

www.easyJet.com/jobs; ☎ +44 (0) 1582 525369
www.easternairways.com
www.emiratesgroupcareers.com

EL AL: www.elal.co.il
www.etihadairways.com
www.emerald-airways.co.uk
www.evaair.com
www.excelairways.com
www.eurowings.de

FARE4U: **www.airmalta.com**
www.finnair.fi
www.firstchoice.co.uk
www.flyana.com
www.flybe.com/jobs
www.flyblu.com
www.flyglobespan.com
www.flyingfinn.fe
www.flyniki.com
www.flyzoom.com

www.garuda-indonesia.com
www.gbairways.com
www.germanwings.com
www.gotlansflyg.se
www.gulfairco.com/About Gulfair/employment

www.hapag-lloyd-express.com
www.hawaiianair.com
www.flyhelios.com

www.iberian.com
www.icelandair.com
www.icelandexpress.com
www.indian-airlines.com
www.iranair.com

www.jal.co.jp
www.jetblue.com
www.flyjet2.com
www.flyjet.com
JMC: Gatwick ☎01293 569555 / 668329 or Manchester ☎0161 489 0646.
www.jetmagic.ie
Jetstar: www.impulse.com.au

www.keenair.co.uk
www.kenya-airways.com
www.klm.com.uk
www.kullaflyg.se
www.kuwait-airways.com

www.lanchile.com
Lauda Airlines: www.aua.com
www.loganair.co.uk
www.lot.com
www.lufthansa.com
www.luxair.lu
www.lyddair.co.uk

www.maersk-air.com
www.malaysiaairlines.com
www.malev.hu
www.meridiana.it
www.midwestairlines.com
My Travel Airways: (was Airtours) ☎0870 243 0739; pilots phone ☎0161 232
6782 www.mytravelairways-careers.co.uk
www.monarch-airlines.com

www.netjets.com
Northwest Airlines: www.nwa.com
www.norwegian.no

www.olympicairways.com

Portugalia: **www.pga.pt**

www.qantas.co.uk
www.qatarairwys.com (recruitment for private Airbuses based at Doha Ccrecru
itment@qatarairways.co.qa)
www.bruneiair.com
Royal Jordanian Airlines: www.rja.com.jo
www.ryanair.com

www.scotairways.co.uk
Singapore Airlines: www.singaporeair.com
www.skyeurope.com.
www.skyward.mb.ca
www.skyways.se

SN Brussels Airlines: www.flysn.com
www.flysnowflake.com
www.spanair.es
www.southwest.com
South African Airways: www.flysaa.com
www.sterling.com
Swiss: (was Swissair); www.swiss.com

www.tap-airportugal.co.uk
www.flytango.com
TED: (United Airlines' low cost arm) www.flyted.com
www.thaiair.com
www.www.thomsonfly.com
www.turkishairlines.com

United Airlines: www.united.com
www.usairways.com

www.varig.com
www.vbird.com
www.virgin-atlantic.com e – recruitment.services@fly.virgin.com
www.virginblue.com
www.virginexpress.com
www.vlm-airlines.com
Volare: www.volareweb.com

www.westjet.com
www.wideroe.no

AIRPORTS

Amsterdam Airport Schiphol: www.schiphol.nl
BAA (British Airports Authority): www.baa.co.uk; ☎ 0141-585 6000
recruitment@baa.co.uk (For jobs at Aberdeen, Edinburgh, Gatwick, Glasgow, London Heathrow, Southampton, Stansted). Terminal 5 construction workers
☎0800 032 0043
www.belfastairport.com
www.berlin-airport.de
Birmingham: www.bhx.co.uk
www.airport-bremen.de
www.bristolairport.co.uk
www.cardiffairportonline.com

Cologne/Bonn: www.airport-cgn.de
Copenhagen: www.cph.dk
www.flughafen-dortmund.de
www.dresden-airport.de
www.duesseldorf-international.de
Frankfurt/Main: www.flughafen-frankfurt.de
Geneva: www.gva.ch
www.ham.airport.de
www.hannover-airport.de
Leipzig: www.leipzig-halle-airport.de
www.londoncityairport.com
Luton: www.london-luton.co.uk
Madrid: www.madrid-mad.com
Malpensa, Milan: www.sea-aeroportimilano.it
Manchester Airport: ☎0161 253 2579 www.manairport.co.uk
Moscow: www.eastline.ru
Munich: www.flughafen-muenchen.de
Munster: www.flughafen-fmo.de
Newcastle-upon-Tyne: www.newcastleairport.com.au
www.flughafen-nuernberg.de
Oslo: www.osl.no
www.flughafen-paderborn-lippstadt.de
Paris Charles de Gaulle: www.adp.fr
Stockholm: www.lfv.se
www.flughafen-stuttgart.de
www.viennairport.com
Zurich: www.uniqueairport.com

In the USA

J.F.Kennedy Airport, New York: www.panynj.gov
Los Angeles: www.lawa.org
Miami Airport: www.miami-airport.com
O'Hare, Chicago: www.ohare.com
For more airports see: www.airports.org

AVIONICS, ENGINEERING AND MANUFACTURERS

American Airlines: **www.aacareers.com**
www.airbus.com
www.augustawestland.com
www.avcraft.com

BAE Systems: **www.baesystems.com**
Boeing Company: Employment Center www.boeing.com/employment; Intern
and Grads website www.boeing.com/employment/college; Employmentoperati
ons@boeing.com, ☎1-800-254-1591.
www.bombardier.com
www.bristowhelicopters.com

www.craneerospace.com

www.dassault-aviation.com
www.diamond-air.at
www.dunlop-aviation.com

www.embraer.com
Emerald Airways Engineering: www.emerald-airways.co.uk ☎01253-404615
www.eurofighter.com
European Space Agency: www.esa.int
Environmental Techtonics: www.etausa.com

Flybe: Training Centre: 1392-266925 engineering.personnel@flybe.com
www.gardner-aerospace.com
www.generaldynamics.com
General Electric: www.gecareers.com
GKN Aerospace: www.aero.gkn.plc.com
www.goodrich.com
www.gulfstream.com

www.honeywell.com/careers

www.jadeair.plc.uk

www.lear.com
Lockhead: www.lmaeronautics.com

Mann Aviation Group: **www.alanmann.co.uk**
www.marconi.com
Martin Baker ejection seats: www.ukspace.com

Netherlands Aerospace Group: **www.aerospacegroup.nl**
www.networkrail.com
Northrop Grumman: www.northgrum.com

www.oxley.co.uk/avionics

www.phillipsaerospace.com
www.pilatusaircraft.ch
www.piper-group.com

www.quinetiq.com
www.pratt-whitney.com

www.racalinstruments.com
www.raytheonaircraft.com
www.rayjobs.com
www.rockwellcollins.com
www.rolls-royce.com
Roke Manor Research: ☎0194-833455 www.roke.co.uk
www.rolls-royce.com

www.saab.com
www.senioraerospace.com
www.sennheiser.com
Shell Aviation: www.shell.com
SKF Aerospace: www.skf.com
www.smiths-aerospace.com
www.snecma.com
Society of British Aerospace Companies: www.sbac.co.uk/careers
SR Technics: ☎+41 1 812 65 67 www.srtechnics.com
Stellex Aerostructures: www.stellex.com
Systems Engineering and Assessment: www.sea.com

www.textron.com
Thales Aviation Group: www.thalesgroup.com
www.thyssenkrupp.com
Toulouse Aerospace: ☎+33 (0)561 294 807 www.esc-toulouse.com

www.ultra-electronics.co.uk
United Technologies: www.utc.com

Virgin Engineering: ☎**0870 444 7057 www.virgin.com/atlanticjobs**
Volvo Aero: www.aero.volvo.se

CARGO AIRLINES

ANA: www.ananet.org.jp

Austrian Cargo: www.1.aua.com
www.capitalcargo.com
www.cargolux.com
www.dhl.com
Federal Express: www.fedex.com
www.tnt.com
www.unitedcargi.com
UPS: www.ups.com

ARMED FORCES

UK
The Army: ☎0845 800 1480; www.army.mod.uk; www.armyofficer.co.uk
Northern Ireland: Armed Forces Careers Office (NI) ☎028 90427040
RAF Careers: ☎0845 605 5555 www.rafcareers.com
Royal Navy and Royal Marines: www.royal-navy.mod.uk

United States:
*U.S. Air Force:*www.airforce.com
U.S. Army: www.army.mil
U.S. Navy www.navy.com

Canada:
Canadian Navy: www.navy.forces.gc.ca
Royal Canadian Air Force: www.rcaf.com

GROUND HANDLING COMPANIES

Airport Group Int. California: www.airportgroup.com
Alysia: (Charles de Gaulle Airport) www.alyzia.com
Aviance: www.aviancehandling.com
Celebi: (Istanbul) www.celebi.com.tr
Eurohandling: Majorca www.fcc.es
Groundstar: ☎0191214 8121 www.groundstar.com
Jet: (Zurich) www.jetaviation.com
Laufer: (☎Aviv) www.laufer.co.il
www.servair.fr.
Servisair/GlobeGround: www.servisair.com, ☎0161 490 5600
Swissport: www.swissport.com. (UK HR-Department paulina.parara@swisspo
rt.com)

OTHER EMPLOYERS

www.airmiles.co.uk/recruitment, ☎01925- 848614.

www.alpha-flight-services.com
Air Traffic Control: ☎020 7832 5413/5564, or email postmaster@nasrecruitm
ent.demon.co.uk
Eurostar: www.eurostar.com
Eurostar catering: Momentum Services Ltd, ☎020 7904 9792.
Heathrow Express: Evolution Recruitment, ☎0207 978 4924
H.M Customs and Excise: www.hmce.gov.uk/about/career/ recruit-contact.htm
Immigration Service: www.homeoffice.gov.uk
USA Air Traffic Control:(See FAA) Currently this is under control of FAA, but
will probably be privatised shortly.

RECRUITMENT AGENCIES AND JOB CENTRES

www.airforce-technology.com
www.angelsagency.com; ☎0118 877 4970
www.aviationjobsearch.com; a recruitment site for people already working in
the industry. However, they occasionally post job details for companies looking
for new entrants, and these give you an idea of salaries.
www.beapilot.com
www.cabincrewdirect.com;
www.delni.gov.uk/doc/careers
www.fish4jobs.co.uk
www.flightinternationaljobs.com;
www.fly-jet.com
www.flightinternationaljobs.com
Globeground: Heathrow employment agency. Room 2024, Terminal 2, Heathrow Airport, TW6 1EZ.
Heathrow Job Centre:☎020 8250 4700
Job Seekers Direct: www.jobcentreplus.gov.uk; ☎0845-6060234
www.jobpilot.com
www.kreatepromotions.co.uk
Line Up Aviation Personnel: www.luap.com
www.manairport.co.uk/content/nsf;
www.raes.org.uk/ims/careers/cabin%20Crew.pdf
www.redhotchilli.co.uk
Springboard: Information and job centre for hospitality, with some info on airlines www.springboarduk.co.uk; ☎020-7497-8654; 3, Denmark Street, London
WC2H 8LP
www.totaljobs.com
www.toxiclemon.co.uk
www.workthing.com;
www.traveljobsearch.com
www.travelvocation.com

www.zoopeople.co.uk, ☎01844-275 199

WEBSITES GIVING BACKGROUND INFORMATION

www.airliners.net: has photos of just about every plane; useful for reference if training courses talk about specific aircraft training.

www.airlinequality.com: background information on airlines.

www.avweb.com: aviation news for civilian, military and commercial discussion groups, which also has useful section on low down on training courses.

www.beapilot.com: constructed by a Skywest pilot with chat boards, message boards and all sorts of info about commercial aviation.

www.dalpa.com: site for Delta Air Lines pilots, giving real flavour of the industry.

www.flightsim.com; a flight simulation website.

Frightened of Flying? This is a minor, but real problem. Check www.amigoingdown.com for latest information on what industry is doing to help.

www.pprune.org: online chatroom that has interesting and helpful gossip, giving insight into industry.

www.travelmole.com: log on for background on what's happening in the industry before you go for interview.

www.willflyforfood.cc: good background info if you are about to have an interview.

Tip: If you are telephoning on BT Option 3 or similar service, you can find alternatives to 0845 and 0870 numbers on www.saynoto0870.com - and still get free calls.

BOOKS AND MAGAZINES

BOOKS

All the World's Aircraft, published by Jane's, is THE book on the industry, and costs over £1,000. However, many specialist libraries have copies.

Airline Passengers' Guerilla Handbook by George Albert Brown is on the desk of the industry's top lawyers, and many people working in the industry. Gives you the 'other' side of the industry – a good read and amusingly informative. You might find it in specialist bookshops in UK, at Airport Bookshops or on the web. $14.95. Blakes Publishing. ISBN 0–924022-04-3.

Air Supply Aviation Store: large selection of aviation books. ☎0113-250 9581. 97, High Street, Yeadon, Leeds LS19 7TA. www.airsupply.co.uk.

Careers in Airlines and Airports: Kogan Page (020- 7278-0433) ISBN 0 7494 370 22. £8.99

Careers in Marketing, Advertising and Public Relations: Kogan Page. ISBN 0-7494-3917-3. £9.99.

Careers and jobs in Travel and Tourism: Kogan Page. ISBN 0-7494-4205-0. £7.99

Commercial Aviation Safety: Alexander T. Wells. $48.56 on Amazon.

General Aviation Law: Jerry A. Eichenberger. $24.46 on Amazon.

Getting into Tourism: Trotman. ISBN 0-85660-459-3. £8.99.

IFCA Flight Catering Book: Published by University of Surrey.

Jane's Aero-Engines, Jane's Air Traffic Control, Jane's Aircraft Component Manufacturers, Jane's Airports, etc. When Fred T. Jane played with toy boats on his local pond, little did he realise he would go on to found a massive publishing empire, with over 200 books and other media devoted to ships, aviation, etc. Jane's All the World's Aircraft is the 'bible' of the industry. They also publish Jane's Airport Review, at a hefty annual subscription of £125. But it is often to be picked up in airline offices, second-hand copies can be found in bookstores, etc. www.Janes.com.

Leisure and Tourism Textbook: helpful introduction to basics of working in tourism industry. ISBN 0 582 27841 4. £12.99. Pearson

Preparing Your Own CV – Rebecca Colfield. Kogan Page. ISBN 0 74943 893 2. £7.99.

Pilot Warehouse: Large selection of books for trainee pilots. ☎01442-851087. www.pilotwarehouse.co.uk.

www.routesinternational.com: has an excellent selection of aviation books, covering everything from airline history, through working in the industry, to aspects of managing airports, etc.

Travel Industry World Yearbook – The big picture is probably the only global destination update and comprehensive, independent reporting and analy-

sis of the worldwide travel industry, including international tourist arrivals. www.berote.com.
Working in Tourism: Vacation Work £11.95 ISBN 1 85458 311 5. ☎01865-241978. www.vacationwork.co.uk. Tells it how it is. Mentions over 350 companies and tel. nos.

MAGAZINES

Aerospace International: (magazine of Royal Aeronautical Society) £120 p.a. E-mail publications@raes.org.uk, ☎020-7670 4300
Airline Business: ☎0208-652 4996; www.airlinebusiness.com. £85 (student rates available).
Air Enthusiast: ☎01780-480404; www.airenthusiast.com. £34.
Air Forces Monthly: ☎01780-480404; www.airforcesmonthly.com. £35.
Air International: ☎01780-480404; www.airinternational.com. £34.
Airliner World: ☎01780-480404; www.airlinerworld.com. £34.
Airports International: ☎01780-755131; www.airportsinternational.co.uk (free to selected readers).
Careerscope: probably the best magazine I have seen giving information about different careers. ☎01276-21188 to ask for supplement relating to aviation.
Crewtips: is a magazine for airline cabin crew, aimed more at those already working in the industry. Adverts such as mortgages and banking are useful if you are flying, and there are articles such as Yoga for Crews, etc. ☎01235-200658; editor@crewtips.com.
Defence Helicopter: ☎01858-438879; www.shephard.co.uk. £72.
Eurograduate: ☎020-7253 2545; www.eurograduate.com.
Flight International: ☎01444-445454; www.flightinternational.com. £89.
Focus on Commercial Aviation Safety: ☎01276-866193; www.ukfsc.co.uk. £16.60 (has links to interesting aviation sites).
Fly Past: ☎01780-480404; www.flypast.com. £35.
Inflight: ☎01858-438879; www.shephard.co.uk. £67 p.a.
Jane's Airport Review: ☎020-8700 3700; www.janes.com. £125.
Momberger Airport Information: Twice a month this incredibly detailed global newsletter gives details of what is happening in the aviation world. Main section covers airport development and forthcoming events, then subscribers choose which modules they want from Airport Operations, Air Navigation, Consultant and Contractor News, Ground Support, Catering and Maintenance. Subscription €320 (£250) per annum. ☎+49 (7152) 51640. www.momberger.com.
Pilot Journal: (US) ☎310 820 1500; www.pilotjournal.com. $20.
Pilot Magazine: ☎01799-544200; www.pilotweb.co.uk. £39.
Plane and Pilot Magazine: (US) ☎800 283 4330; www.planeandpilotmag.com. $12.
Regional Airline World: ☎01858-438879; www.shephard.co.uk. £72.
Skyport: is a weekly newspaper for airport staff and available on sub-

scription to the general public. Lots of information about jobs, aviation news. It can be picked up free in airport staff coffee lounges, canteens, office foyers etc, at Gatwick, Heathrow or Stansted. Subscriptions £60 a year, £30 for six months or £15 for three months. ☎020-8943 5171. **Today's Pilot**: ☎01780-480404; www.todayspilot.co.uk. £29.

Online Magazines

www.airbus.com/airbus4u
Air and Business Travel News; www.abtn.co.uk
www.aviationnow.com
Aviation Security; www.asi-mag.com and www.airsafetyonline.com
www.cageconsulting.com pilot career advice +1 888 899.
www.eurocontrol.int Click on Skyway News
www.faa.gov – click on Aviation News.
www.flightonline.mcmail.com.
www.flighttechonline.com.
www.policeaviationnews.com. (On-line news source for airborne emergency services industry).
www.travelmole.com/news.

GLOSSARY

AAC: Association of Airline Consolidators.

ABC: 1) advanced booking charter. 2) Able-bodied passengers who are permitted to sit by emergency escape exits and capable of assisting evacuation.

Abort: emergency procedure when aircraft is stopped before it takes off because it would be dangerous to continue.

ACI: Airports Council International.

AD75: Abbreviation for 75% discount; IATA allows appointed agents two 75% discounted tickets per year for agents' own use.

Aerodrome: Place where aircraft land and take-off. Smaller than airport and mainly used by Forces and private flyers.

Airbridge: Flexible corridor at airport with extending doorway, brought to the door of aircraft to allow people to exit and enter.

Aircraft: Normally refers to aeroplane (UK) or airplane (US). Can be used for any form of airborne transport.

Aircraft Utilisation: Hours and minutes an aircraft is used in a day.

Aircrew: Pilot and cabin staff.

AFA: (US) Association of Flight Attendants.

AFCAC: African Civil Aviation Commission.

Airfield: Small aerodrome, often privately owned, which generally has no official presence e.g. customs, etc.

Airlane: Officially recognised route through the air used by aircraft.

Airline: Company that provides regular flights for passengers and/or freight.

Airline Codes: Reference letters used to represent airlines on timetables, tickets, etc.

Airliner: Large aircraft designed to carry passengers.

Air Miles: Loyalty points earned by passengers when flying, or buying certain goods, which can be used towards further flights.

Airport: Place where aircraft land and take off, with facilities for passengers and sometimes cargo handling, with official presence e.g. customs, immigration, etc.

Airship: Large elongated balloon, containing a gas that is lighter than air, enabling it to fly. Airships usually have a passenger cabin suspended beneath the balloon, and are powered by an engine.

Airside: Area of an airport entered after check-in and immigration facilities, where passengers wait to board aircraft and can buy duty free goods.

Airspace: The air or sky above a country recognised as belonging to that country. Aircraft have to obtain official permission to enter and fly across a country's airspace.

Airspeed: Measurement in knots (nautical miles) or kilometres that aircraft travels per hour.

Air Terminal: Airport building used for administration and check-in facilities.

Air Traffic: All aircraft in flight or operating on the manoeuvring area of a runway.

Airway: Controlled pathway or corridor through a country's airspace.

Air Waybill: List of goods or people being transported by air.

Airworthiness Certificate: Issued by government aviation authorities to show that aircraft or components work to authorities' satisfaction.

Aisle: Passage between seats in an aircraft.

Alliance: When airlines form group, often to share routes.

Alternative Airport: Any airport to which a flight may be diverted if a landing at the original destination airport is no longer possible (e.g. fog, industrial action, etc).

Altitude: Measurement of the distance aircraft is flying above sea level.

AMASS: Airport Movement Area Safety System.

AMADEUS: Name for computer reservations system used by Lufthansa, Air France, Iberia, etc.

Amenity Kit: Complimentary bag (often known as goodies bag) given free to passengers to encourage loyalty to airline.

AOA: Airport Operators' Association.

AOG: Aircraft on Ground (used when an aircraft has a mechanical fault and means it can't take off).

APEX: Advance Passenger Excursion Fare. Ticket with limitations.

APOLLO: Computer Reservations System for U.S. Airlines, etc.

Approach: Final part of flight when aircraft is about to land.

APRO: Airline Public Relations Association.

Apron: Area at terminal where aircraft park.

Aquaplaning: When an aircraft skids on a wet runway, causing the wheels to lift slightly in the water, losing grip.

Arrivals: Area passengers enter after leaving aircraft, where they go through immigration, claim luggage then go through customs procedures.

ASAP: Aviation Safety Analysis Program.

ASDE-X: Airport Surface Detection Equipment.

ASM: Available seat mile. One seat (occupied or empty) flown one mile.

ASR-WSP: Airport Surveillance Radar Weather System Processor.

ATC: Air Traffic Control. Official authority in charge of aircraft movements. Air Traffic Controller (Person working in air traffic control).

ATS: Air Traffic Services.

ATOL: Air Travel Organisers' Licence.

ATUC: Air Transport Users Council.

Autopilot: Mechanical means of piloting an aircraft, used when plane has reached cruising altitude. Often known as 'George'.

Average Stage Length: average distance an aircraft is flown from point to point.

Aviation Fuel: Turbine jet engines usually use paraffin, or kerosene. Piston engines need a very high octane petrol (gas).

Back to Back: When tour or charter leaves one group of passengers at a destination to start their holiday, while collecting the previous group for return at the end of their holiday.

Baggage: Luggage

Bassinet: Baby's bed fixed to aircraft bulkhead (US).

BARUK: Board of Airline Representatives in UK.

Beacon: Marker or transmitter used for navigation, the system transmits a signal on VHF, radiating a series of bearings which are picked up on an aircraft's radio compass. Every time the aircraft crosses a beacon signal, the co-pilot reports the time it was crossed, height and estimated time for crossing the next beacon. The ATC will not let the next aircraft cross the beacon until the previous aircraft is clear.

Bermuda Agreement: 1946 air service agreement between Britain and USA, relating to services between the two countries, and often used as the basis for other bilateral agreements.

Bermuda Triangle: A section of Atlantic Ocean between Florida, Puerto Rico and Bermuda, where aircraft are said to have disappeared.

Bird Scarer: Many airports have such an official whose job is to scare away birds (often by using birds of prey) which, if sucked into a jet engine, could cause a crash.

Black Box: Flight recorder on an aircraft (actually a bright orange colour) containing records of air speed, altitude, direction, vertical acceleration, flight time and conversations.

Boarding Announcement: Instructions given by airline employee when aircraft is ready for passengers to go on board.

Boarding Pass: Ticket given to passengers to show they have checked in, and their seat number (if allocated). This is bar coded, and presented by passengers when they board aircraft, so providing a check on numbers and bringing up immediate notification if a passenger is not on plane, but their luggage is, thereby posing a security threat.

Budget Airline: Low cost airline.

Bulkhead: Wall inside an aircraft.

Bumped: Off-loaded or denied a seat on an aircraft, because of over-booking by airline.

Bureau de Change: Kiosk or office where money can be changed from one currency to another.

Buying Forward: When a company purchases foreign currency in advance of requirements; used by astute financial analysts when buying aviation fuel if they think the price is going to rise.

Cabin: Seating area for passengers on an aircraft.

Cabin Attendant/Crew: Staff who look after passengers on board aircraft.

Cabin Luggage/Baggage: Small hand-held pieces passengers are allowed to take on board.

Cabin Pressure: Air pressure inside cabin.

CAEP: Committee on Aviation Environmental Protection.

Captain: Person in charge of an aircraft carrying passengers and/or cargo.

CAS: Cost Accounting System.

CASM: Cost per available seat mile. Average cost of flying an aircraft seat one mile (or one kilometre).

CAST: Commercial Aviation Safety Team

CDA: Continuous Descent Approach

CDM: Collaborative Decision Making

Chicago Convention 1944: meeting in city which set up the I.C.A.O., defining the five freedoms of the air: a list of Traffic Rights permitted under government agreement.

CMD: (US). Center for Management Development.

CNS: Communications Navigation Surveillance.

CIMTIG: Chartered Institute of Marketing Travel Industry Group.

Coach Class: US term for Economy Class.

Cockpit: Pilot's cabin on flight deck.

Code Share: Alliance of different countries' airlines using the same airline prefix for agreed routes. Sometimes unpopular with passengers who do not know that they may not be flying on their preferred airline.

CODPIE: Acronym for children, obese, disabled, prisoners, infirm and elderly excluded from sitting in emergency exit seats, as they would not be able to open emergency exit door.

Consolidator: Person or company that has agreement with an airline to sell empty seats at lower than normal rates.

Co-pilot: The assistant to the captain, who sits in right-hand seat in cockpit.

CSA: Customer Service Agent, sometimes known as Passenger Service Agent.

CVR: Cockpit Voice Recorder. See black box.

D&D: Distress and diversion. Air traffic control sections for emergencies manned by Royal Air Force staff (UK).

Days of Service: Many airline services do not operate every day of the week, so their timetables will carry IATA designated codes 1=Monday; 2=Tuesday, etc.

Deadhead: (1) Staff in transit travelling for free. (2) Transport travelling empty for relocation or positioning.

Defibrillator: Machine used to help revive patient with heart problems – now in use on many aircraft.

Dehydration: Condition where skin dries out due to lack of moisture in atmosphere. Particular problem for cabin crew.

Departure Lounge: room or area in which passengers wait before boarding aircraft.

Deplane: To leave an aircraft.

Departure Tax: Tax payable before leaving a country.

De-pressurisation: Emergency situation when the air pressure inside plane cabin drops rapidly.

Descent: downward path of an aircraft.

DHS: Department of Homeland Security.

Disembark: To leave plane.

Ditch: When a land plane makes an emergency landing on water.

Diversion: When a plane is turned away before reaching its destination, and told to land elsewhere.

DOC: Department of Commerce.

DOD: Department of Defense.

Domestic: Internal flight.

DoT: Department of Transportation

Drag: Air resistance on an aircraft.

Dry Lease: when an aircraft is leased without aircrew.

Duty: (1) Work schedule or roster – On Duty=working; Off-duty=not working. (2) Tax on certain goods being bought into a country.

Duty Free: Goods that are sold free of tax.

EASA: European Aviation Safety Agency.

ECAC: European Civil Aviation Conference.

Economy Class: Cheapest seats in an aircraft. In US known as Coach Class.

Elapsed Flying Time: Actual time spent on a flight between two places.

ELFA: European low fares association

Emergency Card: leaflet kept in the pocket of an aircraft seat, giving safety instructions.

Emergency Exit: Door designated as way out of an aircraft in the event of a fire, crash landing or other emergency.

Emergency Landing: When an aircraft has to make a sudden, unplanned landing because of an emergency.

Empty Leg: Journey made with no passengers on board, usually when locating an aircraft at the start or end of a season.

ETA: Estimated time of arrival.

ETD: Estimated time of departure.

e-ticket: Electronic ticket either issued from a machine operated by a passenger, or the e-mail confirmation of a booking.

Evacuate: Leave aircraft in an emergency.

Evacuation Slide: Inflatable slide or chute, usually stored around the door of an aircraft, which inflates automatically in the event of an emergency, so passengers can slide to ground.

Excess Luggage/baggage: more luggage than allowed for in the ticket price. Usually carried at extra charge.

Executive Lounge: Designated room at airport for VIPs, members of airline's executive club, those paying premium fares, etc.

External Checks: Checks a pilot makes of aircraft before take-off.

F: Letter on ticket which designates holder has paid First Class fare.

FAA: Federal Aviation administration

Fare: Cost of airline ticket from one destination to another.

Fast Track: Way through airport checks to enable certain passengers to avoid long queues.

Final Approach: Last four miles of the approach to an airport by an aircraft, during which time the aircraft is in direct line with the runway for landing.

First Officer: Pilot assistant to the Captain of an aircraft.

FIS-B: Flight Information Service Broadcast.

FITS: FAA: Industrial Training Standards.

Flag Carrier: National airline of a country.

Flaps: Moving parts on the wing on an aircraft to increase lift and/or drag.

Flight: Journey by air in an aircraft, balloon, helicopter etc.

Flight Announcement: Notice given via a public address system on an aircraft.

Flight Coupon: Part of an air ticket used by a passenger to travel between points or destinations.

Flight Deck: Room or cabin at the front of an aircraft where the pilot and flight crew control the aircraft. Cockpit.

Flight Number: Official number given to a commercial flight. All flights travelling either north or east have even flight numbers. Those travelling south or west have odd numbers.

Flight Path: Course or direction of an aircraft through the air.

Flight Plan: Detailed form completed by aircraft captain before flight takes off, with information about the course, duration, etc. of an intended flight.

FMA: Final Monitor Aid.

FOB: Free on board. Cargo which is carried free.

Footrest: Bar or support for passengers' feet.

FOQA: Flight Operational Quality Assurance.

Forced Landing: Emergency landing.

Formalities: Official rules that govern procedures at an airport.

Franchise Partner: When a major airline allows another to deliver its product i.e. One of BA's partners is GBAirways, who fly routes to Gibraltar but under BA banner, crew wearing BA uniform, etc.

Frequent Flyer: Those who travel often with an airline and are sometimes rewarded with gifts or privileges.

Frisk: searching a person for firearms, drugs, etc.

Frontier: The area or border between one country and another. Some airports such as Basle in Switzerland straddle two countries' frontiers.

Fuselage: Body of aircraft.

GALILEO: Computer reservation system for BA, Alitalia, Swiss, KLM etc.

Galley: Kitchen on board aircraft.

GAT: General aviation terminal – terminal section used by private planes.

Gate: Exit in an airport departure lounge that leads to aircraft.

Gateway: main airport for entry to a country.

GBTA: Guild of Business Travel Agents.

General Sales Agent (GSA): Agent appointed by airline to act as principal or sole agent.

GMT: Greenwich Mean Time, usually shown by Z after time.

GNSS: Global Navigation Satellite System.

Go Technical: Slang for when an aircraft breaks down.

GPS: Global positioning system which helps aircraft find current location.

GPWS: Ground proximity warning system.

Ground Handler: Company that supplies services at airports on behalf of airline.

Hand Luggage: Small pieces of luggage carried by passengers on aircraft.

Haul: Part or leg of a journey. e.g. short haul, long haul.

Head Wind: wind blowing straight at aircraft which often slows down speed.

Helipad: Landing space for helicopters.

Heliport: Airport only for helicopters.

Hold: Place on an aircraft where luggage and freight is carried.

Holding: When aircraft have to wait in the air for landing clearance approaching an airport.

Horizon: The line that is seen from far distances where the sky seems to meet the earth or sea.

Hot Air Balloon: Large balloon filled with heated air of a mixture that is lighter than air, causing it to travel above ground.

Hot Connection: When minimum connecting for transit passengers is inside the normal time allowed.

Hub: Base or home port for an airline, into which it flies from other airports and passengers connect with other aircraft to fly on.

Hub and Spoke: Feeder services from small airports that are linked to services flying to other destinations.

Hull: main body of aircraft.

Human Resources Department: personnel department.

IATA: International Air Transport Association.

ICAO: International Civil Aviation Organisation.

IFCA: In-flight Catering Association.

IFR: Instrument Flight Rules.

i.d.card/pass: official identification to enter secure area.

IFALPA: International Federation of Air Line Pilots' Associations.

IFE: in-flight entertainment.

ILS: Instrument Landing System. Equipment used at night or in bad weather to help pilots navigate when approaching landing.

Immigration: Official point on arrival in a country where identification and entry visas of passengers are checked.

Inaugural Flight:first flight on a new airline route or the first flight of a new aircraft.

INCAD: Incapacitated Passenger Handling Document. Form used when passenger needs a wheelchair.

In-flight: Taking place during an air journey.

In-flight Catering: Food and drinks served during flight.

Interline: Connections between different airlines.

In Transit: 1) People or goods that are currently travelling. 2) When passengers stay a short time in a country that is not their final destination, without leaving the airport.

IT: Information Technology

J: Business class on airlines

JAA: Joint Aviation Authority.

JAR: Joint Aviation Requirements

Jet: Aircraft propelled by jet engines.

Jet Lag: a feeling of tiredness and sometimes confusion after a long air journey.

Jetliner: Airliner (US).

Jet Stream: strong wind that blows in the earth's atmosphere.

Jetty: Movable corridor brought to the doors of an aircraft to allow passengers to enter and leave aircraft.

JSC: Joint Safety Committee.

Jumbo Jet: Boeing 747 aircraft.

Jump Seat: Crew seat in an aircraft.

Kiosk: Small shop used for bureaux de change, selling newspapers, etc.

Knock-on-effect: When an initial action or event causes several other events to happen e.g. bad weather can build up aircraft delays.

Knot: Measurement of one nautical mile per hour (also used in aircraft).

Landing: When an aircraft touches down on runway after flight.

Landing Card: Form filled in by passengers and handed to immigration on arrival in a country.

Late Booking: Booking made at the last minute, sometimes incurring extra charge.

Latitude: Distance measured in degrees north or south from Equator.

Layover: Compulsory stop for aircrew who otherwise would be working more than officially permitted hours. When passengers break a journey due to lack of connecting flights.

LDR: Labor Distribution Reporting System.

Leg: Section of a journey.

Let Down: When the wheels on the undercarriage of an aircraft are lowered, ready for landing.

Life Jacket: Inflatable, buoyant clothing which keeps a passenger afloat in water.

Life Raft: Inflatable boat carried for rescue if aircraft ditches.

Light Aircraft: Small aircraft that only carries a few passengers.

Load Factor: Percentage of a plane filled with paying passengers or space for cargo.

Loading Bay: Area where luggage and cargo is put onto aircraft.

Logistics: Planning of movement of equipment and/or people.

Long Haul: Long distance flight, usually over six hours flying time.

Lounge: Seating area (usually with some privacy) apart from general areas in airport.

MA: Mid Atlantic.

Manifest: List of passengers or cargo.

Mayday Mayday: International distress call.

MCO: Miscellaneous charges order. Airline voucher used for payment.

MCT: Minimum connect time (between two flights).

Medical Kit: Pack containing basic medical necessities that by law has to be carried in aircraft. Today, many airlines issue extremely sophisticated equipment for use on board.

Meet and Greet: Service meeting arriving passengers.

MEL: Minimum equipment list.

Meridian: line on a map passing through the North and South Poles.

Mishandled Luggage: Luggage damaged while in transit.

Misrouted Luggage: Luggage that has been lost or sent to wrong destination.

Mule: person who smuggles illegal goods through customs.

NA: North Atlantic

NASA: National Aeronautics and Space Administration

NAS: National Airspace System

Necessities Bag: a small goodies bag given to airline passengers whose luggage has been misrouted.

Negative: no

NNEB: Nursery Nurse Examinations Board qualification for Nursery nurses.

No Show: passenger who does not claim their reserved place.

NOTAMS: Notice To Airmen

NP: North or Central Pacific.

Nose: Front end of aircraft.

Nozzle: Outlet delivering cooled air or liquid.

NTSB: National Transportation Safety Board.

OAG: Official Airlines Guide.

Off Duty: When someone is officially not working.

Off Loaded: When people or goods are taken off aircraft.

Onboard: When person or goods are on aircraft.

One Way: Single journey.

OPEC: Organisation of Petroleum Exporting Counties, who set rates which govern how much airlines pay for fuel.

Open Date: Return portion of ticket that can be used on any date.

Open Jaw: On a return flight you fly in to one destination, and return home from another.

Open Skies: Air space that is not regulated by any country. Free movement of aircraft.

Outward: Departing leg of a return journey.

Overbooking: When seats booked exceed the number available.

Overhead Lockers: Installed above seats to provide containers for passengers' possessions.

Ozone: Form of oxygen found especially in upper atmosphere of the earth.

P: Premium or First Class fare.

Part Charter: When only some of the seats on an aircraft are chartered by a tour operator.

Passenger: A person travelling – abbreviation: pax.

Passport: Official identity document generally used to enter another country.

Passport Control: Place at an airport controlled by Immigration service,where passengers have to show their passports.

Pax: (abr) Passenger/s.

Pilgrim: Person who travels for religious reasons.

Pilot: Crew member whose job it is to fly the aircraft.

PIR: (Property Incident Report). Official form to be filled in at airport when luggage is missing.

Pitch: Distance between the back of aircraft seat in front and back of your seat.

Plonky Kit: Pack carried by cabin crew containing working necessities such as corkscrew etc.

Pooling: When two or more airlines agree to share revenue on a route.

Port: Left hand side of aircraft.

Porthole: Small window in aircraft's fuselage.

Pre-assigned Seats: Seats allocated beforehand.

Pre-boarded Passengers: Passengers allowed onto aircraft in advance of others.

Premium Traffic: Passengers paying higher fares.

Pressurised: When the air pressure in an aircraft cabin is kept at a certain level.

PRM: Precision Runway Monitor.

Pull: Slang meaning removing voucher from airline ticket.

Punctual: To be on time.

Purser: Person in charge of cabin crew.

Q/C aircraft: Quick Change Aircraft that can easily convert between carrying passengers or freight.

Quarantine: Period of time during which humans or animals are kept away from others to reduce the risk of disease spreading.

Radar: System of radio signals used to discover the position of objects and/or their speed when they cannot be seen.

Ramp: Access to aircraft.

Reclining Seats: Seats that have an adjustable back which can be tilted back or upright.

Reconfirm: To confirm or check a booking that has already been made.

Refreshments: Food and drink.

Revalidate: Officially reconfirm or re-instate a ticket or booking.

Reverse Thrust: Push or thrust of a jet engine when it is reversed on landing to act as a brake.

Roster: Official list of staff and their duties.

Rotation/s: Number of round trips or return flights an aircraft can perform in one day.

RPK/M: Revenue passenger kilometre/mile. One paying passenger flown one mile.

RQ: On airline ticket it means holder must re-confirm flight.

Rudder: Vertical moving surface, attached to the upright fin at the rear of an aircraft tail, to control the horizontal movement of aircraft.

Runway: Landing and take-off strip for aircraft.

RVSM: Reduced vertical separation minimum.

SABRE: Computer reservation system for American Airlines.

Safety Announcement: Verbal instructions given by cabin crew member at start of each flight.

SAGE: System for assessing aviation's global emissions

SAR: Search and Rescue mission.

Schedule: Timetable.

Seat Allocation: When CSA assigns passenger a designated seat on check-in.

Seat Belt: Strong, adjustable strap to secure passengers in their seats during take-off and landing. etc.

Seat Only: Sale of seats only on a charter aircraft with no accommodation included.

Seat Pitch: Distance between rows of aircraft seats.

Sector: One part of a flight between one airport and another, without stops.

Security: Procedures to ensure protection and safety of passengers and staff, etc.

SFAR: Special Federal Aviation Regulation

Shoulder: Period in timetable between high and low season fares.

Shuttle: Short, frequent scheduled aircraft routes, usually no booking required.

Sick Bag: Heavy paper bag used if passenger is sick.

Skyjack: When an aircraft is hijacked during flight.

Slide: Shute used as emergency exit from aircraft.

Slot: Pre-booked time for a flight to take off, fly through every segment of airspace a safe distance from other aircraft, and finally time booked to land on the destination airport's runway.

Smuggler: Person who secretly and illegally brings banned goods into a country.

SMS: Safety Management System

SOPs: Standard Operating Procedures.

SP: South Pacific.

Split Charter: When two or more companies share charter of aircraft.

Standby: Passenger who has to wait to see if everyone checks in, before they know if they can obtain seat on aircraft.

Starboard: Right side of plane.

Steward/stewardess: Male/female member of cabin crew.

Stop-over: Break in a long journey when passengers/crew stay en-route.

Stowaway: Person who hides and travels illegally on aircraft.

Subsonic: Below the speed of sound.

Supersonic: Faster than the speed of sound.

Tail Wind: Wind behind aircraft that can often make for faster journey times.

TDWR: Terminal Doppler Weather Radar.

Technician: Expert – usually mechanical.

TFM: Traffic Flow Management.

Thin Route: Airline route where demand for seats is low.

Three Letter Codes: Abbreviated identification codes used by cities and airports as quick means of identification.

Thrust: Force from a jet engine that propels the aircraft forward.

Time zone: Area of the world where time is calculated as being a particular number of hours ahead/behind Greenwich Mean Time. These areas are across 15° of longitude.

Timetable: Table of times of scheduled flights.

TOD: Ticket on departure.

Tourist Class: Least expensive class of travel.

TRANSEC: Transport Security Department of the Department for Transport – DfT.

Transfer: Move passengers from one aircraft to another.

TSA: Transportation Security Administration.

Travicom: Air flight information and reservation computer terminal system.

Trolley: Movable wheeled machine used for serving food on board.

Trolley Dolly: Slang term for cabin crew.

Turn Round/around: Time when passengers leave aircraft and it is made ready for incoming passengers.

UATP: Universal Air Travel Plan: IATA's credit card facility.

Unconfirmed: Not officially agreed.

Undercarriage: Part of an aircraft, including wheels, that supports it when it lands and is on ground.

Unpressurised: When the air inside an aircraft is not pressurised.

Upgrade: When more expensive seats are offered free to passengers, usually because they are good customers of airline.

VFR: Visual Flight Rules.

VIP: Very important person or passenger.

Visa: Official stamp or paper in a passport to show holder can enter and/or leave another country.

VTOL: Vertical take-off and landing aircraft.

Wait Listed: passengers on waiting list for aircraft that is already fully booked.

Warsaw Convention: Conference held in 1929 to establish agreement on the extent of airline's liability for death, injury or loss of luggage to passengers.

Waybill: List of passengers or goods being transported.

Wet/dry Lease: When aircraft is leased with/without crew.

Wide-bodied Jet: Aircraft with extra wide body capable of taking more seats.

X-Ray: Radiation that can pass through most solid materials, and highlight illegal or dangerous goods.

Yellow Card: International record of vaccination and immunisation against disease.

Z: Used to signify Greenwich Mean Time.

Zone: A defined area of earth's surface.

Vacation Work Publications

Distributors of:
Summer Jobs in the U
Internships ....
World Volunteers ....
Green Volunteers ....
Archaeo-Volunteers ....

Vacati

Visit us o

tr